Didaktik and/or Curriculum

American University Studies

Series XIV
Education

Vol. 41

PETER LANG
New York • Washington, D.C./Baltimore • Boston
Bern • Frankfurt am Main • Berlin • Vienna • Paris

Didaktik and/or Curriculum

An International Dialogue

Edited by

Bjørg B. Gundem
& Stefan Hopmann

PETER LANG
New York • Washington, D.C./Baltimore • Boston
Bern • Frankfurt am Main • Berlin • Vienna • Paris

Library of Congress Cataloging-in-Publication Data

Didaktik and/or curriculum: an international dialogue / [edited by]
Bjørg B. Gundem & Stefan Hopmann.
p. cm. — (American university studies, XIV; v. 41)
Articles from a conference held at the Institute for Educational Research,
the University of Oslo, in August 1995.
Includes bibliographical references.
1. Curriculum planning—Cross-cultural studies—Congresses. 2. Teaching—
Cross-cultural studies—Congresses. 3. Curriculum change—Cross-cultural
studies—Congresses. 4. Critical thinking—Cross-cultural studies—
Congresses. 5. Education—Cross-cultural studies—Congresses. I. Gundem,
Bjørg Brandtzæg. II. Hopmann,Stefan. III. Series: American
university studies. Series XIV,Education; vol. 41.
LB2806.15.D54   375'.001—dc20   96-23784
ISBN 0-8204-3385-3
ISSN 0740-4565

Die Deutsche Bibliothek-CIP-Einheitsaufnahme

Didaktik and, or curriculum: an international dialogue / Bjørg B. Gundem
& Stefan Hopmann. –New York; Washington, D.C./Baltimore; Boston;
Bern; Frankfurt am Main; Berlin; Vienna; Paris: Lang.
(American university studies: Ser. 14, Education; Vol. 41)
ISBN 0-8204-3385-3
NE: Gundem, Bjørg B. [Hrsg.]; American university studies / 14

The paper in this book meets the guidelines for permanence and durability
of the Committee on Production Guidelines for Book Longevity
of the Council of Library Resources.

© 1998 Peter Lang Publishing, Inc., New York

Printed in the United States of America.

Table of Contents

Acknowledgments

We are grateful to the Faculty of Social Sciences and to the Institute for Educational Research at the University of Oslo for supporting the conference which gave rise to this publication as well as for the support granted to the publication itself.

We also wish to express our thanks to Ian Westbury of the University of Illinois at Urbana-Champaign for his extensive and indispensable help and advice throughout the preparation of this volume. William Pinar gave us crucial help at an important point in this project and we must express our gratitude for that assistance.

We also thank the people who helped preparing the manuscript: Research Assistant Kirsten Sivesind, and the graduate students Sigtona Halrynjo and Yngve Lindvig, all at the Institute for Educational Research, the University of Oslo.

We are also grateful to our colleagues who so willingly agreed to contribute. It is thanks to them that this publication was made possible.

The University of Oslo, August 1996

Bjørg B. Gundem
Stefan Hopmann

Introduction

Didaktik Meets Curriculum

Bjørg B. Gundem
Stefan Hopmann

Didaktik meets Curriculum: The Starting of a Dialogue

With the increasing interdependence and harmonization of education systems, and of expectations for their achievement outcomes, the necessity is growing for cooperation across national borders in curriculum research and development. An important obstacle to such work, although one that is hardly recognized, results from differing attitudes towards curriculum planning and implementation. Here we will be considering two basic models and two sets of attitudes representing ideals that pose major problems of intercultural communication: the Anglo-Saxon tradition of *curriculum studies* and the Central and North European tradition of *Didaktik*. These models rest on distinct traditions of teacher education and of national-local relationships. The Didaktik-centered teacher education of continental Europe is clearly different from the method-centered teacher education of the US; the European pattern of a centralized education system with state control over curricula and syllabi is also different from the locally initiated and controlled curriculum development found in many Anglo-Saxon countries.

Surprisingly there has until recently never been a systematic comparison between these two strands of tradition with regard to possible consequences for international understanding and cooperation, even though in Scandinavia and a few other European countries both variants have co-existed for many years (Gundem 1992, 1995; Kansanen 1995).

One problem in the search for such mutual understanding is the fact that many of the meaning-conveying educational concepts, terms and words of the German-Scandinavian language area lack counterparts in English—and resist exact translation. Indeed the term *Didaktik* itself with its comprehensive intertwining of action and reflection, practice and theory is one such untranslatable concept. The most obvious translation of Didaktik, *didactics*, is generally avoided in Anglo-Saxon educational contexts, and refers to practical and methodological problems of mediation and does not aim at being an independent discipline, let alone a scientific or research program. (We use the spelling *Didaktik* throughout this volume in order to emphasize the Central and Northern European connotations of the concept.)

The same problem of translation also relates to many of the key terms of Didaktik. It suffices to mention the word "Bildung" in German, "bildning" in Swedish, and "danning" in Norwegian. No term in English conveys the meaning of this concept—which refers to the process and product of personal development guided by reason. A parallel process, formation by external influences like parents and teachers, is expressed by the German word "Erziehung" and the Scandinavian word "oppdragelse". Both terms, Bildung and Erziehung, are generally translated as "education". And even when we think that we have found a word which matches a specific term well, like translating the Norwegian "undervisning" as "teaching", there is a great risk that we do not transfer the same sense of meaning—and in fact we do not. In short, linguistic proliferation means that the central concepts of both Didaktik and curriculum cannot be translated in any literal sense without risking serious misunderstandings.

Needless to say, this makes comparative research and cooperation, and mutual exchange of traditions and approaches, the more important and such work has been at the heart of the international research co-operation that we called "Didaktik Meets Curriculum—Didactical and Curricular Theories and Patterns: An International Comparison". The project group consists of Walter Doyle, University of Arizona; Sigrun Gudmundsdottir, University of Trondheim; Bjørg B. Gundem, University of Oslo; Stefan Hopmann, University of Trondheim and University of Oslo; Rudolf Künzli, Didaktikum Aarau, Zürich Universität; Roland Lauterbach, University of Leipzig; Peter Menck, Siegen Universität; Kurt Riquarts, Christian-Albrechts-Universität, Kiel; and Ian Westbury, University of Illinois at Urbana-Champaign. The aim of the project is to improve communication between the mainland European and Anglo-Saxon traditions by facilitating dialogue through mediating personal encounters and translations of classical texts (JCS 27 (1); Westbury 1994).

The conference at the Institute for Educational Research, University of Oslo, in August 1995, *Didaktik and/or Curriculum–A Continuing International Dialogue: The Didaktik and Curriculum of the 1960s into the 1990s*, the source of the essays in this book, was a follow-up of earlier symposia that our project group helped initiate. Perhaps the most significant of these events was a symposium, "Didaktik and/or Curriculum," that took place at the Institute for Science Education, Christian-Albrechts-Universität, Kiel, in 1993. There the question of Didaktik and/or curriculum was related to topics like "their common roots," teaching and teaching content, research, teacher training, school practice, etc.. Contributions from scholars like Wolfgang Klafki (Marburg), Klaus Schaller (Bochum), Lee Shulman (Stanford), Max van Manen (Alberta) and David Hamilton (Liverpool) made possible some first steps towards bridging the misunderstandings between the two traditions (see Hopmann & Riquarts 1995; Hopmann et. al 1995). The intention of the Oslo conference was to continue the dialogue begun at Kiel and especially to focus on developments and changes in both Didaktik and curriculum from the 1960s to the present and to discuss the consequences for both traditions of the educational developments of the 1990s.

The Dialogue Continued:
The "Didaktik" and Curriculum of the 1960s into the 1990s

From the 1960s into the 1990s Didaktik and curriculum faced rapidly changing conditions and constraints within turbulent societies, and both have been challenged, and changed from within by developments in related fields like educational research, schooling and teacher education and in the teaching profession itself. This book examines some of the changes which have had an impact on both Didaktik and curriculum as well as on the relation between them, dealing especially with how those working in each field have seen their missions changed. Each section features contributions from both the Didaktik and the curriculum traditions.

The 1960s were years of fundamental change within both traditions, seeing the breaking up of old patterns of research, curriculum making, and teacher education, and the introduction of a wide range of new models and methods. Inside the academic fields there was a growing impact by the social sciences and empirical research. At the same time, and culminating in the late 1960s, political, social and cultural tensions challenged traditional views on the functions and impact of schooling, raising questions about the social and professional legitimacy and significance of what Didaktik and curriculum had been. Part I of this book focuses on these developments in both a historical perspective and as a starting point for a critical appraisal of the state of the art today. The theme of Part I, *Changing Views of the Curriculum*, is approached from two perspectives: *Moving Commonplaces* and *Changing Paradigms*.

From the perspective of *Moving Commonplaces*, important contributions to the description and discussion of these changing views of curriculum and Didaktik are offered by William A. Reid, UK, Rudolf Künzli, Switzerland, Ian Westbury, USA, and David Hamilton, UK. In his *Systems and structures, or myths and fables? A cross-cultural perspective on curriculum content* Reid emphasizes the reality that issues of curriculum and Didaktik are always rooted in the particularities of national histories, of national habits, and national aspirations. In his *The common frame and the places of Didaktik* Künzli follows up Reid's argument, illuminating especially the context and frames of reference of Didaktik. Westbury's *Didaktik and curriculum studies* offers a comparative analysis aimed at elucidating the way curriculum studies and Didaktik may complement each other, but also underlines the important differences in how the planning process has been approached and seen within the two traditions.

David Hamilton's essay, *Didaktik, deliberation, reflection (In search of the commonplaces)*, links the perspective of *Moving Commonplaces* to the perspective of *Changing Paradigms* as well as linking the discussion on curriculum and Didaktik to an important topic in contemporary teacher education, deliberation and reflection of teachers. Hamilton's paper is a contribution to the understanding of teacher reflection and challenges the way this issue has been dealt with within educational research.

The second perspective *Changing Paradigms* is represented by the contributions of O. L. Davis, Jr., Ewald Terhart and Erik Wallin. In his *The theoretic meets the practical: The practical wins* Davis portrays in a vivid and convincing manner some unknown and unappreciated—in any case, to most Europeans—dimensions of the picture of curriculum development in the US. Terhart offers a critical and revealing analysis of German developments seen as *Changing concepts of curriculum: From "Bildung" to "learning" to "experience"*. In Wallin's essay, *From educational technology of the 1960s into the curriculum theory/ Didaktik of the 1990s*, the focus is on curriculum and Didaktik in Sweden and the essay contextualizes the developments of the period from two perspectives: from psychology/behavioral technology to social science, and from the modernity project to critical theory and neopragmatism.

The themes of Part II, *Dealing with Change*, are foreshadowed by Wallin's discussion of educational technology as an influencing factor during the 1950s and early 1960s. The 1960s left nothing unchallenged in the field of education; however, it is debatable whether or not this challenge has affected underlying institutions and behavioral patterns. This is especially true for curriculum-making and teaching. Curriculum-making was where Didaktik and Curriculum first met in Europe, viz., in a context of massive imports of Anglo-Saxon curriculum theories and models to European countries where, until then, Didaktik had dominated. Didaktik was not really pushed aside, but social changes and new theories brought the challenge to take a new look at the classical topics of Didaktik.

Two perspectives are highlighted: *The Making of Curriculum-making* with contributions by Frances Klein, U.S.A., Ulf P. Lundgren, Sweden, Carlo Jenzer, Switzerland, and Lars Løvlie, Norway; and *The Essence of Teaching* with contributions from Peter Menck, Germany, Tomas Englund, Sweden, and Erling Lars Dale, Norway.

Ulf Lundgren's *The making of curriculum-making: Reflections on educational research and the use of educational research* explores the development of curriculum research in Sweden, focusing especially on two research concerns: a theoretical interest linked to systemic reform and policy decisions, and a practical interest linked to teacher education. The analysis and overview of Frances Klein's *Approaches to curriculum development in the United States* together with Carlo Jenzer's *The making of curriculum-making: Switzerland* give valuable examples of curriculum-making in different contexts. While the concern of Klein relates curriculum reform to the possibilities of realizing curriculum change, Jenzer's contribution gives an account of recent curricular innovations in Switzerland. Løvlie's *Paradoxes of curriculum reform: The case of Norway*, applies critical philosophical analyses to recent curriculum reforms in Norway.

From the point of view of the perspective *The Essence of Teaching*, Tomas Englund's *Teaching as an offer of (discursive?) meaning*, argues that the ultimate goal of the curriculum is to convey meaning. Peter Menck approaches the same topic from what may seem a different angle. His *The formation of conscience: A lost topic of German Didaktik* argues that the task of Didaktik is the formation of conscience, that is the cultivation of a moral authority that enables young people to see the difference between good and evil, between use and abuse, and to choose one and condemn the other. The last essay in this section, *The essence of teaching* by Erling Lars Dale, deals with the question of rationality in the communicative act of teaching.

Part III of the book, *Reconceptualization*, with contributions by Wolfgang Klafki, Germany, and William F. Pinar, U.S.A., deals with two different but closely-linked issues: *The Emergence of Critical Thinking* and *Towards New Issues*. The changes in Didaktik and Curriculum have led to their "re-thinking". Two fundamental motives have played a major role. One is the self-commitment to "critical- constructive" relations between school and society. The other is the active participation of educators in social movements and conflicts. Both have led to similar reconceptualizations of both Didaktik and curriculum.

The contributions in this section highlight both of these perspectives. In the essay *Understanding curriculum: A postscript for the next generation* Pinar and his co-authors argue that the curriculum field has achieved a new identity, one based on understanding rather than curriculum development and pointing to the importance of both self-realization and society. Klafki's *Characteristics of critical-constructive Didaktik* presents the critical version of modern German Didaktik—underlining especially the importance of a Didaktik conveying self-determination (autonomy), co-determination (participation) and solidarity.

Finally in *Didaktik meets Curriculum: Towards a New Agenda,* Stefan Hopmann and Bjørg B. Gundem underline three perspectives. First there is a return to the problem of "What are we talking about" approached in the introduction and dealt with throughout the volume. Second, the question concerning differences between Didaktik and curriculum is highlighted. Third, a new research agenda is envisaged and tentatively outlined.

References

Gundem, B. B. (1992). Notes on the Development of Nordic Didactics, *Journal of Curriculum Studies*, 24, (1), 61–70.

Gundem, B. B. (1995). The Role of Didactics in Curriculum in Scandinavia, *Journal of Curriculum and Supervision*, 10 (4), 302–316.

Hopmann, S. & Riquarts, K. (Eds.) (1995). *Didaktik and or Curriculum.* Kiel: Universität-Karl-Albrechts: IPN.

Hopmann, S.; Klafki, W.; Krapp, A. & Riquarts, K. (Eds.) (1995). Didaktik und/oder Curriculum. Beiheft 34 der *Zeitschrift für Pädagogik.* Weinheim: Beltz.

Journal of Curriculum Studies, 27(4).

Kansanen, P. (1995). The Deutsche Didaktik. *Journal of Curriculum Studies,* 27 (4), 347–352.

Westbury, I. (Ed.) (1994). *The German Didaktik Tradition: Implications for Pedagogical Research.* Final Report to the Spencer Foundation. Urbana, IL: University of Illinois at Urbana-Champaign, College of Education.

PART 1

CHANGING VIEWS OF THE CURRICULUM

Moving Commonplaces— Changing Paradigms

Chapter 1

Systems and Structures or Myths and Fables?
A Cross-Cultural Perspective on Curriculum Content

William A. Reid

Introduction

Structures of schooling are both complex and familiar. Perhaps this is why thinking about them in conceptual ways can be so difficult; perhaps it is why opportunities to engage in international conferences on curriculum are so appealing. Often, I think, we come to such occasions entertaining the expectation that, if only we could put a little distance between ourselves and the cultures in which we are enmeshed, if only we could meet with scholars who work with interestingly different perspectives, we might at last begin to see and understand the bigger picture that, most of the time, so teasingly eludes us.

Well, that is the bright promise that a new conference holds out. But, all too often, reality fails to keep up with our eager expectations. The larger picture that seems to be coming into focus can, after a while, become even more blurred, as we get embroiled in the particularities of 'band' in the USA, 'assembly' in the UK, and 'joiking' in Norway; as we come to realize that 'skole' does not mean 'school', and 'læreplan' does not mean 'curriculum'. The fundamental problem about curriculum obstinately refuses to go away. How learning is organized, how it is perceived, how issues about it are debated are always rooted in the particularities of national histories, of national habits, and of national aspirations. However, rather than simply making claims of this sort, I should produce some supporting evidence.

American and European Traditions of Schooling

Let us, then, consider two short and rather parallel extracts from two official documents on curriculum, one from Europe and one from the United States. How easy is it to decide which is which?

> (1) The teaching of *social studies* . . . should be designed to: (a) enable students to fix their places and possibilities within the larger social and cultural structure; (b) understand the broad sweep of both ancient and contemporary ideas that have shaped our world; (c) understand the fundamentals of how our economic system works and how our political system functions; and (d) grasp the difference between free and repressive societies.[1]

> (2) Education has a number of seemingly contradictory aims: to convey our culture's moral commonality, with its concern for others—*and* to foster the ability to plot one's own course; to provide familiarity with our Christian and humanist heritage—and knowledge of and respect for other religions and faiths; to develop independent and autonomous personalities—and the ability to work and function as (a member of) a team; to overcome self-centredness and belief in the right of the strongest—*and* to inspire strength to stand alone.[2]

The first quotation is from the US Department of Education document *A Nation at Risk,* and the second from a recent Norwegian report on Core Curriculum.

Of course, a strong pointer to the sources of my quotations is provided by the reference to 'our Christian heritage'. Even if such an expression found its way into the draft of an official US report on education, it would very likely be excised before publication. American public education is constitutionally required to be independent of any religion.

Such an observation is at once trivial and profound. Constitutional arrangements, like the separation of education and religion in the United States, or the conflation of Church and Education in a single Ministry in Norway, are not accidental. They reflect deep and enduring cultural traditions which are determinative of the part which schooling plays in modern societies. Such an idea perhaps comes more readily and more compellingly to Europeans who have been reared in the consciousness of national differences, between England and France, between Norway and Sweden, and so on, than it does to North Americans whose history is more closely woven into Enlightenment universalism.

But the essential contrast between my two quotations rests more in what needs a little excavation, than in what is immediately obvious.

Most fundamentally, I would say that, for American students, the world that education should help create is presented as objectified, and for European students, as subjectified. For the American student, on the evidence of our quotation, the social and cultural world is an objective *structure*, consisting of *systems* (such as the economic system or the political system). The task of curriculum will then be to present this structure to students, and help them determine what place they will occupy in it. The premises behind such reasoning are firstly that culture and society can be rendered into facts to be learned, and secondly that, for students, the question of how they are to relate to society and culture is one that they have complete freedom to answer for themselves. The only point at which values enter overtly into the prescription is in the final reference to 'free' and 'repressive' societies. And here there are no shades of grey. Societies, apparently, fall quite clearly into one category or the other. That too we can learn.

The Norwegian view, again on the evidence of the quotation, is quite different. There are things to be learned, such as knowledge of other religions and faiths, and students *should* be encouraged to 'plot their own course'. But these proposals are set within a recognition that students are themselves the *product* of tradition, and that the tradition is something to be cherished. There is also recognition that being a member of a traditional society in the modern world provokes tensions and contradictions; that, in the end, questions about one's place in society are as much about the management of dilemma as about rational choice based on objective knowledge. Here too there is a problem about freedom and repression; but it is presented as a complicated question, affecting the character of the individual as well as the nature of society. In short, what we have in this document is an account of learning which sees it as intensely implicated in the subjectivity of the student as member of a culture, rather than as an affair of instruction in factual knowledge.

All of this is rather predictable. American society is republican and secular; European society, in varying degrees, religious and monarchical. Revolution in America, a young country, could be real. Revolution in European countries had thousands of years of tradition to contend with. Though far more people attend church in the United States than in any European country that I know of, the influence of religion is here deeper and more pervasive. And though monarchs have disappeared in many European states—or have been relegated from state coaches to bicycles—the mindset of monarchy persists. What religion and monarchy, in the European tradition, have in common is that they are both important sources of authority.

By that, I do not mean that they present us with sets of established beliefs—far from it. What they offer is a paradox: on the one hand, the assurance that culture and society are exceedingly complicated, even contradictory; on the other, the ability to assume supreme confidence in making judgments about complicated and contradictory cultural and social questions. Religion and monarchy are comfortable with the idea of mystery. Why should things be clear? Why should they be capable of analysis of reduction to facts and hypotheses? *Core Curriculum* states:

> education must clarify and justify ethical principals and norms, These in turn can be elucidated by Biblical similes . . . by illustrations from other religions, from history, fiction, biography, and from *legends, parables, myths and fables* (p.9, my emphasis).

Legends, parables, myths and fables! What sort of stuff is this for a curriculum! First of all, if we are to get into the territory of myth, whose myths are we going to hear about? This is not seen as presenting a difficulty. On page 7 we read:

> Education shall be based on fundamental Christian and humanistic values. It should uphold and renew our cultural heritage to provide perspective and guidance for the future.

But, secondly, how do we assess learning in this curriculum? What meaning do we assign to achievement, when what is at issue is how well students have gleaned meanings from myths and fables? Well, that too need not be a problem. That is what teachers and examiners, by virtue of their roles, are equipped to do. If they are asked to assign grades, they will assign grades, and they will be seen to have a perfect right to do so. Never mind that what they are judging cannot be reduced to measurable objectives, to numbers and percentages, to right and wrong answers. Just as monarchy gave monarchs the right to rule their whole domain, so it gave to their subordinates the right to rule their piece of it. And if monarchs no longer rule, governments do. With few exceptions, curricula in Europe are determined by national or regional agencies, and often defined by Acts of national parliaments.

On the other side of the Atlantic, however, in republican America, such things are barely imaginable. When monarchy, aristocracy and religion have been set aside as sources of authority, questions of who decides what, on what grounds and by what right are not so easily settled. Republicanism raises its own paradoxes, which have been identified by Eva Brann[3] as relating to utility, tradition and rationality.

First, let us consider utility. As soon as traditional sources of authority are cast aside, so that things are no longer learned because socially, culturally, historically, they are *good* to learn, the question of *why* anything should be learned becomes perplexing. It would seem that removal of the encrustations of tradition should be a great opportunity for curriculum, which is now free to focus on what is central, fundamental and enduring. But, paradoxically, this cannot be the case, since everyone is now their *own* authority on what should be learned. The commonest solution to this problem is to say that what will be learned is that which is 'useful'. And the sub-text of my quotation from *A Nation at Risk* is that the Social Studies curriculum should primarily aim to teach what it is *useful* to know. There is practical utility in knowledge about social, economic and political systems, since this enables learners to become individually successful as workers and citizens (while, at the same time, a little instruction in good republicanism is added through warnings about repressive societies). As Brann explains:

> Frankly and hardheadedly useful training has been an educational preoccupation of this Republic from its inception. Early republican college charters regularly made *usefulness and reputation* the educa-

tional aim. . . . Over a century later, precisely the same efforts were made at "introducing into our educational system the aim of utility, to take its place in dignity by the side of culture, and to connect education with life by making it purposeful and useful."[4]

And in a 1991 Report *What Work Requires of Schools*, we read:

Whether they go next to work, apprenticeship, the armed services, or college, all young Americans should leave high school with the know-how they need to make their way in the world. . . . Parents must insist that their sons and daughters master this know-how and that their local schools teach it.[5]

We also note that useful knowledge is eminently testable. And that this solves the problem of how grades can be assigned. Authority is shifted from the teacher to the test; verdicts can be supported by arithmetic, and the question of who has the right to sit in judgment on students is avoided.

Secondly, and related to utility, there is the paradox of tradition. Modern republicanism was a 'literary' invention; certainly, the founders of the American republic were steeped in the classics and in the 'great books' generally. Yet, once again, it is the new beginning that must be given emphasis.

Although an understanding of the founding means understanding classical texts, texts in the republican curriculum are almost entirely replaced by textbooks. Let Brann explain:

By a *textbook*, as opposed to a text, I mean manuals of prepared, convenient teaching material written in conventional technical language. Textbooks, then, are opposed to works that are original in both senses of the term, in being the discoveries or reflections of the writer . . . , and in taking a study to its intellectual origins, using the original language of discovery (p.100).

Textbooks are, of course, the natural allies of useful learning. What we 'need' to know is best detached from its intellectual origins. All school systems use textbooks. But it is important to inquire into the centrality of the textbook in the curriculum, and into how 'textbooky' as opposed to how 'texty' they are. One assumes that legends, myths, parables and fables either arrive as *texts*, or in textbooks which are rather different from those setting out 'fundamentals of how our economic system works'.

The third paradox relates to rationality. Since, in the republic, citizens must not rely on received wisdom, but think for themselves, exercise of rationality becomes the highest virtue. But this has the consequence that each thinker's personal views must seem to be true, whereas all others views are merely opinions. The implications of this final paradox are, Brann explains, 'tremendous'

> . . . there can be no authoritative teaching concerning the necessity, hierarchy, or even the content of studies. No faculty must "impose its ideas" on students or "tell them what to think." Inasmuch as human beings have not yet learned to live without reference to truth, truth is retained, but as a private possession, a nonuniversal, uncontrollable, unarguable, unteachable truth, a truth "true for me" alone (p.126).

Thus, the Social Studies in America are concerned with 'structure' and 'systems', with 'broad sweeps' and 'fundamentals', and it is up to students to fix their own "places and possibilities" within this grossly sketched social arena.

Such are the political and cultural realities that lie behind theoretical pronouncements about the nature of the content of schooling, and these we have to bear closely in mind as we embark on the perilous enterprise of seeking for convergences between European theoretical traditions which talk about *Didaktik*, and North American traditions which talk about Curriculum.

Curriculum and *Didaktik*

In the light of these comments, let us now look at two theoretical statements about the content of learning; again, I have chosen one from Europe and one from the USA.

As the 'paradoxes of education in a republic' are fresh in our minds, we will turn first of all to the comprehensive statement entitled 'The translation of curriculum into instruction', published by Johnson in 1969.[6] This I offer as a classical exposition of what Philip Jackson[7] has described as the 'dominant perspective' in American curriculum theory.

Here is an example of how Johnson discusses curriculum:

> It is useful to think of curriculum development as occurring in two phases. The first entails a process of selection from the cultural reser-

voir, followed by an ordering or structuring of the selected elements, resulting in what might be called a *curriculum matrix* or master curriculum ... The curriculum matrix consists of all the cultural content selected from the disciplines and practical enterprises, with indications of priorities, structural relationships, and type of outcome ... The second phase involves a further selection from this matrix ... of a *curriculum* for a specific program. Even after this second phase, the product still consists of *intended learning outcomes*. without reference to the instructional means of attaining them (pp. 118–119).

The first point to note is that what is being discussed here is a universal procedure. The concern is not so much with the worthwhileness of particular content, as with how a multiplicity of varied contents can be selected, processed, and packaged into programs (Johnson refers to what comes out of his second phase as a 'product', and elsewhere in his paper describes the translation of curriculum into instruction as the development of 'instructional *packages*'). Set against the background of my earlier discussion, this is, of course, entirely appropriate. As Brann suggests, 'There can be no authoritative teaching concerning the necessity, hierarchy, or even the content of studies'. What is *authoritative* in the dominant tradition of American curriculum theory is not so much content as proposals for how content can be assembled, sifted, itemized and made available for selection by or on behalf of students.

Secondly, we can see that this is, *par excellence*, a proposal for curricula that must be conveyed through the medium of the textbook. The content of the curriculum is to consist of an ordering of selected elements, available in a variety of packages, and specified in terms of learning outcomes. This is far removed from anything that could be accomplished through exposure to texts, which take 'a study to its intellectual origins, using the original language of discovery'

Thirdly, the fact that curricula are to be tailored to specific programs suggests that a criterion of individual utility is to be invoked. This is indeed the case, though, in this case, crude definitions of utility are modified to accommodate the idea of the importance of general education, which entails acquaintance with academic disciplines. 'In lieu of a task analysis', Johnson suggests, 'what is required is a disciplinary analysis using internal selection criteria of *significance* and *power* for further understanding of the discipline rather than the external criterion of specific utility' (p.121).

Johnson next discusses instruction, which he differentiates from curriculum:

> Some instructors are competent, he says, to read a properly formulated curriculum and from it to devise an appropriate instructional plan. If the curriculum reveals the type of outcome, . . . and provides structuring or ordering information, the instructional planner is faced with the task of selecting "instrumental content" to be displayed, choosing or creating the media for displaying it, and deciding the general strategy by which the instructee's responses to it are to be controlled (p.129).

Instructors, or teachers, then, need to have some understanding of content but their expertise is different from that of curriculum planners. Their job involves selection from the total content available to be learned, 'display' of that content, and 'control' of the learning process. Again, what is being discussed is a universal procedure. Instructional skills of selection, display, and control could, in principle, be applied any imaginable content—to science, to driver education, to home economics, to cinematography. Moreover, for teacher as well as student, the textbook, or curriculum package, supplemented by teaching aids, is a fully adequate source of instructional material.

Now let us turn to a contrasting view from the *Didaktik* tradition. Klafki, in his much referenced 1958 paper 'Didactic analysis as the core of preparation of instruction (*Didaktische Analyse als Kern der Unterrichtsvorbereitung*),[8] also addresses the question of the content of the curriculum. The term he uses is Bildungsinhalt, which we must translate as 'content of education'. Klafki points out that there is no consensus on the exact meaning of Bildung, but also suggests that there can be general agreement around broad definitions such as that proposed by Litt:

> When we refer to a person as educated (*gebildet*) . . . we mean at least that this person has succeeded in establishing a certain degree of order in the whole of his existence . . . However, a person can never, never create order within himself, unless he has regulated his relations to the world in an appropriate manner. If we regard the one side by side with the other, we may use the term . . . (*Bildung*) for any state of mind of a person which puts him in a position to impose order upon himself, as well as upon his relations to the world.[9]

Now this is a totally different conception of curriculum content from one which talks about selection from cultural reservoirs. Center stage is given not to a curriculum matrix, but to the *person* whose attainment of a state of *Bildung* depends on development of an orderly relationship with the world. Implicit in this notion is an assumption that it is possible to identify the essential components of learning which will bring about this desirable condition. On this point, Klafki quotes Willman:

> Within the whole of the contents to be acquired there is the essential and the inessential, fruit and leaves, the interior and the exterior. From among the whole of an object of instruction, we distinguish its educational substance (*Bildungsgehalt*) (p.19).

This idea of *Bildungsgehalt* is central to the whole enterprise of *Didaktik*; it says that, faced with the total possible range of cultural content, we can identify those elements which have the potential to bring about the state of *Bildung*. Just as religious traditions can tell us what beliefs and activities can lead us to salvation, or to a state of grace, so the tradition of *Didaktik* can tell us what knowledge and capabilities we should address in order to become educated. Within the tradition of *Didaktik*, the selecting and ordering of content depends on a process which also includes identification of that specific content which has the capability of achieving the goals of *Bildung*.

This implies, of course, that students do *not* have an untrammeled right to pursue their own definitions of belief and rationality. Within the *Didaktik* tradition, it is indeed possible for there to be 'authoritative teaching concerning the necessity, hierarchy, or . . . content of studies'. This is the whole point of the enterprise. It does not envisage a situation where all opinions are relative, all personal perceptions to be equally esteemed.

Conversely and concomitantly, teachers occupy a position of power and authority. There is no question of them being merely instructors:

> In this perspective, [says Klafki,] teachers must be willing to be moved by the subject-matter during preparation, honestly and seriously. They can only fulfill their task of educating and instructing their children if they *represent* the content which is to be acquired . . . if they themselves personify it and credibly reflect it. The poem the teacher is to present the next day, and which he or she will interpret with the children and render with the feeling it inspires, this poem must 'enchant' anew the teacher herself, shake her up, delight her, affect her (p.18).

The teacher here is not so much a technician, deploying skills of display and control, as a committed academic, enthused by the original insights which first-hand inquiry yields. Such a teacher would be rather comfortable with legends, parables, myths and fables. In this connection, I am also reminded of Rothblatt's remark that:

> Whereas in Europe, high school teachers . . . valued their ties to universities and identified with the academic community above them . . . in the United States the identity of high school teachers remained closer to that of teachers in the lower schools.[10]

Curriculum Theory and Cultural Traditions: The Press for Convergence

Thus far, my presentation has pursued a theme of comparison and contrast, in which Curriculum has appeared as the antithesis of *Didaktik*. Yet we know that each tradition is anxious to learn from the other. Already, in the 1960s Scandinavians and other Europeans were collaborating with North American curriculum theorists to explore ways in which American ideas could be adopted into research and policy-making in their own countries. Why did this happen? It might easily be assumed that what we were seeing was simply the effect of a kind of curricular imperialism. America, in the post-war period, was economically and ideologically dominant on the world stage, with scholars and administrators ready to accept the mission of coming to the aid of less privileged countries struggling with a legacy of neglect, impoverishment, or outdated institutions. But European—especially Scandinavian—countries have a proud record of independence and self-sufficiency. If they chose to look to the United States for inspiration and ideas, it was not through any sense of inferiority; it was because they identified new social and educational demands to which their existing traditions could not provide satisfactory answers.

In pursuit of contrast, I have characterized the European countries as conservative in their cultural instincts; as happy with ideas of common heritage, of enduring values, of the natural authority of teachers as well as of intellectual leaders, as opposed to the conception of the curriculum as a repository of 'useful knowledge'. To a large extent this is true. But it is not as true as it was. Already, in the 1960s, Scandinavia, ahead of the rest of Europe, was seriously exercised by questions of how educational institutions which had been designed for the preparation of an elite could be adapted to accommodate the entire school population up to the equivalent of 12th. grade. The motivation for this was partly political, and partly economic. Kallós and Lundgren explained it as follows:

> A new ideological concept of schooling emerged, firmly anchored in the idea that education is intrinsically beneficial and that educational systems play an important role in economic and social development. ... The trend of post-war economic and industrial development required new skills and qualifications among workers. Education was conceived of not only as an important means towards the implementation of these new qualifications, but also as a promoter of social and political justice in terms of social mobility, equality of opportunity, and economic equality.[11]

This raised for them exactly the kinds of paradoxes with which American high schools had been wrestling since the turn of the century: how can notions of utility be accommodated to traditions of liberal education? How can authority in curriculum matters co-exist with a diverse population, not all of whom would see themselves as sharing a common cultural heritage? If schools are to be seen to be democratic, how can assessments be made to which all will assent? How can a common curriculum be made accessible to all students when, for some, parts of it are hard to understand and, for others, parts of it are unrewarding?

The American curriculum, the curriculum of useful knowledge, tailored to the preferences of individual students, offered answers to these questions. It showed how inclusiveness could be coupled with choice, universality of assessment with varied levels of engagement, utility with goals of general education— no mean achievements. But Europe was only to a limited degree impressed; countries such as Sweden and Norway compromised by expanding the framework of the traditional curriculum to include new subjects, and by creating opportunities for a choice of 'tracks' within this expanded framework, while at the same time preserving a high level of commonality in the curriculum of all students, and a distinct disciplinary focus in subject matter.

But my characterization of curriculum in the United States has also been seriously one sided. I have emphasized the pursuit of utility, the dominance of the textbook, the elevation of the individual to be the arbiter of what is worth learning. But there were other contrasting concerns which have been given a strong stimulus by the critique of high profile national reports like *A Nation at Risk*. The burden of this criticism is that, while the American tradition has been successful in meeting some of the challenges of modernity, this success has been bought at the expense of other valuable attributes of a well designed curriculum.

> Secondary school curricula, we are told, have been homogenized, diluted, and diffused to the point that they no longer have a central purpose. In effect, we have a cafeteria-style curriculum in which the appetizers and desserts can easily be mistaken for the main courses.[12]

This kind of criticism has been around for a long time, but it has recently been sharpened by the perception that failures of disciplinary teaching, especially in Mathematics and Science, are having serious consequences for American competitiveness in world markets. The 1991 report *America 2000* warns:

> the rest of the world is not sitting idly by, waiting for America to catch up. Serious efforts at educational improvement are under way by most of our international competitors and trading partners. Yet while we spend as much per student as almost any country in the world, American students are at or near the back of the pack in international comparisons. If we don't make radical changes, that is where they are going to stay.[13]

It is hardly surprising, then, that convergence is now also occurring in the other direction. Americans are becoming interested in European curriculum traditions which appear to be better at maintaining coherence, at fostering achievement in the disciplines, and at retaining public confidence in standards of performance. We are now engaged in a two way convergence, a two way dialogue, expressed in the title of this conference as '*Didaktik* and/or Curriculum'.

Conclusion

So should it be 'and', or should it be 'or'? It would be attractive to believe that we can pick and choose from both traditions. That perhaps we could perform some kind of needs analysis of what we would like curriculum in the United States or Norway or Germany or the UK to achieve, and then select pieces of curriculum theory from here and from there in order to achieve those purposes. That, it seems to me, would be altogether too simplistic. As I have stressed in my discussion, we are not dealing with a scientific problem, where we can agree about the relevant data, then try out various theoretical explanations of those data, perhaps in the process seeing how alternative theories can be reconciled with one another, or subsumed one within another. Traditions of curriculum theory grow out of long-standing cultural habits. They are adapted to educational institutions which are also outgrowths of cultural habit, and which produce schools and teachers, bureaux and administrators, each having their own unique characteristics. 'Skole' is not 'school' and 'læreplan' is not 'curriculum'. The state board of education is not the Royal Ministry of Church, Education and Research. If Europeans are to make sense of North American curriculum theory, or Americans are to make sense of *Didaktik*, the approach has to be made in a humanistic, culturally appreciative spirit which is as sensitive to uniqueness as it is to commonality.

Having said that, there is no question that each tradition has a lot to learn from the other. They are interestingly complementary. What one tends to do well, the other tends to do badly, and vice versa. Europeans tend to worry that their curriculum is too demanding, and compromises their democratic ideals. Americans worry that the ability of their curriculum to reach everyone means that no one learns very much. But in both cases, I think, the problems arise not from lack of vision, but from an excess of vision. '*Didaktik*' and 'Curriculum' are both, in their own ways, visionary. To believe that *Bildungsgehalt* can enable us to impose order upon ourselves, as well as upon our relations to the world is visionary. The idea that, through curriculum, we can, as Jefferson proposed,

> illuminate . . . the minds of the people at large . . . that they may be enabled to know ambition under all its shapes, and prompt to exert their natural powers to defeat its purposes[14]

is equally visionary.

We can readily comprehend that legends, parables, myths and fables are the stuff of vision. Yet, in a curious way, systems and structures, units and grades are also the stuff of vision. Visions are powerful, but they are also limited. Their focus on one goal above all others sharpens their intensity, but restricts their range. Kallós and Lundgren in their 1977 paper complained that the Swedish comprehensive school was failing to serve all children; that what it offered was still, fundamentally, the curriculum of the old 'realskola'. Such complaints are still to be heard today, while, on the other side of the Atlantic, complaints of a different kind also go unanswered. A 1983 report, *Educating Americans for the 21st. Century*, promised a 'plan of action for improving mathematics, science and technology education for all . . . students so that their achievement is the best in the world by 1995'.[15] In 1991, *America 2000*, has now postponed the same goal to the next century. Essentially, the effect of thinking within one curricular tradition or another is to determine which way the balance will fall, when finely balanced decisions must be made.[16] American curriculum theory inclines us to a democratic bias. The problems of mathematics and science are indefinitely postponed. *Didaktik*, on the other hand, inclines us towards the claims of the disciplines. Better that some students be labeled 'remedial' than that we sacrifice standards of achievement.

So, I tend to believe that, most of the time, it has to be '*Didaktik*' *or* 'Curriculum'. But it is good that those who have been reared in the virtues of systems and structures should open themselves to the enticements of myths and fables. And it is also good that those whose traditions are mythic and fabulous should, in their turn, be able to understand that systems and structures have their own possibilities for turning visions into realities.

Notes and References

1. United States Department of Education, National Commission on Excellence in Education (1983). *A Nation at Risk*. Washington, DC: US Government Printing Office. [Reprinted in Gross, B. & Gross, R. (Eds.). (1985). *The Great School Debate: Which Way for American Education?* New York: Simon & Schuster, p.39.]

2. Royal Ministry of Church, Education and Research (1994). *Core Curriculum for Primary, Secondary and Adult Education in Norway*. Oslo: Akademika, p.39.

3. Brann, Eva T.H. (1979). *Paradoxes of Education in a Republic*. Chicago: University of Chicago Press.

4. *Report of the Commission on National and Vocational Education* (1914). [Quoted in Brann, op.cit., p.36.]

5. Secretary's Commission on Achieving Necessary Skills (1991). *What Work Requires of Schools: a SCANS Report for America 2000*. Washington, DC: US Department of Labor, pp. vi-vii.

6. Johnson, M. (1969) The translation of curriculum into instruction. *Journal of Curriculum Studies*, 1:2, 115-131.

7. Jackson, P.W. (1992) Introduction. In P.W. Jackson (Ed.), *Handbook of Curriculum Research*. New York: Macmillan.

8. Klafki, W. (1995) Didactic analysis as the core of preparation for instruction. *Journal of Curriculum Studies*, 27: 1,13-30 [This is an abridged and revised version of Klafki, W. (1958). Didaktische Analyse als Kern der Unterrichtsvorbereitung. *Die Deutsche Schule*, pp.450-471].

9. Litt, Th. (1963). *Naturwissenschaft und Menschenbildung*. [4th. Edn.]. Heidelberg, p.11.

10. Rothblatt, S. (1988). General education on the American campus: a historical introduction in brief. In Westbury, I. and Purves, A.C. (Eds.), *Cultural Literacy and the Idea of General Education, 87th.Yearbook of the NSSE*. Chicago: University of Chicago Press, p.15.

11. Kallós, D. and Lundgren, U. P. (1977). Lessons from a comprehensive school system for curriculum theory and research. *Journal of Curriculum Studies*, 9:1 (3-20).

12. Gross & Gross, op. cit ., p. 34.

13. United States Department of Education (1991). *America 2000: An Educational Strategy*. Washington, DC: US Dept. of Education, p.5.

14. Brann, op. cit., p.40.

15. National Science Board Commission on Precollege Education in Mathematics, Science and Technology (1983). *Educating Americans for the 21st. Century*, Washington, DC.

16. Reid, W. A. (1991). The ideology of access in comparative perspective. In Chitty, C. (Ed.), *Post-16 Education: Studies in Access and Achievement* (33–45), London: Kogan Page.

Chapter 2

The Common Frame and the Places of Didaktik[1]

Rudolf Künzli

I

It is not particularly novel to say to English-language curriculum scholars that curriculum problems are practical problems and that the appropriate method in dealing with them is *deliberation*. From Joseph J. Schwab's (1978) "Practical" papers to William A. Reid's *Pursuit of Curriculum* (1992), this has become a well established view—at least in principle. Many of us will also agree with Reid's (1992: 86) further proposition that "curriculum problems are not just practical, but uncertain and moral".

In a similar manner, but under different preconditions and following different theoretical influences, the curriculum approach adopted and developed in German-speaking countries became a mutual enterprise among school administrators, researchers, teachers and politicians. Rationality in argument, transparency in decision making and participation of the persons involved have become the main criteria of validity in curriculum making. These principles undergird the great school development project carried out under the leadership of Wolfgang Klafki (1982) as well as the model of the curriculum conference worked out and implemented by Karl Frey (1982). In Germany the deliberative method of curriculum problem solving was transformed into a view of curriculum as *public* negotiation. And as they articulate such a perspective on cur-

riculum making most authors concerned with this process acknowledge their obligation to critical theory and to the hermeneutic tradition in pedagogy—and, therefore, to its deeper roots
in rhetoric.

It was Schwab's "Practical" that first allowed me to redis-
cover the underlying flow of rhetoric in European pedagogy,
particularly in the tradition of the so-called humanistic pedagogy (*Geisteswissenschaftliche Pädagogik*). In my opinion, Rhetoric, and especially the classical *topical* rhetoric, provide firm
ground on which to discuss and compare curriculum and
Didaktik. In this chapter I will explore this ground by outlining a rhetorical or—to be more precise—a "topical" perspective
on Didaktik.[2] By topical I understand, first, the Aristotelian
method of argument in fields of uncertainty, probability or
plausibility, in short, in areas of human practice and, second,
the relationship of "topic" to a well-organized stock or resource
of viewpoints, cases, examples, schemes and patterns of deliberation, the so-called *topics* or *commonplaces*. (The German word
Erörterung offers a compelling metaphor of deliberation as
going through all the relevant places of the subject under
consideration.)

What we know as the "German Didaktik" is a professionalized
art of argument and deliberation—but in order to secure a
deeper understanding of this aspect of Didaktik, we must recognize its often-overlooked and latent character as rhetoric. I
will suggest that Didaktik should be understood as an art of
practical rhetoric, whose appropriate methodology is topical.
To demonstrate this connection and context of German
Didaktik I will briefly examine some of the elementary "places,"
or topics, of Didaktik reasoning. Furthermore, the elaboration of a deliberative or rhetorical perspective on the German
tradition of curriculum making leads necessarily to an historical examination of the stock of patterns and places used in
Didaktik. Any examination that focuses solely on currently used
commonplaces (viewpoints, cases, examples, etc.) and their role
in school as well as in public discourse cannot be sufficient in
that we are also looking towards the moral foundation in
Didaktik reasoning. Legitimacy in deliberation arises not only
from the full participation in the present but also in the relevant past. Using the stock of teacher knowledge passed on as

a heritage of the teaching profession invites us to consider the history of their effects (*Wirkungsgescshichte*), not only in a deconstructivist sense but also in the light of the hermeneutic methodology elaborated, for instance, by Gadamer (1965) or—more usefully I believe—by Blumenberg in his *Metaphorology* (1960).

I will, first, take a look into the history of pedagogy and search for the elementary places of Didaktik. I will then attempt an explanation of the usefulness of one of the most common and widespread schemes of Didaktik—the Didaktik triangle. Finally I will use this triangle to claim that understanding means realizing the significance—related explicitly or latently—behind what has been said.

II

We can identify three main streams of thought within the historical roots of Didaktik as we know it today: rhetoric, catechetics, and method. Following these three streams I will outline three elementary modes of Didaktik: a mode of *representation*, a mode of *intercourse* (a serious and caring relationships with others) and a mode of *learning experience*.

First a short look at the heritage of *rhetoric*. It begins with Isocrates' program for the public use of reasoning and argument as a human ideal and is elaborated upon by Cicero and Quintilian. Cicero testified to his own existence and his publications as an example of the educated man, and Quintilian, in his *Institutio Oratoria*, reformulated a rhetorical ideal, not only for public education, but also for mankind. He did this at the end of the era of classical education at the point in time when the ideal of rhetoric lost its real political importance.

Within this tradition of rhetoric, the rhetorical approach is seen as an ideal of human existence and as an ideal of teaching processes. The persuasive power of the teacher/speaker is mainly seen to result of his or her competence in the area of the topic being spoken about. In his *De Oratore* Cicero has Crassus and Antonius dispute this very issue. Cicero's own preference is for Crassus' position. In the ideal of *vir vere orator* (an orator is truly a man), real rhetorical competence is the deeply interwoven and inseparable combination of two things: the knowledge of one's subject and the art of its presentation.

Teaching processes were understood as the ability to speak convincingly.

This is not the place to elaborate upon the historical development of the rhetorical tradition and its underlying patterns of thinking and argument in pedagogy.[3] In the late 18th and early 19th centuries, when rhetoric disappeared from the official curriculum as a university subject (at the same time pedagogy became established at universities)[4], the two sides of rhetorical competence (knowledge of the subject matter and its art of presentation) became divided institutionally into two tasks and two areas of responsibility:

— The selection and organization of subject matter worthy of educational processes became the task of universities and higher administration (*Lehrplanarbeit*); and
— The arrangement and presentation of subject matter became the essential task of teachers themselves. The freedom to teach became the well secured privilege of the teaching profession.

Herbart's theory of educative instruction (*erziehender Unterricht*), and especially his model of articulation, became the most influential master plan for the professional arrangement of school instruction. His four steps of articulation and their affinity to classical rhetorics becomes apparent to anyone familiar with the rhetorical tradition: on one hand the steps of elaboration and preparation of a speech: *inventio* (discovery), *dispositio* (organization), *elocutio* (delivery), and on the other hand the dispositional parts of speech itself : *exordium* (introduction), *narratio* (narrative), *argumentatio* (argument) (with the two parts of *probatio* or *apodeixis* [proof] *refutatio* or *elenchos* [refutation]) and *peroratio* (conclusion) (see Prange 1989, 21–41).

No other scheme of instruction or teaching has had more influence upon teacher training than this one. The method of articulation—a universal psychological mechanism of learning processes—was used in teacher training as an instrument for lesson preparation seen as an organization of subject matter. In this way, an over-dominant subject matter orientation was lessened and yet the Didaktik approach remained. Didaktik

became established within the German tradition as a professional technique for explication of what the state curriculum
(*Lehrplan*) suggested be taught, i.e., subjects and themes. The
re-thinking of what curriculum-makers had intended, while at
the same time selecting and organizing the cultural objectives
(knowledge, values, symbols, skills, etc.) worthy of being taught
in schools, became the main subject of Didaktik, and thus the
real task and duty of a teacher (Klafki 1968).

The second main stream in the process of what we call
Didaktik, *catechetics*, had its roots in the specialized form of
rhetoric practiced by the early propagandists of Christianity
and the Fathers of the Church. Their mission to preach and
convert pagans to the true faith created new problems of presentation and communication. Early Christianity had to find
an inner and interpersonal approach to the transfer of ideas,
not a public form of reasoning and argument. Augustine elaborated this new rhetoric in his small booklet, *De catechizandis
rudibus*, for catechists in their work as missionaries.[5] The core
concept of this catechetics lay in viewing teaching processes as
a personal communication between the teacher and the learner.
The quality of the process made the difference and this process had to be grounded in friendly and personal care: Augustine used the word *amor* (love).[6]

In the early days of professionalized teacher training we re-
discover this catechetic method of teaching as a main topic of
philanthropy (Salzmann is a good example) and later on we
find it in the German followers of Pestalozzi, Dinter and
Deisterweg with their strong emphasis on the teacher's personality as the key to a teacher's effectiveness. But this trace
of catechetics did not lead to a new technique of teaching or
to a variant form of Didaktik. It merely stressed the moral demand of the professional ethos and this has become a broadly
discussed topic in the field of pedagogical anthropology.

The roots of the third main stream contributing to what we
now know as Didaktik, *method*, can be found in areas and situations where the problem of teaching has become a problem of
subject matter itself because of an explosion of new knowledge
and skills, forcing a reorganization of paradigms, or a withering or a decrease in the validity of old knowledge, forcing a
formalizing view. Under these conditions teaching becomes a

mode of ordering facts and terms and an instrument for a methodical acquisition of knowledge. Rhetoric and catechetics look at subject matter as a given corpus worthy to be learned; method on the other hand looks at subject matter as the experience of a well-prepared subject. In other words subject matter has to do with learning about the processes of production of knowledge, of organization, and of how to evaluate and legitimate knowledge.

In the 11th century a situation arose which is an exemplar of such situations: Aristotle's corpus was rediscovered; monasteries, agriculture and crafts developed, and universities were founded. In his *Didascalicon de studio legendi* (Taylor 1961) Hugh of Saint Victor elaborated an answer to then-new problems which were arising in the educational system. The center of his proposed order and method for teaching is his concept of *disciplina* which can be taken as the organizing idea of the educational system during the Middle Ages. *Disciplina* covered the four central aspects of teaching: First, the order of the subject matter. Second, in Hugh of Saint Victor's system of the *septem artes liberales* (seven liberal arts), *disciplina* means the methodical or disciplinary way of studies. Method here is seen as an inherent character of a subject, it is a logic of the discipline. Third, *disciplina* expresses a behavioral demand upon the students. It is a condition which is preliminary to fruitful studies. Finally, *disciplina* covers the very goal of every study: the forming of a habit. It is a moral seriousness. Here teaching problems are thus solved by fixing a focus on what students have to do—on *how* they learn (see Künzli 1986: 30-35).

III

The roots of Didaktik[7] I have been exploring can be easily portrayed by means of the Didaktik triangle. Systems, mainly in the forms of tables and figures but with strongly explanatory qualities, are essential elements of German Didaktik and their use as simple formulas or recipes for teaching is therefore a much discussed problem. Yet, in spite of their sometimes misleading quality, such models and systems of presentation are useful intellectual crutches.[8] The Didaktik triangle seems to me to be such a useful tool. Its origin in history is dark and, to me at least, unknown. The triangle was used in an extended form with theoretical intentions, by Harm Paschen (1979) in his *Logik der Erziehungswissenschaft* (Logic of Pedagogy). It was philosophically interpreted as a measure of good teaching by Klaus Prange (1986) in *Bauformen des Unterrichts* (Architectonic of Teaching).[9]

The Didaktik triangle[10] is the most appropriate schematic representation of the various models of Didaktik (and its roots) (see Figure 1). It is an explanatory and classifying arrangement and relates the general elements of any teaching—the teacher, the subject matter and the student—to each other. In all teaching there is, first of all, a *subject* to be taught and learned. Second, there is a *learner* to whom the subject is offered; and, third, teaching requires a *teacher*, a person or an agent who serves as

Fig. 1

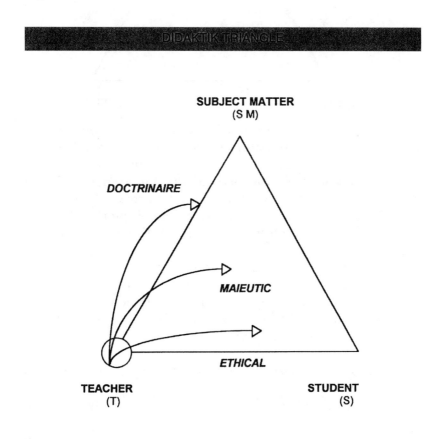

DIDAKTIK TRIANGLE

SUBJECT MATTER
(S M)

DOCTRINAIRE

MAIEUTIC

ETHICAL

TEACHER
(T)

STUDENT
(S)

Fig. 2

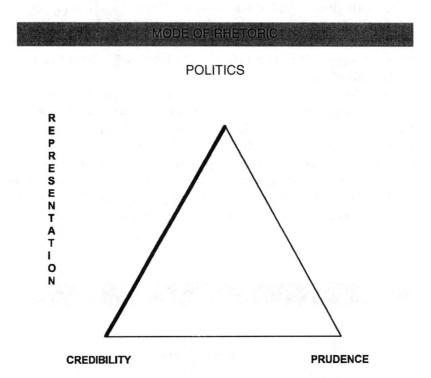

a bridge between the learner and the subject. Teachers have to be knowledgeable of the subjects they teach. Following Prange, I call this the doctrinaire *dimension* of teaching. Teaching also comprises a knowledge of the students' knowledge, skills, interests, needs and abilities; this is called the *maieutic dimension* of teaching. Finally, teaching requires the teacher's full awareness of his doings and interactions; this is the *ethical dimension* of teaching.

Three basic strands, represented by the three variants of Didaktik, can be discerned here, each having its own emphasis in theory and in practice. The emphasis depends on the different viewpoints of reference. Thus the *representation axis—* "*teacher-content*"—can be interpreted in two ways:

— as a *doctrinal interpretation* giving content priority over the teacher; or
— as a *magisterial interpretation* giving the teacher priority over content.

Fig. 3

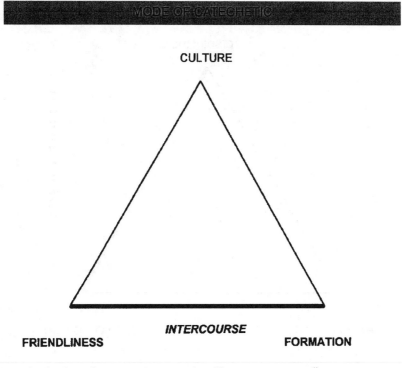

CULTURE

FRIENDLINESS *INTERCOURSE* FORMATION

Similarly for the *experience axis*—*"learner-content:"*

— an *objective interpretation* can be adopted where the objects of experience are rated high, or
— a *subjective interpretation* can be preferred bringing the learner to the fore.

The *catechetic axis*—*"teacher-student"*—may be subject to

— a *charismatic interpretation* where the teacher as a role model is emphasized, or
— to a *democratic interpretation* where the asymmetry of the teacher- student relationship is transformed (with pedagogical intentions) into a quasi-symmetrical relationship.

With the Didaktik triangle in front of us, it is easy to recognize and reconstruct the connections and intervals between the magisterial interpretation of representation and the charismatic

Fig. 4

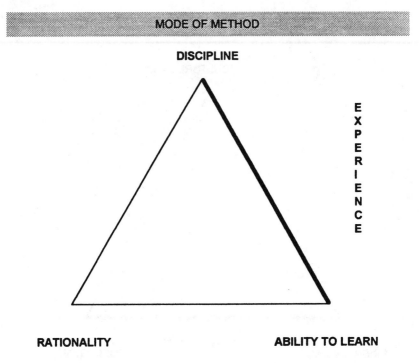

interpretation of classroom intercourse, to compare and contrast the objective interpretation of experience and the doctrinal interpretation of representation, or the democratic interpretation of classroom intercourse and the subjective interpretation of experience.

Subject matter can further be specified according to the predominant roots of teaching as *politics*, in the broadest sense of the Greek word, as *culture*, in the sense of the hermeneutic tradition, and as *discipline*, in the sense of disciplined knowledge and science. According to the three main modes of teaching, the intention of teaching focuses in the case of rhetoric on *wisdom*, or prudence (*prudentia* as an appropriate behavior), in the case of catechetics on *individual formation*, and in the case of method on the *ability to learn*. These intentions normally indicate only an option preferred in a characteristic, but not exclusive, meaning. In the same sense we can distinguish *credibility*, *friendliness*, and *objectivity* as attitudes of the teacher's

Fig. 5

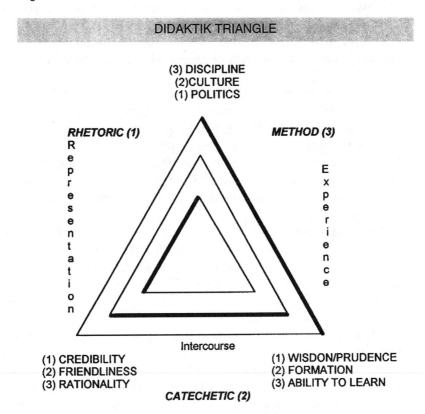

DIDAKTIK TRIANGLE

(3) DISCIPLINE
(2) CULTURE
(1) POLITICS

RHETORIC (1)
Representation

METHOD (3)
Experience

Intercourse

(1) CREDIBILITY
(2) FRIENDLINESS
(3) RATIONALITY

(1) WISDON/PRUDENCE
(2) FORMATION
(3) ABILITY TO LEARN

CATECHETIC (2)

role in the three modes of teaching. Balancing the triangle is its own Didaktik challenge and becomes a measure or standard of teaching.

IV

Finally, I would like to make some remarks on the special field of German Didaktik. It was not by pure chance that we placed *subject matter* at the top of the triangle. We can more or less explicitly proclaim the predominance of content over any other aspect of instruction to be a fundamental characteristic of German Didaktik. This point holds true despite frequent debate.[11]

A didactician looks for a prospective object of learning (here education is seen as *Bildung*, which is an all encompassing term) and he asks himself what this object can and should signify to the student and how the student can experience this significance. Education (*Bildung*) is a *code* in traditional Didaktik and its concern is to synthesize everything that occurs within instruction into a consistently coherent whole (see Diederich 1988: 239 ff).

All other questions and problems—other than the significance of the learning content—such as class management, individual and social learning, learning control, individual learning speed, appropriate representation, etc.—are subordinate to this central concern and gain significances only when the question of educative substance (*Bildungsgehalt*) is at issue. Educational psychology and instruction research tend to be peripheral phenomena.

Looking back on the constitutive elements and history of German Didaktik[12] it becomes clear that subject matter is given a dominant position, but it is also a teacher-centered perspective. Didaktik holds it to be within the teacher's scope—and his duty—to be able to reflect and organize and foster the learning of something known to him.

This differs from the "curriculum approach" which stresses the same corner of the triangle, but focuses on an institutional perspective of schooling rather than the persons who sustain it. From the very onset German Didaktik was opposed to the establishment of an educational system. And it was exactly at this point of separation—between teaching as personal intercourse and teaching as an institutionally organized practice—that Didaktik emerged. It was a professional framework or system with which teachers could bridge the gap between experience and system, enabling them to prepare for and reflect upon their practice. Thus, Didaktik belongs more to the traditional stock of teachers' knowledge than to the body of a scientifically-oriented discipline. Suffice it to say that this teacher-centered reflection on teaching, as the very core of the Didaktik tradition, does *not* imply a teacher-centered method of instruction.

It is within the concept of *Bildung* that both subject matter and teacher orientation are bound together in the program of humanistic pedagogy. Pedagogical work revolves around a theory of the assets of education (*Bildungsgüter*) and a theory of pedagogical action. The question of the mediation or mediator between theory and practice—indeed the question of Didaktik itself—becomes the question of the educated personality (*gebildete Persönlichkeit*). It was Erich Weniger who stated this Didaktik manifestation of pedagogy most clearly. For him Didaktik is "the theory of intellectual encounters between the generations"(Weniger 1975: 205) and this requires "existential concentration" of the teacher.

Since the 1960s there have been two major efforts to correct or to balance the predominance of subject matter and teacher orientation in German Didaktik. One is the curriculum movement, the other a recent division between general Didaktik and subject-matter Didaktik.

Thus it was, in my view, precisely on this issue that the curriculum movement in German-speaking countries of the 1960s and 1970s was focused. The institutional dimension of teaching was emphasized, and social conditions, organization and administration came into the view of Didaktik. Curriculum was the right answer to these problems but it was a solution on quite a different level and did not lead to a new or better balance between rhetoric, catechetics, and method. At least in the German-speaking countries the curriculum movement was a failure at the level of teaching.

Recently another tendency in German Didaktik can be observed. It seems that there is a new division of labor on the institutional level between general Didaktik (*Allgemeine Didaktik*) and subject-matter Didaktik (*Fachdidaktik*). In teacher education, and also in higher educational schools, Didaktik has become a discipline and a training in social engineering guided by a broad humanistic psychology in which subject matter can be seen as a loosely-given opportunity to deal with the social behavior of students and teachers. Subject-matter Didaktiks have taken over the task of analyzing, organizing and preparing the subjects of teaching. Perhaps we can see in these tendencies the demise of human science pedagogy, a demise, note carefully, first announced in 1968 at the very beginning of the curriculum movement.

Notes

1. Although the concepts, ideas and interpretations of the following were produced and developed in close cooperation with Stefan Hopmann within the context of our university seminars held together in Zürich, the following observations and arguments are my own responsibility.

2. Interestingly, the meaning of "topic," which comes from the Greek, means "place." The adjective was derived from it and meant "of the place" which came then to mean "commonplace," and metaphorically speaking "to be relevant." Aristotle used it in his treatise, *Topica*, which contains commonplace arguments. The meaning of topic as "subject" or "theme" arose only in the 18th century. The original meaning "of place" is preserved, e.g., in "topography."

3. Cf. the programs of the *artes liberales* (liberal arts), the establishment of the new Scholar and Latin Schools during and since the period of European Humanism, and at a later date, Schools of Higher Education.

4. Cf. Lohmann, I. (1993) *1750 und 1850*.

5. Augustine (1925) De catechizandis rudibus. In A. Augustinus, *Ausgewählte praktische Schriften homiletischen und katechetischen Inhalts*. Ed. S. Mitterer (München: Kösel, Pustet).

6. This catechetics has, of course, nothing to do with the ping-pong question and answer method in church practice well known since the 18th century: the famous preformulation of great questions and the right answers, the popular theological doctrine *ad usum delphini*. In contrast, the original focus of catechetics is a vivid interaction in the search for the right faith and the reception of the Holy Scriptures. Cf. f.i. Felbiger *Vorlesungen über die Kunst zu katechisieren*. 1774

7. The Greek root of the word Didaktik is cognate with "deik" and means the action of showing and indicating. *Didaktike techne* or Didaktik would thus be the art of showing, of pointing and drawing attention, of allowing something which does not simply demonstrate itself, or cannot be understood, seen, perceived and recognized. In keeping with this original meaning of the word, Didaktik can be used to mean the science of such actions of demonstrating, or more specifically, as a science of instruction—Didaktik as theory of instruction and the embodiment of knowledge about instruction. On the other hand, it can also be used to refer to the more or less binding set of rules governing skilled teaching and reflecting the professional ability of the teacher. No strict delineation is made between the meanings, i.e., between "theory of instruction" and "art of instruction." There is, therefore, some justification for saying that the *Great Didactic* of Comenius and Wolfgang Ratke's

Neue Lehrart, together with J. F. Herbart's decisive *Allgemeine Pädagogik aus dem Zweck der Erziehung abgeleitet* have continued to influence German pedagogical approaches in their scope and in their claim to synthesize the theory and the craft. In view of the Herbartian concept of "educating instruction," the two concepts of Didaktik and Pedagogy can be read to a great extent as synonymous, which is what happened in Herbartian teacher education. Cf. Adl Amini *et al.* (1979).

8 Models are tools (forms, heuristics, rules, schemata, classification patterns and interpretational views) for the design and possibly also for the analysis of instruction, its planning and preparation. Their instrumentality varies, as does the level of instruction planning at which they aim. Models range from theorization about general education of the future, to the structuring of curricula and teaching media, to the daily preparation work of the individual teacher.

9 I am indebted to the work of both of these scholars in the interpretation of the Didaktik triangle that follows.

10 The theoretical significance of the Didaktik triangle was last explained by H. Paschen.

11 An overall view of the German controversy—which has become notorious—can be found in *Didaktik-Methodik* compiled by B. Adl. Amini. The two main opponents are Klafki on one hand and the so called "Berlin School of Didaktik," centered around P. Heimann and his students and colleagues, W. Schulz and G. Otto. Their Berlin model of Didaktik has had a determining influence on teacher training programs in Germany in the recent past and even to the present.

12 I use the word "German" here to embrace the so called *Geisteswissenschaftliche Didaktik.*

References

Adl Amini, B. (Ed.). (1981). *Didaktik-Methodik*. Weinheim: Belz.

Adl Amini, B.; Oelkers, J & Neumann, D. (1979). *Didaktik in der Unterrichtspraxis. Grund-legung und Auswirkungen der Theorie der Formalstufen in Erziehung und Unterricht*. Bern and Stuttgart: Haupt.

Blumenberg, H. (1960). *Paradigmen zu einer Metaphorologie*. Bonn: Bouvier.

Diederich, J. (1988). *Didaktisches Denken, Eine Einführung in Anspruch und Aufgabe, Möglichkeiten und Grenzen der Allgemeinen Didaktik*. Weinheim and München: Juventa.

Frey, K. (1982). Curriculum-Konferenz: ein Ansatz für Curriculumentwicklung. In: *Gruppen*, Kiel: IPN.

Gadamer, H. G. (1965). *Wahrheit und Methode*. Tübingen: Mohr.

Klafki, W. (1968). *Didaktik*. In H. Heiland (Ed.). *Didaktik*. Bad Heilbrunn: Klinkhardt.

Klafki, W. (1982). *Schulnahe Curriculumentwicklung und Handlungsforschung–Forschungsbericht des Marburger Grundschulprojektes*. Weinheim: Beltz.

Künzli, R. (1986). *Topik der Lehrplandenkens*. Kiel: Mende.

Lohmann, I. (1993). *Bildung, bürgerliche Öffentlichkeit und Beredsamkeit. Zur pädagogischen Transformation der Rhetorik zwischen 1750 und 1850*. Münster and New York: Waxmann.

Paschen, H. (1979). *Logik der Erziehungswissenschaft*. Düsseldorf: Schwann.

Prange, Klaus (1986). *Bauformen des Unterrichts*. Bad Heilbrunn: Klinkhardt.

Prange, K. (1989). Zillers Schule. In: P. Zedler & E. König (Eds.). *Rekonstruktion der pädagogischen Wisschenschaftsgeschichte* (21-41). Weinheim: Beltz.

Reid, W. A. (1992). *The Pursuit of Curriculum: Schooling and the Public Interest*. Norwood, NJ: Ablex.

Schwab, J. J. (1978). The practical: A language for curriculum. In I. Westbury & N. J. Wilkof (Eds.). *Science, Curriculum, and Liberal Education: Selected Essays* (287-383) Chicago: University of Chicago Press.

Taylor, J. (Tr. & ed.). (1961). *The Didascalicon of Hugh of S. Victor.* New York, London: Columbia University Press.

Weniger, E. (1975). Theorie der Bildungsinhalte und des Lehrplans. In: E. Weniger (Ed.). *Ausgewählte Schriften zure geisteswissenchaftlichen Pädagogik.* Weinheim: Beltz.

Chapter 3

Didaktik and Curriculum Studies

Ian Westbury

This essay is speculative. It is a contribution to a discussion of
the relationship between my own (American) tradition of curriculum studies and the German tradition of Didaktik as two
distinct ways of thinking about teaching, schooling, and educating and, more important for my purposes here, two traditions of educational practice. Wolfgang Klafki has suggested
that "curriculum" and Didaktik are not far apart, not least
because they are concerned with a parallel set of issues or
questions:

- the question of teaching and learning goals;
- the question of the topics and contents that follow;
- the question of organizational forms, teaching and learning methods and procedures;
- the question of teaching and learning media;
- the question of prerequisites, disturbing factors, and un-
  intentional auxiliary effects;
- the question of the way in which learning results and forms
  can be controlled and judged.

I, on the other hand, will argue here that while Didaktik and
curriculum studies do address parallel questions, the ways in
which traditional American curriculum theory and Didaktik
have posed and sought to answer these questions have been
very different. In the American case the answer has been intimately associated with the idea of building *systems* of public
schools in which the work of teachers was explicitly directed

by an authoritative agency which had as part of its larger program a curriculum containing both statements of aims, prescribed content (and, in the American case, textbooks), and methods of teaching which teachers are expected to "implement". In the German case the state's curriculum-making has not been seen as something which could or should explicitly direct teaching, but rather as an authoritative selection of traditions that must become embedded, for realization in the classroom in the self-determined work of teachers and in the forms of teacher thinking represented by Didaktik. Didaktik is not, therefore, centered on the school system, but on the expectations associated with the tasks of a teacher working within both the values represented by the concept of education as *Bildung* and the framework of an authoritative state-mandated curriculum (*Lehrplan*). Didaktik seeks models of teacher thinking—seen in terms of the quality and character of the *rationales* which they yield and which teachers, in their turn, can use to thoughtfully justify their teaching in terms of both its contribution to *Bildung* and the mandates of the *Lehrplan*.[1]

In other words the "traditional" American curriculum theory and research which I will be considering here and the German tradition of Didaktik have been and are embedded in very different practical, cultural and structural contexts. They are very different intellectual systems developed out of very different starting points, and seek to do very different kinds of intellectual and practical work. Let me try to make this argument by, first, describing briefly each of the traditions and, then, comparing them. I will conclude this essay by outlining a framework which offers a way of seeing a constructive complementarity between the two traditions. At least from the American side of the coin, such complementarity promises a great deal in that Didaktik offers ways of thinking about what has been to this point virtually a void in the curriculum theory tradition.

Curriculum Theory and Research

If we start our analysis with the American field and stay close to the dominant form of curricular thinking in the world of the schools, "curriculum" can be readily described within the framework associated with the three clusters of concerns which lurk around the fundamental icon of the American curriculum field, Ralph Tyler's (1949) *Basic Principles of Curriculum and Instruction*, the Tyler *Rationale*. In the text itself but, more explicitly, in the praxis symbolized by the Tyler *Rationale*, there are two distinct themes. While these aspects of curriculum thinking are fused within the framework of the *Rationale*, they reflect different strands, or rather strata, in the evolution of American curriculum theory—and become different issues in practice.

First, there is the assumption of a *managerial* framework for curriculum development and specification and, later, for the control and evaluation of educational "service delivery". The classical curricular "technologies" of curriculum planning, objective-writing, course and curriculum development, "instructional" development, curriculum implementation, test development and testing, curriculum evaluation and assessment follow from the larger framework. Second, this structure is highly *rational* (or seemingly rational) in that it specifies a set of orderly steps through which a school system's or school's curriculum can be developed and its implementation assessed. This rationality is framed in the *Rationale* by the notion of the "needs" of students and society as the basis for developing the larger goals for the school, the transformation of these goals into potentially attainable immediate objectives—from which instructional methods and evaluation follow. It is the task of evaluation to provide feedback to curriculum developers and teachers about the quality and appropriateness of their work. Finally, the notion of analyzable and determining "needs" yields Tyler's prescription that curriculum planners consider subject traditions, contemporary life outside the school, and the worlds of students as together constituting the *sources* of the curriculum as propositions that come from these arenas are passed through the "screens" of psychological and philosophical theory.

The lowest of the strata forming the framing assumptions of traditional curriculum theory and practice reflects the most basic assumptions of American public education—and of educational systems in other societies which were formed in the same era. Thus Kaestle (1973 a) notes that when the monitorial instruction[2] that became the hallmark of New York City's schools in the first half of the 19th century was first discussed the term "monitorial system" was seen as a way of organizing instruction in a single school. Later "system" was seen as "new concept . . . , as a way of regulating a whole group of schools" (Kaestle 1973 a: 164, 171).

For our purposes several features of this early 19th-century system development in New York City are important: It was a response to a ten-fold population increase between 1800 and 1850 with a consequent increase in the scale of social problems which the prior structure of independent school-mastering and schools seemed unable to respond. Systematization of schooling proved to be a way in which the scale of the emergent problems could be addressed: "Once the system was established, it was recursive. No matter how many new children appeared, poor or rich, immigrant or native, the system would simply provide more identical schools and train more identical teachers." (Kaestle 1973 a: 166). This system was hierarchical, and necessarily standardized in all respects, and particularly in its curriculum which was the same in all schools and carefully regulated across levels. It was a system which offered careers for teachers along with a "sense of security and common enterprise, bought at the price of subordination within the system" (Kaestle 1973 a: 176). Decision-making about the curriculum was out of the hands of teachers as the people who dealt with the system's clients, i.e., pupils and, as a consequence, the relationship between teachers and students was (to use Kaestle's word) "depersonalized".

In developing his account of the emergence of New York's system of schools between 1800 and 1853, Kaestle makes two related points which are critical to an interpretation of the nature of American curriculum work. First, the course of development that he observed was a response to urbanization and drew heavily for the inspiration for its institutional development both on the notion of a school based on universal, general rules about how human affairs might be ordered and on the imagings, and the practices, of the industrial and organizational revolution of the 19th century (see Kaestle 1973 b: 9–17).[3]

The system applied collective decisions to a large mass of people; it promulgated detailed procedures and then attempted to ensure quality by eliminating deviation from those procedures. The system's governors employed supervision, inspection, punishments, and rewards to encourage uniform performance, and they made explicit the relationships between levels in the authoritative hierarchy for teachers and the curriculum hierarchy for students (Kaestle 1973 a: 182).

Second, it was a system developed within an institutional context which offered common direction from a single authoritative center. This center directed and provided the organization within a bureaucratically organized, monopolistic provision of "public" education. Almost all of the forms of the modern American school system can be seen encapsulated in the early 19th century school system that Kaestle describes.

"Curriculum-making", seen as the creation of detailed guides that would prescribe and control the work of this public system of schools, was a fundamental part of this institutional development. This curriculum work consisted of developing graded and differentiated courses of study and manuals of practice for approval by (typically) elected school boards and their agents and their use in the school system. The assumptions and prescriptions that circle around the Tyler *Rationale* about how operational curricula might or should be most effectively written reflect, and only extend, 19th-century procedures of systemic curriculum-making. Most importantly, they do not change the assumptions that the systemic thinking of the 19th century made about the roles of teachers as *agents of the system.*

The second stratum in the Tyler *Rationale*, and in American curricular thought more generally, emerged in the 1920s and 1930s. This second stratum contained two disparate strands— and a shift in the social role of some of the central actors in the curriculum "field". On the one hand, there was the movement for the "progressive" reform of pedagogy in the elementary school. On the other hand (and for Tyler whose focus was on the emerging comprehensive secondary school, it was this second strand which was more important), there was the set of tasks associated with the emergence of mass terminal secondary education as distinct from the élite preparatory secondary education of the 19th and early 20th century (Trow 1961). This

1961). This transition required both ideological and public legitimation of the curricular changes that were seen as the necessary concomitants of a "new" school intended to serve new classes of pupils and the communication of the social inventions that accompanied the new school, particularly the emergent comprehensive high school. It was this communicative task, one that necessarily involved some apartness from the existing institutional categories and organization of the then-school, that was taken up aggressively by the new class of curricular "intellectuals" like Tyler who worked in universities. In this new mutation curriculum work became an activity which supported, rationalized, directed and sought to legitimate the changes being undertaken in the schools, and a source of authority vis-à-vis publics for the emerging professional, administrative "leadership" of such social change. It was "movement" which sought sanction for its prescriptions in new versions of "science" (i.e., Tyler's "psychology"), the systematic ("scientific") analysis of social "needs", and images of a "modern" school; and while it identified itself with the curriculum, and with the school programs and teacher practices that would support the new schools, its target of concern was still the "system" (see Clifford and Guthrie 1988).

The history of the curriculum field, and of curriculum policy-making, since the 1930s has seen only a playing out of concerns that, as I have suggested, derive from the institutional characteristics of the larger school system. Thus, from the origins of curriculum work in the urban school bureaucracies of the 19th century, through the period of reform of the 1920s and 1930s which created the modern comprehensive high school, through the curriculum reforms of the Sputnik era to the concerns of today with nation-wide "systemic reform" and the national curriculum, the focus has been on public needs and on the adjustment of the system to the perceived public "needs" of each time (see Westbury 1988).[4] Within the perspective of curriculum, teachers are always, as I have suggested, the invisible *agents* of the system, to be remotely controlled by that system for public ends, *not* independent actors with their own visible role to play in the schools. They are seen as "animated" and directed *by* the system and not as sources of animation *for* the system.

Three themes circling around all discussion of curriculum follow, in a sense, from this institutional matrix. First, and as I have suggested, as the formal plan-of-work for a publicly- determined and centrally-managed, community- or nation-wide *service delivery system,* all discussion of the curriculum is framed in terms of conceptions of public "needs"—with the school being seen as the agency for satisfying those "needs" by way of its program. The system, at least rhetorically, is always turned towards such *public ends,* whether these be the inculcation of the values of obedience, thrift, etc., of New York's 19th-century monitorial schools or the more recent economic productivity, environmental awareness and the like (see Westbury 1979). *Other models of the school are not available for discussion within the dominant formal curriculum tradition or its policy-making analog.* Second, as a by-product of the modernizing task of curriculum-making, curriculum is a field whose work is inextricably associated with notions of "modernization" and "reform" of the schools. The systemic technologies that are the focus of much curriculum theory exist to change and redirect schools, not to maintain and support them as institutions or to nurture or support the on-going day-to-day work of their teachers! Finally, and given this point of view, the curriculum and its transmission, teaching, is ideally "teacher-proof". Thus both traditional curriculum theory and "practical" curriculum work have seen the abstracted teacher as a (if not the) major brake on the necessary innovation, change, and reform that the schools always require, a "problem" which must be addressed by highly elaborated theories and technologies of *curriculum implementation.* Teachers are seen as the conservative source of the "failure" of much innovation. It is the task of teacher education to prepare teachers as effective vehicles for delivering the curriculum and its goals to students by equipping them with the most effective methods for delivering that content. *It was and is not their task to reflect on that content.*

As I have been foreshadowing, it is their view of the teacher, and the role of the teacher within their theoretical and institutional systems, which represents the most dramatic difference in viewpoint between Didaktik and curriculum studies. As I will suggest in the concluding pages of this essay, it is its view of the teacher which represents one of the major sources of internal tension within contemporary American curriculum theory.

Didaktik

The institutional origins of the "model" of the German school system were, as Hopmann (1990) has emphasized, very different from those of the United States. Moreover, the German idea of professionalism is, as Jarausch (1990) has likewise emphasized, very different both ideologically and institutionally from the American ideal. Just as I have attempted to present an idealized image of the traditional American curriculum field and its institutional and cultural context, I will attempt to describe what seem to be the contexts that have framed the Didaktik tradition; I will do this in a way that highlights the differences between the American and German traditions.

I have suggested that the emergence of the institutional form of the American (public) school system, and therefore the institutional context for curriculum, emerged in the large cities of the United States in first half of the 19th century—and was, in a real sense, a response to the problems associated with mass elementary education in a context of rapid urban development. On the other hand, the structure and institutional context of the German school system are associated with the 18th century and the first decades of the 19th century and predate both Germany's urbanization and the emergence of the educational and curricular "systems" of the Anglo-American world.

The German states had developed a systematized educational administration in the 18th century and, in the first decade of the 19th century, had extended their administration to curriculum. But these educational and curriculum administrations did not assume responsibility for the management of the pre-existing network of schools but, rather, their focus of concern, the *Lehrplan* was a set of guidelines for the local selection of topics to be taught in schools sponsored and administered by a wide variety of agencies. Schools, and later teachers, were *licensed* to teach the topics of the syllabus; instructional planning at the school or classroom level was thus decoupled from the state curriculum and state administration. Thus, for example, the Lutheran, Reformed and Roman Catholic churches and clergy, town authorities, charitable foundations, and owners of estates were free to support and direct *their* schools while some central regulation was achieved, via the *Lehrplan*, over the timetable and what was taught in one or another kind of school.

Given the prior existence of long-sanctioned networks of schools which the state did not have the power or the desire to control, administrative expediency played an important role in the development of the institutional patterns of the German school system. But, at the same time, the patterns and traditions associated with the larger context of the German professions also played an important role in determining the framework of understandings within which modern *Didaktik* emerged. Thus, the emergence of all the German professions, which included 19th century *Gymnasium* teachers, was heavily dependent on the legal and professional notion of professional licensing by the state. Such licensure conferred an autonomy for the professions—which were heavily represented in the various state bureaucracies—to practice within the state's legal and administrative frameworks. Just as the law provided a frame for professional interpretation by lawyers, the emergent "didactics" provided languages within which "professional" teachers could discuss and defend the appropriateness of their interpretations of the *Lehrplan* as the authoritative administrative frame for teaching.[5]

The rationale for such licensing of the German professions was embedded in the forms of education of professionals and pervasive structure of state examinations which, in Jarausch's (1990: 14) words,

> imparted the general liberal education (*Bildung*) that is necessary for an elevated social position, a modicum of the abstract scholarly knowledge (*Wissenschaft*) that is necessary for generalized problem solving, and some degree of trade training (*Ausbildung*) facilitating subsequent practical learning. The complex system of two tiers of state examinations, with the first testing scientific information and the second checking its application to practice, elevated all German academic vocations above lesser pursuits.

The form and manner of this intertwining of the state, the professions, and the university also meant that the *akademische Berufstände*, and particularly Gymnasium teachers, were influenced, in a way not found in American schooling, by "cultural" issues. This context became important in the formation of the culture of German teachers and teaching and played a decisive role in the creation of an intellectual, professionalizing framework around teaching that was to support the emergence of modern Didaktik. One strand of this influence is quite fundamental!

La Vopa (1990) notes that in the last years of the 18th century *Pädagogik* was seen as an inductive science that sought to refine understanding of the universal principles governing human growth and the "art" of applying those principles. By the end of the 1780s this rationalist conception of *Pädagogik* had hardened into a rigid orthodoxy which lead to a vision of a life and work which was to become increasingly unappealing to the *akademische Berufstände*. As a result the ideology of this utilitarian *Pädagogik* was abandoned in favor of a "new" classically-based neohumanism which celebrated the "particularity" (*Eigentümlichkeit*) of each "personality" as a unique embodiment of human moral force (see Klafki 1987). Gymnasium teachers were, of course, at the heart of this movement.

Several aspects of this neo-humanist movement were important for the future of German thinking about teaching and schooling. Thus, institutionally, this 19th century neohumanism can be seen as an attempt to legitimate the authority of state officials as professionals, and of the professional office and license, over both the claims of a local community or patron and the routinizing demands of state structure. But, more fundamentally for what was to emerge, this 19th-century neohumanism located authority in philosophical, spiritual, and moral frames, in the "educated" or cultivated personality, rather than in public or bureaucratic frames. Such an ideology, with its emphasis on "life, the 'experiential fullness of human existence in the world' rather than 'antiseptic rationalism'" (Palmer 1969: 101), was fundamentally inhospitable to the "new" *Pädagogiks* that emerged during the later half of the 19th century—of the kind found, for example, in the American search for sociological and psychological foundations for a "rational", scientific basis for effective institutions, and in American thinking about the curriculum.

In the first half of the 19th century the ideology of neohumanism, and particularly its core conception of *Bildung*,[6] provided an overwhelmingly attractive vision which could be turned to legitimate the social and cultural pretensions of middle class professionals (see Ringer 1990). But the *ideal* of *Bildung* as this had emerged in the last decades of the 18th century (see Klafki 1987) persisted in German thought and was a language which even "modernists" could continue to refashion in new directions. Thus in Weimar Germany "The modernists asked themselves, for example, how the ideal of self-cultivation might be relevant to the experience of a factory worker, or to a much enlarged system of secondary schooling, or to sources of *Bildung* other than those of classical antiquity (Ringer 1990: 18; see also Klafki 1995). In post-War Germany didakticians worked within the human science (*Geisteswissenschaft*) legacy left by Wilhelm Dilthey and refashioned by his disciples into *Geisteswissenschaftliche Pädagogik* to effect what Jarausch (1990: 64; see also Lüth 1990) calls an "unusual juxtaposition of neo-humanist rhetoric and reforming post-war conceptions". The post-war didakticians reformulated and extended the legacy as a vital tradition which could direct thinking about new forms of both elementary and secondary schooling and new ways of thinking about the Didaktik task.

Thus the inter- and post-war *Geisteswissenschaftliche Pädagogik* sought to appropriate and creatively extend to a newly emerging *akademische Berufstände* of elementary school teachers both progressivism and the forms of thinking about teaching associated with the neo-humanist image of an idealized Gymnasium *Oberlehrer*. Modern *Didaktik* is intimately associated with this reforming and professionalizing social movement. It is centered on the teacher as a "professional" practitioner who works within, but is *not* directed by, the framework provided by the "text" of the *Lehrplan*. It seeks to model forms of teacher thinking that might direct the teacher to systematic hermeneutic reflection about the ways in which classroom environments might support a personal subjective encounter, or relationship, with the educative "content" represented in the curriculum, the ultimate forms of social life, and the like. This post-war Didaktik fused the "educational" concerns of Germany's inter-war reform pedagogy, *Reformpädagogik,* and elementary education with the professional ideologies of an idealized teacher in a search for models of teacher thinking, forms of *Didaktik analysis*, which can be institutionalized in the teacher training and certification structures and to embrace consideration of both the purposes, "content", and the means of teaching. The result is, as I have suggested, a tradition of educational, i.e., curricular and pedagogical, thought which addresses questions and problems that have no analogs in the American tradition.

Didaktik and Curriculum Theory

Curriculum development is . . . the construction of and revision of a programme of ordered sequences of learning experiences, related to intended objectives.

Robinsohn (1992)

The Didaktiker does not begin by asking how a student learns, how a pupil can be led towards a body of knowledge, nor does he or she ask what a student should be able to do or know, but instead asks wherein the character-forming significance of the knowledge and skills lies which a culture has at its disposal. . . . The Didaktiker looks first for the point of prospective object of learning in terms of education (Bildung), asks what it can and should signify to the student, and how students themselves can themselves experience this significance.

Künzli (1994)

To this point I have attempted to set out the context and character of the curriculum and Didaktik traditions separately. Now let me sketch the differences I see between the two systems more systematically. The two traditions are, I have suggested, very different in the contexts, in the starting points and methods, *and in the work they seek to do*–but mapping these differences lays out a richly-textured territory.

Let me begin by summarizing the argument of the previous sections about the institutional contexts of curriculum theory and Didaktik. In the American world the legacy of the institutional origins of the educational system have resulted in a vision of a system of schools with strong and overt formal controls over teachers as *employees* of the system. Thus, in the US the "curriculum" is an authoritative and directive manual of teaching tasks to be undertaken and procedures to be used. It is the responsibility of the governing authorities of each school system to determine that curriculum in order to instantiate (and symbolize) the educational values and goals of the community—

although more recently external testing has been the preferred mechanism of organizational and symbolic control. Traditional American curriculum thought has found its problems, and derived its language, from the framing assumptions that this context creates—as is symbolized by its preoccupation with the problem of "curriculum *implementation*" and control.

In Germany, on the other hand, secondary teaching was "professionalized" by the turn of the 20th century. Crucially for the purposes of comparison with the American tradition, the German professional ideal centers, as Jarausch (1990 c; emphasis added) observes, on an effort to establish a "middle ground of *expert self-determination*" against bureaucratic, i.e., systemic, regulation. Like lawyers and engineers, teachers

> expected autonomy of practice, with their "professional" decisions reviewed not by clients or employers, but by peers in a system of self-discipline. To justify such privileges, these callings embraced an ethos of public service, which was linked to central social values such as law, knowledge, and progress.

Didaktik is the institutionalized framework within which teachers and the profession of teaching has pursued, and pursues, its aspiration to a professional self-determination based on expertise. While the *Lehrplan* as the state's framework for teaching provides the context for the teacher's work, the *Lehrplan* is actualized and set alongside the more fundamental values that inhere in the teaching situation through and by way of each teacher's reflection, as an expert professional, on what he or she should be doing for these ends, with this material, in this setting, and with this class and these students. Didaktik, as a body of theories and frameworks which can assist *planning for teaching*, provides the language for such reflection and, as such, is the core focus of formal teacher education. Thus every German teacher must, as part of his or her Second State Examination, present a thesis which demonstrates facility in sustained, theory-based reflection on teaching using one or another of the topics or themes of the *Lehrplan* as an example. They must demonstrate how they marry, using the language provided by Didaktik, the values represented by the teachers' role as a public servant working within the framework of the *Lehrplan*, understandings of the ideal embedded within autonomous tradition of *Bildung*, and the "needs" of the students—and then justify their decision-making in these same terms.

These institutional contexts of the American and German worlds also provide the starting points within which curriculum and Didaktik *as intellectual traditions* have found their tasks. We can see what these differences mean when we compare these traditions using as the framework for the analysis the elements of a slightly modified version of the classical Didaktik formulation of the *Didaktik Triangle*: the topic of *agent* replaces the "teacher" of the traditional formulation. I will suggest that the different understandings of enveloping topic of *subject-matter* seen in the two traditions lead to very different interpretations of the meaning of the elements of the triangle (see Figure 1).

For *Geisteswissenschaftliche Didaktik*, with its human science, hermeneutic, and neo-humanist roots, there is a basic distinction between the external, objective aspects of the subject matters to be taught in the school and their inner meaning. In the words of Heinrich Roth (1994: 21, 22–23)

> An entity is educative if it leads to an experience of values, creates intellectual needs, spiritualizes vital drives, forms attitudes, sparks moral understanding. . . . The educative moments of the object are those which attract vital interests, which capture feelings and emotions, but which in the dealings with the object—and this is the crucial point—transform: direct and bind them to higher values, in other words moralize and spiritualize.

Education (*Bildung*) is, in Künzli's (1994) words, "the character-forming surplus beyond mere knowledge and skills" that is at the center of Didaktik. Thus from the point of view of the Didaktik tradition, while the decisions about content that underlie the *Lehrplan* prescribe the traditions and topics that will be taught by the teacher, these traditions and topics must be understood by each teacher in the contexts both of "higher" values that they represent, reflect, and might nurture, and the embeddedness of both curricular topics and cultural values in the subjective individuality that education seeks to support. In Menck's (1994) words:

> There are many metaphors for those activities which help to bring together the general and the individual, the objective and the subjective, for example, "reciprocating", "exchanging", "unifying", or "encountering". . . . The objective side is perceived as factual, as indepen-

Views of subject matters of education

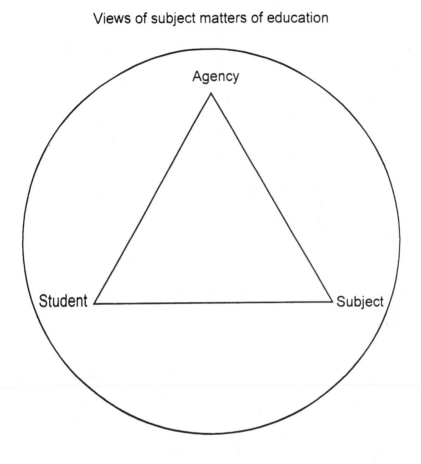

Figure 1 The Pedagogical Triangle

dently valid; the subjective side is spontaneous in the acquisition of reality. It is these two factors which enable the teacher to function as a link.

It is the teacher who is the only agent for the realization of a *Bildungsideal*. In Künzli's (1994) words:[7]

The Didaktiker looks first for the point of a prospective object of learning in terms of education (*Bildung*), and then asks what it can and should signify to the student and how the students can themselves experience this significance

For curriculum theory, on the other hand, the curriculum, and school subject matters—the "objects of learning" in Künzli's terms—do not have the dualism that derives from the German concern with *Bildung* as subjective "formation" The subjects and topics of the curriculum are objectified bodies of information, repositories of skills and objective understandings, or ways of knowing that can be specified, stand apart from the learner and the teacher, and can be "taught" using appropriate methods of instruction—and the efficacy of the transmission by teachers and schools can be tested and evaluated. The task of the curriculum maker is to build an organizational and/or curricular framework or program that optimizes the match between the educational and social goals of the school system, subject matters and topics, the "needs" of the social order and students, and outcomes—while minimizing the problems that the idiosyncrasies of individual teachers pose for the effectiveness of the total system.

Thus, for curriculum the central construct is the school *system* as an agency for the institutionalized teaching of a "content", seen unproblematically in terms of this or that view of and selection from a subject matter. The agent of "education", or more correctly instruction, is the school system, and the central question is how might the most appropriate and effective curriculum be determined and, once determined, implemented in a school system. Thus the core (normative) foci of curriculum thinking center, first, on calibrating "programs" to the "needs" of students of different capacities and in different contexts and, second, on the "effectiveness" of the work of the system or the curriculum in achieving an appropriate and common "learning". As such systemic program planning and evaluation is undertaken, a fourth key topic becomes added to the three terms of the Didaktik Triangle, *milieu*: the work of effective curriculum-building seen in this way needs to understand the appropriate functional matches between the "purposes" of education and the larger social and economic context or milieu and the school's programs. Figure 2 seeks to summarize this interpretation of the central concerns of curriculum theory.[8]

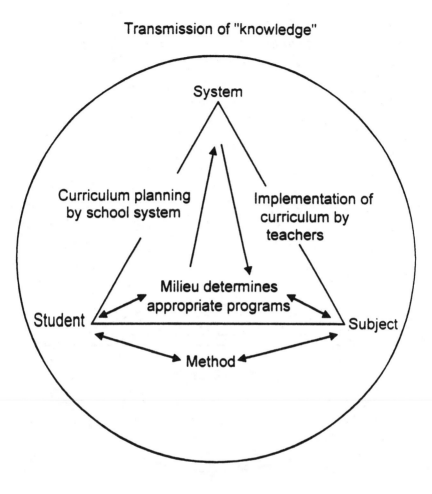

Transmission of "knowledge"

System

Curriculum planning by school system

Implementation of curriculum by teachers

Milieu determines appropriate programs

Student

Subject

Method

Figure 2 The Curriculum Theory Triangle

For Didaktik, on the other hand, it is the teacher—and of course the interaction between a particular teacher and his or her students—who nurtures the character-formation which is at the center of education seen as *Bildung*. Human individuality can only be nurtured by people—and no abstracted and institutional "system" can support such individual, interior *formation*. The *reflective teacher* and reflective teaching are then

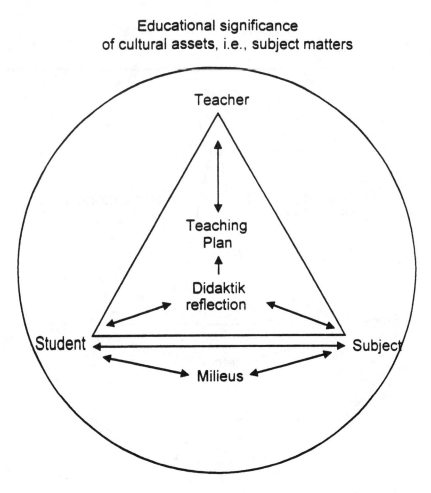

Educational significance
of cultural assets, i.e., subject matters

Teacher

Teaching
Plan

Didaktik
reflection

Student   Subject

Milieus

Figure 3 The Didaktik Triangle

the key terms in Didaktik's interpretation of the pedagogical triangle, the only possible agent and agency of formation. Thus in contrast to curriculum, where the development of effective methods for *curriculum delivery* is the school system managers' obligation and responsibility—and their implementation through "instruction" the duty of teachers as agents of the curriculum—*Didaktik* gives to each teacher the expert tasks both of discerning what formative value is available for his or her students in this or that element of the state curriculum and of developing an overall teaching plan to instantiate those values. Thus *subject matter*, as the second key term in the framework of Didaktik, is seen broadly as a set of conditions and means which the individual teacher works within and with, necessarily independently, in his or her classroom. The teacher must thoughtfully explore, by way of hermeneutic reflection, the relationship between topics of the curriculum and their educative potential, these topics and "larger" cultural forms, and the lifeworlds of a particular group of students. The core of the teacher's professional work is to discern in what way, and how, such a web of potential interactions might be productively engaged.

Didaktik seeks to assist teachers in this complex deliberation by offering frameworks and models to crystallize "appropriate" patterns of thinking. Whereas the core task of curriculum centers on thinking about building and managing a controlling institutional (curricular) delivery system, Didaktik seeks to explicate, and then turn into a usable framework, deliberation about the educational (in the largest sense) problems which teacher reflection must and might engage. Figure 3 summarizes this interpretation of the central concerns of Didaktik.

Conclusion

If the analysis summarized in Figures 2 and 3 succeeds in capturing something of the core of the curriculum and Didaktik traditions, these two traditions represent related, but very different, frameworks for thinking about the educational work of the school and of classrooms. But the key (and the interesting) question is not *Are curriculum and Didaktik the same or are they fundamentally different?* but, rather, *What can be learned from the understanding that these two traditions have coexisted without knowing each other well?*—each addressing "curriculum" in its own way but not, to this point, in ways that might be potentially complementary. But before seeking to address this question directly I must first explicate the elusive term "curriculum". I will try to do this in a way that covers the clusters of issues that both American curriculum studies and Didaktik face.[9]

In broad terms, the term "curriculum" can be seen occurring at two distinct levels of schooling: *institutional* and *classroom*. At the institutional level, curricular discussions emerge in two basic arenas:

- the intersection between schooling, culture and society, the *policy level*, and
- the technical analysis of "content" as school subjects and the construction of forms of "content" for classroom use, the *programmatic level*.

In such institutional curricular discussions, we can see two major foci of concern:

- the form of the abstract or ideal curriculum that is seen as defining the connection between schooling and both a culture and a society, the *symbolic curriculum*, and
- the nature and character of the curriculum structures and programs that translate the abstract curriculum into frameworks that are the ultimate basis for an organization of schooling and the work of the school, the *organizational curriculum*.

Discussion of the symbolic curriculum centers on images or metaphors. Such images are, however, fundamentally important because they embody conceptions of what is desirable in social and cultural orders, what is to be valued and sought after by members of a community or nation. The *organizational curriculum* as a framework for schooling as a service delivery system involves sets of complex processes through which curricular visions are translated into frameworks for systems of schools and for what social and cultural images mean for work in classrooms. And, at bottom, such processes depend on a view of "curriculum" as a *theory of content* with respect to both the aims of education and schooling as a service delivery system. Thus, the process of constructing curriculum is grounded in arguments that rationalize the selection and arrangement of subject matter content for schools of particular types and character and the transformation of that content into school subjects appropriate to those schools or school types. In other words, formal curricula, as a theory or set of theories of contents appropriate both to overall schools and school types as well as particular schools, link the abstract curriculum to schools and to the programs, classrooms and teachers of those schools.

> At a *classroom level*, "curriculum" is an event, initiated by the teacher and jointly developed by the teacher and the students, that reflects a view of subject content as an educative experience for students. Such events depend on societal, teacher, and student curricular interpretations *and* understandings of culture and schooling, how they are constructed, and how they affect what the curriculum actually comes to be in the events of teaching. Classrooms are contexts in which teachers and students act with respect to theories of education, society, culture and content.

> From this perspective, it is the inevitable task of teachers to "author" curriculum events to achieve one or more effects on students. In this sense, teachers are "curriculum makers" and interpreters of the curriculum who shape the views of that curriculum that are allowed in a school or classroom, and, importantly, define the tasks that students are to accomplish – which, in their turn, define the classroom curriculum.

Seen from this perspective, curriculum and Didaktik address very different images of "curriculum"—with traditional curriculum studies of the kind I have discussed here centering its sights on the institutional curriculum while Didaktik has centered its sights on the classroom curriculum. Traditional American curriculum studies seeks to provide, for example, a structured framework for thinking about institutional issues, a way of thinking about issues like school change and reform, and of the ways in which institutional aspirations might be "implemented" in organizational worlds. It is this way of thinking which explains the role that American curriculum theory assumed in Sweden in the 1950s and 1960s at the point at which a "new" school and a new social and educational order was being sought and symbolized by the new comprehensive system. American "curriculum theory " assumed the same role in the late 1960s and 1970s in the Federal Republic in the thinking of that period about how a new German secondary school system might be conceived. In both cases curriculum was seen as providing a way of thinking about the *institutional* task of building of a new school system. These were then-urgent tasks of the modernization of the school which Didaktik seemed not to be able to address (see Terhart 1995).

Thus the term "curriculum" with its multiple meanings provides, a way of gathering the threads of this speculative essay together and points very directly to the relevance of Didaktik in, at least, the American system. The assumptions that have traditionally dominated American understandings about how curriculum thinking and practice should be conceived have meant that the classroom curriculum has been neglected *and, in particular, the role of the teacher as an interpreter of the curriculum has not been systematically addressed.* And in recent years traditional curriculum theory in the US as I have described it in this paper has been subjected to sustained criticism and the focus of much curriculum theory has moved towards the notion of the teacher as an active maker of the classroom curriculum rather than seeing the teacher as the agent for the institutional curriculum (see, for example, Hansen 1996, Pinar *et al.* 1995). As Doyle (1994; emphasis added) writes reflecting one aspect of this shift in concern and its rationale:

> teaching and teacher education can never be treated solely as a matter of technical proficiency. Teaching is, at its core, an interpretive process grounded in conceptions of what one is teaching and what value that content has for students and society. And the choices teachers make with respect to their content have enormous consequences for the lives of students and the health of the society. *To teach effectively, teachers must be responsible curriculum theorists.*

Such a starting point, with its focus on the classroom curriculum *and not the system,* has been at the heart of Didaktik. Using Doyle's language, both the "theory" and the practice of Didaktik represent a sustained attempt to work out what it means for teachers to be "responsible curriculum theorists", and a development of ways of embedding that aspiration in the institutional world of schooling. And in doing so Didaktik has sought to solve, many of the problems that are endemic to all American attempts to relate educational and curriculum "theory" to classroom "practice"— in a way that honors practice. In Künzli's (1994) words, within *Didaktik* "practice itself [is] the starting point and the referential framework for theory (*réflexion engagée*) and . . . the mediation of both theory and practice [is transposed] into the educated (*gebildet*) individual [teacher]. . . . The concept of education (*Bildung*) has proved to be a stable source of orientation for this approach." While there are, as I have emphasized, real problems—which must be acknowledged—in directly mapping the specifics of German interpretations of the categories that Künzli outlines into an American (and Anglo-Saxon) conceptual frame, the *general* framework that underlies Künzli's concept map of Didaktik does address the issues that the contemporary shift in American curriculum theory opens *but has not resolved.* Didaktik addresses frontally and head-first Doyle's assumption and assertion that "teaching is, at its core, an interpretative process"—and shows what such a conception can mean.

Thus, if we return to the issues which circle around the relationship between curriculum and Didaktik, it is clear that Didaktik does offer an intriguing complementarity to the traditional American curriculum tradition with its focus on the institutional and organizational curriculum. Didaktik seeks to work out the implications of the understanding that the classroom curriculum is an outcome of a curriculum theory, of the *réflexion engagée* of the teacher—"Its objects are . . . children, youth, growing young people, in so far as they need education, *Bildung*, vocational training" (Flitner in Menck 1992).

Thus while Didaktik and curriculum as institutionalized traditions reflect a continuum of concern—and are, therefore, clearly complementary—they are nevertheless in fundamental tension because of they seek to do their work from different starting points. Any attempt to yoke Didaktik and curriculum too firmly within the common framework suggested by a notion of a curriculum continuum engages these tensions—with the result that, were the two traditions to be seen merely as two sides of the same coin, they would be in tension at almost every point at which they might connect. Nevertheless as an American I cannot but observe that there is an important set of "lessons" to be learned by American curricularists and teacher educators from Germany's Didaktikers. *Because* it is very different from our curriculum studies Didaktik offers an important vantage point for seeing and ways of thinking about what has been, to this point, a void in American educational theory.

Acknowledgments

This paper is a substantial revision of a paper entitled "Didaktik and Curriculum Theory: Two Sides of the Same Coin" in Stefan Hopmann and Kurt Riquarts (eds.) *Didaktik and/or Curriculum* (Kiel: IPN, 1995). Both papers represent an extended reflection on conversations in an ad hoc international working group on Didaktik meets Curriculum (*see* Introduction this volume). The errors of understanding in this paper are, however, my own and should not be attributed to my colleagues. The work of this group has been supported by our institutions, the *Deutsche Forschungsgemeinschaft*, and the Spencer Foundation, Chicago.

The work reported in this paper was supported in part by a grant from the Spencer Foundation, Chicago. Needless to say, the opinions expressed here do not necessarily reflect the views of the Spencer Foundation. Walter Doyle, Tomas Englund, Stefan Hopmann, William A. Reid, Francis Schrag and Max van Manen provided very helpful comments on the early drafts of the paper. Needless to say, none of these colleagues is responsible for what I have made of their help!

Notes

1   As Hopmann and Riquarts (1995) write, "From Dörpfeld's first curriculum theory (1872) to Rein's first theory of curriculum development
(1897) to contemporary models of didaktik, there can hardly have been
a didactical conception which does not determine the task of the teachers as interpretation, explication, transposition, etc. of predetermined
curriculum making'.

2   'Monitorial' instruction refers, of course, to the methods of school or-
ganization and teaching associated with the work of Andrew Bell and
Joseph Lancaster. Hopmann (1990: 15) summarizes the features of the
Bell-Lancaster system as follows:

   • pupils were used as assistant teachers (monitors)
   • all pupils in a school were organized by achievement level in small
     groups for instruction in each subject matter being taught so that
     each group could be taught by one monitor
   • Such grouping required careful organization of subject matter into
     small 'units'
   • since all pupil groups worked simultaneously, there was constant ac-
     tivity in the school which required careful attention to discipline
   • the classroom and teaching materials had to be carefully arranged
     both spatially and pedagogically (see also Kaestle 1973 b).

   Hopmann notes that the monitorial system led to the careful stan-
dardization of subject-matter in order to make the curriculum which, in
turn, facilitated control by supervisors of teaching and supported indi-
vidualization in that students could leave and later re-enter school, pick-
ing up their schoolwork where they had left off.
   The monitorial school was followed in much of the Anglo-American
world by the 'classroom system' (see Hamilton 1989) which persists to
the present as the dominant form of school organization. The relations
between the monitorial and class systems await sustained investigation
but, clearly, the structures and technologies of class teaching and organization depended on the inventions of the earlier system.

3   Hopmann (1990) adds to this the notion that the governing institutions
must have the capability, i.e., ways and means and the ability of develop
appropriate ways and means, to administer a *system* of schooling. His
observation that Prussian state did not, for reasons that might be thought
of as political and administrative, choose to develop this capability becomes important in assessing the role of *Didaktik* in the German educational system (Hopmann 1990: 26–27).

4   The notion that education should serve public needs has been an enduring theme of American educational ideology since the Revolution.

As Yazawa (1991: 410–411) writes of the conception of education in the Revolutionary period, "Educated citizens . . . might advance the common good and prolong the life of the Republic". As Gonon (1995) points out, such a conception of education as advancing public purposes was a hallmark of 18th century revolutionary ideologies.

5   In Gundem's (1993: 257; emphasis in original) words, in Norway, which shared to some extent the German tradition, "teachers were 'licensed' to *implement* the decisions taken at the state level, making them morally, but not juridically, responsible for the final realization of educational aims and objectives".

6   For a comprehensive discussion of the elusive (for Anglo-Saxons) concept of *Bildung*, see Lichtenstein (1971); see also Burrow (1969), Menck (1995) and Gonon (1995).

7   For a discussion of *Bildung* as the starting point of modern educational inquiry in Germany, see Lichtenstein (1971); see also Willmann (1909, 1930).

8   While the topics of subject-matter, milieu and students, as well as the curriculum-making aims and objectives, instruction, and learning, are highly elaborated within curriculum theory, *they are conceived as abstractions and as representing organizational roles, categories, and tasks.* Subject matter in the sense of the disciplines, is considered as an objective body of 'content' which may be distributed in different ways across tracks or streams, i.e., as a component of an overall 'curriculum' of a school system or school, as something which may be conceived of as a whole, and as something that may be taught or tested more or less appropriately. The idea of the curriculum does not receive any sustained elaboration as a complex construction which may be considered a resource for 'education' after transformation through teaching.

9   I draw this analysis of 'curriculum' in the most generic sense from work by Walter Doyle of the University of Arizona. See Doyle 1993; see also Riquarts and Hopmann 1995.

References

Burrow, J. W. (1969). Editor's introduction. In Wilhelm von Humboldt *The Limits of State Action*. Ed. J. W. Burrow. Cambridge: Cambridge University Press, vii–xliii.

Clifford, G. C. and Guthrie, J. W. (1988). *Ed School: A Brief for Professional Education*. Chicago: University of Chicago Press.

Doyle, W. (1993). Curriculum theory in the preparation of teachers. Paper presented to the seminar "Didaktik meets Curriculum", University of Kiel: Institute for Science Education, October 1993.

Doyle, W. (1994). Why Didaktik might be of interest to Americans. Paper presented to the annual meeting of the American Educational Research Association, New Orleans, April 1994.

Doyle, W. and Westbury, I. (1992). Die Rückbesinnung auf den Unterrichtsinhalt in der Curriculum- und Bildungsforschung in den USA. *Bildung und Erziehung*, 45 (2), 137–157.

Ermarth, M. (1978). *Wilhelm Dilthey: The Critique of Historical Reason*. Chicago: University of Chicago Press.

Gonon, P. (1995). The German concept of Bildung and schools in the 19th century. *Nordisk Pedagogik*, 15 (2), 66–71.

Gundem, B. B. (1993). Rise, development and changing conceptions of curriculum administration and curriculum guidelines in Norway: the national-local dilemma. *Journal of Curriculum Studies*, 25 (3), 251–266.

Hansen, D. T. (1996). *The Call to Teach*. New York: Teachers College Press.

Hopmann, S. (1990). The monitorial movement and the rise of curriculum administration: A comparative view. In H. Haft and S. Hopmann (Eds.) *Case Studies in Curriculum Administration History*. London: Falmer, 13–30.

Hopmann, S. and Haft, H. (1990 a). Systems in formation and transition: Curriculum administration for Schleswig and Holstein. In H. Haft and S. Hopmann (Eds.) *Case Studies in Curriculum Administration History.* London: Falmer, 64–80.

Hopmann, S. and Haft, H. (1990 b). Introduction: Comparative curriculum administration history: Concepts and methods. In H. Haft and S. Hopmann (Eds.) *Case Studies in Curriculum Administration History.* London: Falmer, 1–12.

Haft, H. and Hopmann, S. (1990). Curriculum administration as symbolic action. In H. Haft and S. Hopmann (Eds.) *Case Studies in Curriculum Administration History.* London: Falmer, 159–173.

Hamilton, D. (1989). *Towards a Theory of Schooling.* London: Falmer.

Hopmann, S. and Künzli, R. (1992). Didaktik-Renaissance. *Bildung und Erziehung,* (45),117–135.

Hopmann, S. and Riquarts, K. (1995). Didaktik and/or curriculum: basic problems of comparative Didaktik. In S. Hopmann and K. Riquarts (Eds.) *Didaktik and/or Curriculum.* Kiel: Institut für die Pädagogik der Naturwissenschaften [IPN].

Jarausch, K. H. (1990 a). The German professions in history and theory. In G. Cocks and K. H. Jarausch (Eds.) *German Professions, 1800-1950.* New York and Oxford: Oxford University Press, 1990, 9–26.

Jarausch, K. H. (1990 b). "Bildungsideale", society and politics: some critical considerations. In W. Nijhof (Ed.) *Values in Higher Education: "Bildungsideale" in Historical and Contemporary Perspective.* Enschede, The Netherlands: University of Twente, Department of Education, 60–70.

Jarausch, K. H. (1990 c). *The Unfree Professions: German Lawyers, Teachers, and Engineers, 1900-1950.* New York: Oxford University Press.

Kaestle, C. F. (1973 a). *The Evolution of an Urban School System: New York City, 1750-1850.* Cambridge, MA: Harvard University Press.

Kaestle, C. F. (1973 b). *Joseph Lancaster and the Monitorial Movement: A Documentary History.* Classics in Education, No. 47. New York: Teachers College Press.

Klafki, W. (1987). The significance of the classical theories of education for an up-to-date concept of general education. *Education,* vol. 36. Tübingen: Institut für Wissenschaftliche Zusammenarbeit, 7-31.

Klafki, W. (1995). On the problem of teaching and learning contents from the standpoint of critical-constructive Didaktik. In S. Hopmann and K. Riquarts (Eds.) *Didaktik and/or Curriculum.* Kiel: Institut für die Pädagogik der Naturwissenschaften [IPN].

Künzli, R. (1994). *Didaktik: Models of Education, of Intercourse and of Experience.* Aarau, Switzerland: Didaktikum Aarau.

La Vopa, A. J. (1980). *Prussian Schoolteachers: Profession and Office, 1763-1848.* Chapel Hill, NC: The University of North Carolina Press.

La Vopa, A. J. (1990). Specialists against specialization: Hellenism as professional ideology in German classical studies. In G. Cocks and K. H. Jarausch (Eds.) *German Professions, 1800-1950.* New York and Oxford: Oxford University Press, 27-45.

Levine, D. N. (1971). Introduction. In G. Simmel *On Individuality and Social Forms.* Edited by D. N. Levine. Chicago: University of Chicago Press, ix-lxv.

Lichtenstein, E. (1971). Bildung. In J. Ritter (Ed.) *Historisches Wörterbuch der Philosophie,* Band 1 Basel/Stuttgart: Schwabe & Co. Verlag, 922-938.

Lüth, Ch. (1990). Integration Allgemeiner und Beruflicher Bildung - zur Revision einer Deutschen Tradition. In W. Nijhof (Ed.) *Values in Higher Education: "Bildungsideale" in Historical and Contemporary Perspective.* Enschede, The

Netherlands: University of Twente, Department of Education, 43–59.

Menck. P. (1992). "Pedagogical responsibility"—a clue to German Didactics. Siegen: Universität-Gesamthochschule Siegen.

Menck, P. (1994). Content—still in question? In K. Riquarts (Ed.) *The German Didactic Tradition: A Discussion of Texts from the Tradition* Kiel: IPN.

Menck, P. (1995). "Bildung"—A core concept in German Didaktik. Siegen: Universität-Gesamthochschule Siegen.

Palmer, R. E. (1969). *Hermeneutics: Interpretation Theory in Schleiermacher, Dilthey, Heidegger, and Gadamer.* Evanston, IL: Northwestern University Press.

Pinar, W.F., Reynolds, W. M., Slattery, P., and Taubman, P.M. (1995). (Eds.) *Understanding Curriculum.* New York: Peter Lang.

Ringer, F. (1990). "Bildung" and its implications in the German Tradition, 1890-1930. In W. Nijhof (Ed.) *Values in Higher Education: "Bildungsideale" in Historical and Contemporary Perspective* Enschede, The Netherlands: University of Twente, Department of Education, 1–22.

Riquarts, K. and Hopmann, S. (1995). Brave new world: review of Benchmarks for Science Literacy. *Journal of Curriculum Studies,* 27 (4), 455–461.

Robinsohn, S. B. ([1969] 1992). A conceptual model of curriculum development. In S. B. Robinsohn, *Comparative Education: A Basic Approach.* Ed. H. Robinsohn. Jerusalem: Magnes, 125–144.

Roth, H. (1994). The art of lesson preparation. In *The German Didaktik Tradition: A Discussion of Texts from the Tradition.* Kiel: Institute for Science Education.

Siebert, H. (1967). Humboldt and the reform of the educational system. In Joachim II. Knoll and Horst Siebert, *Wilhelm von Humboldt: Politician and Educationist.* Bad Godesberg: Inter Nationes, 28–54.

Terhart, E. (1995). Changing concepts of curriculum: From "Bildung" to "Learning" to "Experience": Developments in (West) Germany from the 60s to 1990. Paper presented at the Conference on "Didaktik and/or Curriculum—A Continuing International Dialogue", University of Oslo, August 1995.

Trow, M. (1961). The second transformation of American secondary education. *International Journal of Comparative Sociology*, 1961 (2), 144–166.

Tyler, R. W. (1949). *Basic Principles of Curriculum and Instruction*. Chicago: University of Chicago Press.

Westbury, I. (1979). The curriculum: What is it and how should we think about it? In M. Bloomer and K. E. Shaw (Eds.) *The Challenge of Educational Change: Limitations and Possibilities*. Oxford: Pergamon Press, 129–158.

Westbury, I. (1988). Who can be taught what? General education in the secondary school. In Alan C. Purves and Ian Westbury (Eds.) *Contemporary Culture and the Idea of General Education*. 87th Yearbook, Part 2, of the National Society for the Study of Education. Chicago: NSSE and University of Chicago Press, 171–197.

Westbury, I. (1992). Curriculum studies in the United States: Reflections on a conversation with Ulf Lundgren. In D. Broady (Ed.) *Education in the Late 20th Century: Essays Presented to Ulf P. Lundgren on the Occasion of his Fiftieth Birthday*. Stockholm: Stockholm Institute of Education Press, 117–140.

Westbury, I. (1994). Deliberation and the improvement of schooling. In J. T. Dillon (Ed.) *Deliberation in Education and Society*. Norwood, NJ: Ablex, 37–65.

Willmann, O. (1909). *Didaktik als Bildungslehre nach ihren Beziehungen zur Sozialforschung und zur Geschichte der Bildung*. Braunschweig: Verlag Friedrich Bieweg und Cohn.

Willmann, O. (1930). *The Science of Education in its Sociological and Historical Aspects*. Trans. F. M. Kirsch. Latrobe, PA: The Archabbey Press.

Yazawa, M. (1991). The impact of the Revolution on education. In J. P. Greene and J. R. Pole (Eds.), *The Blackwell Encyclopedia of the American Revolution*. Cambridge, MA: Blackwell, 409–417.

Chapter 4

Didaktik, Deliberation, Reflection (In Search of the Commonplaces)

David Hamilton

As a 'discussant' at the Oslo conference on 'Didaktik and/or Curriculum' (August, 1995), I spoke briefly against the strong dualist claim that the realms of curriculum and Didaktik are irreconcilable. Among other things, I felt that it is possible to identify a convergence between modern Didaktik theory (cf. Klafki) and curriculum theories that emphasize deliberation (cf. Schwab) or reflection (cf. Schön). This essay is devoted to further exploration of that claim.

Didaktik

Wolfgang Klafki describes his ideas as 'critical constructive Didaktik'. The critical element is a fusion of nineteenth century Didaktik theory (cf. hermeneutics/ Geisteswissenschaft) and twentieth century critical theory associated with the Frankfurt School. Critical constructive Didaktik sets itself a hermeneutic task: to elicit a Didaktik 'text' (Lundgren, 1983) that, in turn, can be realized through the subsequent classroom processes.

In the sense used by Lundgren, a curriculum or Didaktik text is not the same as a statement of aims, objectives and procedures. It denotes a much more diffuse set of phenomena that includes written and unwritten, explicit and implicit, and visible and hidden elements of education and schooling. In short, a Didaktik text is embedded in the warp and weft of a culture and, by the same token, Didaktik analysis is also cultural analysis.

A classical curriculum analogue of Didaktik analysis is Herbert Spencer's question 'What knowledge is of most worth?' (1859). Yet, modern Didaktik theory is more than the selection of bodies of knowledge. Klafki's work also has a critical element. It asks questions like 'How should classroom life relate to the world beyond schooling?'; 'How might a Didaktik text be cut, supplemented and tailored to fit the exigencies of the historical moment'; and 'How can it also be a statement about citizenship, democracy, sustainable development, and peaceful coexistence?'.

The constructive element in Klafki's Didaktik theory—the difference between what is and what might be—is also rooted in earlier German practice—especially Bildungstheorie. The Bildung notion—which came to prominence in the Enlightenment—relates to the transformative potential of education. It assume that individuals can shape themselves and, in the process, contribute to wider social progress. If a reasonable curriculum question is 'What should they know?', the equivalent Bildung question is 'What should they become?'. Thus, Klafki's critical constructive Didaktik theory seeks to confront historical circumstances in a interpretative, transformative manner. The future is to be designed on the basis of a review of the past, an appraisal of the present and a projection of the future.

A Didaktik text, therefore, is more than a body of knowledge or a cluster of school subjects. It is not an organizational statement about schooling; it is a programmatic statement about the future of culture and society. Accordingly, a Didaktik text is not a curriculum guide. It is long on cultural significance and short on bodies of knowledge. A recent Norwegian publication—*Core Curriculum for Primary, Secondary and Adult Education in Norway* (1994)—illustrates this difference. It is a 40-page illustrated preamble to curriculum practice. It does not feature school subjects. Instead, it projects a range of curriculum principles that include:

> Society is responsible for ensuring that equality of educational opportunity is a reality;

> Education shall be based on fundamental Christian and humanistic values. It should uphold and renew our cultural heritage to provide perspective and guidance for the future;

The ultimate aim of education is to inspire individuals to realize their potential in ways that serve the common good; to nurture humanness in a society in development. (Royal Ministry of Church, Education and Research, 1994)

The Norwegian core curriculum does not stand alone. As a preamble, it is complemented by extension documents. These include curriculum or pedagogic guides for subject and class teachers, and even a curriculum guide for school students in the upper levels of the national school system. In Norway, too, production of these ancillary documents remains a responsibility of the central Ministry of Education. But there is no reason why Didaktik texts cannot be complemented with pedagogic materials produced by other agencies (e.g. municipalities, subject associations, local teachers' groups and school-based teams).

In fact, a national initiative to separate the centralized production of a Didaktik text from the devolved production of pedagogic guides is a current and contrasting feature of curriculum development in Sweden (facilitated by an agency led, incidentally, by another participant in the Oslo conference, Ulf Lundgren). It may be no accident that one of Lundgren's curriculum statements identifies 'the process of making a curriculum' as straddling two social contexts: 'the context of formulation and the context of realization' (Lundgren, 1983, p. 13). At the same time, Lundgren also implies that a Didaktik text need not, in principle, differ from a curriculum text. Both can be equally sensitive to social, cultural and historical circumstances. Nevertheless, recent curriculum practice in England suggests otherwise—a phenomenon that, it seems, also obtains in the USA (cf. Pinar *et.al.*, 1995). European Didaktik texts, like the Norwegian *Core Curriculum*, appear to be so different from their Anglo-American counterparts (e.g. NCC, 1992). If Didaktik texts are about cultural vision, curriculum texts are about classroom minutiae.

Deliberation

But where does Klafki's Didaktik theory intersect with Joseph Schwab's notions of deliberation? My own feeling is that deliberation is also a hermeneutic activity. At the risk of oversimplification, it focuses upon interpreting a Didaktik text to yield pedagogic practices:

> It treats both ends and means . . . as mutually determining one another. It must try to identify, with respect to both, what facts may be relevant. It must try to ascertain the relevant facts in the concrete case. It must try to identify the desiderata in the case. It must generate alternative solutions. It must make every effort to trace the branching pathways of consequences which may flow from each alternative and affect desiderata. It must then weigh alternatives and their costs and consequences against one another, and choose, not the *right* alternative, for there is no such thing, but the *best* one. (Schwab, 1978, pp. 318–9)

Deliberation, therefore, relates to the realization of a Didaktik text in a specific context (my classroom, not classrooms in general). And it is this last point—Schwab's prioritization of pedagogic practice over Didaktik theory—that also provides a bridge between the ideas of Wolfgang Klafki and Donald Schön. In effect, Schwab's curriculum practice is the same as Klafki's pedagogic practice; and both take shape in Lundgren's 'context of realization'. Indeed, Schwab's 'the practical' (p. 288) operates at the same level as Lundgren's 'context of realization'. Its 'subject matter' is 'always something taken as concrete and particular and treated as indefinitely susceptible to circumstance' (p. 289). Schwab also identifies the context of realization in terms of curriculum commonplaces. His 'language for curriculum', that is, embraces the 'co-ordination' of 'four commonplaces of *equal* rank: the learner, the teacher the milieu and the subject matter' (pp. 371–2).

Reflection

Donald Schön also starts from practical matters. But he replaces the contemplation of deliberation with the dynamism of 'reflection-in-action'. Or does he? Schön's terminology is problematic. Michael Eraut has recently argued that it is illusory: 'Most [of Schön's] examples fail to provide evidence of reflection-in-action and none of them relate to crowded settings like classrooms' (1995, p. 9). These latter settings, Eraut feels, are the site of 'hot' reflection whereas much of Schön's writing, like that of Dewey (1933), relate to 'cool' reflections conducted beyond the immediate contexts of practice (cf. hermeneutic deliberation). In Schwab's terminology, Eraut feels that Schön's reflection is conducted with reference to curriculum commonplaces but not within curriculum commonplaces.

But there is another, contrasting, source of Schön's view of reflective practice. His defense of reflection also arises from his critique of 'technical rationality'. His view of professional practice is that it cannot validly be steered by the 'canons' of technical rationality. It should, instead, be considered not from the 'high ground . . . of research-based theory and technique' but from the 'indeterminate, swampy zones of practice' (1987, p. 3).

Schön, like Schwab, feels that practice takes place within indeterminate, open systems. Teaching, therefore, cannot be envisioned as a uni-linear activity. It is never possible to define or control the contingencies surrounding its realization. Necessarily, so the argument runs, teaching is suffused with branching pathways whose selection requires deliberation and/or reflection-in-action.

Schön's writings have been important in the United Kingdom. They are consonant with the feelings of practitioners. Their teaching, so they believe, is constantly buffeted by irritating contingencies; and much of their time is taken up with accommodating and overcoming these contingencies (or commonplaces). As a result, many teachers feel that an ability to surmount such difficulties is the touchstone of their professional practice.

Quick-witted, reflection-in-action may make them a professional; but does it also make them a good professional? Returning to Schwab's terminology, professional practice can be traced in two ways: (1) as the following of 'multiple pathways'; and (2) as the weighing of 'alternatives and their costs'. In the first case, there is the danger that schoolteachers become automatons. Their practice is routinized, rutted, and thus relatively insulated against new contingencies. Insofar as they cease to weigh alternatives against desiderata, they are run-down professionals whose practice is only sustained by the curriculum and pedagogic commonplaces of yesteryear. Their 'reflection in action' is conservative. It is reactive rather than reflective, 'phenomenological' rather than 'hermeneutic' (Uljens, 1995, p. 16).

Hot Reflection

Deliberation *for* curriculum is not reflection *in* action; just as knowing schoolteaching is not the same as doing schoolteaching. Hot reflection, in Eraut's sense, arises from three classroom contingencies. First, that pedagogic practices are routinely subject to classroom disruption. Secondly, that teachers take counter action to refocus classroom activities. And thirdly, that this responsive action entails reflection-in-action.

Experienced teachers may anticipate disruptions, accepting them as both irritants and opportunities. Inexperienced teachers, on the other hand, may be displaced by such disruptions, regarding them merely as irritants. In the first case, experienced teachers have 'situational understandings' that, Elliott suggests, prefigure 'possibilities for action' (Elliott , 1993, pp. 73, 75, following Dreyfus). Indeed, experienced professionals may deliberately exploit such procedural indeterminacy. Their lesson plans are based on starting points, with the rest of the lesson left to the intervening possibilities of classroom life.

Such an improvisational, yet professional, model of lesson planning should not, however, be regarded as procedurally aimless and goal-free. Deliberate recourse to 'possibilities for action' is itself a lesson goal which, in its turn, can serve strategic goals beyond the limits of a single lesson. Thus, professional deliberation and professional reflection are inseparable yet different. They are both cool and hot. Indeed, this dialectic of (cool) deliberation and (hot) reflection is also embodied in the distinction between 'Pädagogik' and 'Bildungstheorie'. It is also equivalent to the contrast between a curriculum plan of reachable goals and a Didaktik vision of transcendent goals. The Norwegian *Core Curriculum* also acknowledges this tension. It prefaces its principles with the statement: 'Aims in this connection are a) something to work towards [and] b) something one can know whether one approaches or not' (p. 4).

In an important sense, the dialectic of transcendent and short-term educational goals is trivial: schooling has always served different purposes. Yet, an appreciation of these differences, gained through attendance at the Oslo conference, helps me to understand why some German University Departments of Education have Pädagogik in their titles while others prefer

Didaktik. From a cross-national comparative perspective, it helps to explain the juxtaposition of the words 'curriculum' and 'instruction' in university departmental labels in the USA (e.g. the departments of 'Curriculum and Instruction' at the University of Wisconsin and Teachers College, Columbia University). On a more parochial level, too, it might also explain the bemusement that greeted my suggestion that the name of Liverpool University's Faculty of Education and Extension Studies be changed to the Faculty of Pedagogics and Didactics!

References

Dewey, J. (1933). *How We Think,* (2nd ed.). Boston: Heath.

Elliott, J. (ed.) (1993). *Reconstructing Teacher Education.* London: Falmer Press.

Eraut, M. (1995). Schön schock: a case for reframing reflection-in-action. *Teachers and Teaching: Theory and Practice, 1,* 9–22.

Lundgren, U. (1983). *Between Hope and Happening: Text and Context in Curriculum.* Geelong: Deakin University Press.

NCC (1992). *Starting Out with the National Curriculum: An Introduction to the National Curriculum and Religious Education.* York (UK): National Curriculum Council.

Pinar, W.F., Reynolds, W.M. Slattery, P. & Taubman, P.M. (1995). *Understanding Curriculum: An Introduction to the Study of Historical and Contemporary Curriculum Discourses.* New York: Peter Lang.

Royal Ministry of Church, Education and Research (1994). *Core Curriculum for Primary, Secondary and Adult Education in Norway.* Oslo: Royal Ministry of Church, Education and Research.

Schön, D.A. (1987). *Educating the Reflective Practitioner: Toward a New Design for Teaching and Learning in the Professions.* London: Jossey-Bass.

Schwab, J. J. (1978). Science, Curriculum, and Liberal Education. In I. Westbury & N.J. Wilkof (Eds.) *Selected Essays.* Chicago: University of Chicago Press.

Uljens, M. (1995). School didactics and reflective pedagogic practice. Paper presented at the 'Didaktik and/or Curriculum conference', Oslo, August 9–13th, 1995.

Chapter 5

The Theoretic Meets the Practical: The Practical Wins

O. L. Davis, Jr.

Curriculum may be defined easily if not comfortably. On the other hand, to understand the school curriculum in the United States seems seldom helped by simple reference to definitions. Understanding remains elusive, difficult, and problematic, not just for American scholars, but for school practitioners and citizens alike. Pursuit of understanding, nevertheless, persists as task and opportunity. The present analysis displays the current state of one continuing pursuit of increased understanding. It seeks to foster clarity and to freshen awareness about the curriculum.

Six Fundamental Features of the American Curriculum Scene

At the outset, several matters must be recognized. They should not be accepted uncritically. Some of their dimensions continue to be contested vigorously. Others are known largely in outline or impression and await further exploration. To some unknown extent, also, they may be unique to the American experience of curriculum. Still, they provide a convenient and responsible basis for the analysis that follows.

The American school curriculum has never served to certify qualifications of its graduates. Some current versions of school offerings, to be sure, are promoted as "preparation" for subsequent specific work experience or entrance into further

education. These programs and substantial contemporary public rhetoric advocate an increase in "school-to-work" schemes.
However, few actual programs exist to "qualify" graduates for
post-school occupations. Many firms, to be sure, set a high
school diploma as a screen by which to restrict the number
of applicants for jobs. Thus, the diploma has become a kind
of business "qualification", but one unrelated to the school
curriculum.

In only one sense is the American school curriculum perceived properly as a qualification. High school graduation has
been and is a common but certainly not a sufficient prerequi-
site for university entrance. The general liberal high school
curriculum, without ties to special qualifications, remains
a standard feature of American elementary and secondary
schooling.

American public schools, moreover, were *not* established to
educate any elite group within society, neither ones of intellectual talent, social position, race, or parents' financial success
or misfortune. Today's American public schools continue to
include or be open to what some have called "all the children
of all the people." In fact, until very recently, only a very few
non-public schools were established to favor special groups of
children and youth. The number of schools that serve elites
and other special groups admittedly has risen during the past
40 years. This development, in no small measure, has occurred
as a response to legal requirements for desegregation of public education, to an increase in the number of parents who
seek a deliberately religiously-oriented (currently, mainly fundamental Protestant) education for their children, and to a
swelling perception that public schools are inadequate and
unsafe. Nevertheless, the vast majority of American public
schools flourish and continue to welcome all students undifferentiated by talent, social prestige, ethnicity, or career goals.

American public schools were established and have been
maintained and expanded for purposes neither specifically
intellectual nor social. Still, they have served both these secondary goals as they have pursued their central aim. The central purpose for American public education has been to foster
children's entry into participation in the *civic* enterprise of
American society. Certainly, this purpose routinely has been

contested. It is under severe stress at the present time. However, it has *not* been overturned. This robust *civic* purpose, recognizably, has been and will be revisited, reconsidered, and renegotiated from time to time. Its relative strength has varied over the years and should be expected to wax and wane in the future. Its durability, however, testifies to this purpose's potency among the shared sentiments that constitute the American culture.

American public schools and their curriculum were *not* and *are not now* the creatures of state or federal governments. Originally, local community groups or local governments created schools. Now, under state statutes, local governments or taxing districts create and manage schools for children residing in the area encompassed by the local authority. Within the past century, public schools within the 50 states came under the increased regulation of and received increased financial support from those state governments. Within the past several decades, the percentage of state government support has dropped precipitously. Concurrently, yet incongruously, the amount and type of state regulation appears to be withering as well as increasing. The *local community* nature of public education continues to have minor federal or national financial support and even less governance.

The essential point here is that American public schools and their curricula continue to be governed and supported mainly at the local level. Commentary and reports and proposals for national initiatives, including national curriculum standards, consequently, exist primarily as rhetorical appeals. These advocacies, regardless of their attractiveness, magnitude, and volume, cannot be implemented unless they are processed through discussion and decisions in thousands of individual school districts and many thousands of individual school units. American public education continues to be a local enterprise.

Two additional features merit recognition. Neither represents fixed positions. Both present in early American society, they continue to exist as elements of tension. They appear to be most accurately understood as expressions about *emphasis* and *direction*.

Across their history, American public schools and their curricula *have not been* guided mainly by the *theoretic*, that is, grand

schemes of educational and, even, economic and political philosophy. The persisting ideal of public schooling's contribution to *civic virtue* or *purpose* represents the principal exception to this historical interpretation. American schools have
been and are understood primarily as altogether practical institutions intended for the education (service) of children and
youth of the entire society. Additionally, their change over time,
especially their curricular changes, however inconsequential
or substantial, has proceeded largely on practical grounds. That
is, American schools have been and are agencies of action. This
claim does not dispute the influence of a number of theoretic
advocacies on American schools and their curricula, especially
during the 20th century. These rhetorical proposals ranged
from Deweyian child-centered notions to business management
justifications and procedures to rigidly behaviorist proposals
and programs. Many rejected ideas have been discovered anew,
if not reborn, and, repackaged and marketed, they have enjoyed short periods of popularity. At times, their influence has
been insistent and vigorously asserted. Nevertheless, the practical routinely has survived and the theoretic appears to have
disappeared except for its residue of emptied slogans and imagined presence.

The last of these six important understandings about the
American school curriculum may be more arguable even than
the claim for its essential practicality. Still, the point merits
explicit assertion. Over time, concern for individual students,
their personal meanings, and their individual potentialities has
remained a continuing and prominent emphasis of American
education. The rise and persistence of bureaucracy is only one
pressure to have exacted fearsome consequences on this profound sense of person. Bureaucracy's vigor and its ruthless
concern for efficient production has failed, however, to extin-
guish the resilient American concern and respect for human
individuality.

Of these six features of American public schools and their
curricula, the first four represent widely accepted received wisdom. The last two, however, seem to be understood inadequately or simply unknown by most Americans, citizens and
scholars alike. Without question, these two features—practicality and individuality—have been obscured or underrecognized

if not hidden by the conventional rhetoric about curriculum in American schools. This missed understanding characterizes standard histories of that curriculum (e.g., Kliebard, 1986; Tanner and Tanner, 1980). Robust analysis of proposals ordinarily substitutes for reasoned and interpreted story of curriculum commonplaces. The essential error in understanding lies in the general acceptance of the rhetoric of advocacy as an accurate, responsible, and sufficient rendering of curriculum realities. This flawed historiography must be corrected by interpretations based upon thick descriptions of the nature and experience of curriculum realities in ordinary practice, with mindful consideration of their complexity and convolutions (Davis, 1977, 1991).

The remainder of this analysis focuses on the American experience of the practical in curriculum. This major focus lies at the heart of the views or images of the contemporary curriculum and efforts to improve or to change it.

The Real and Illusory Triumph of Bureaucracy, the Factory, and Efficiency in the American Curriculum

According to standard American educational history, bureaucracy and the factory model of schooling triumphed in the early part of this century (e.g., Callahan, 1962; Tyack, 1974). Increasingly professionalized superintendents and their enlarged staffs of administrators led the educational bureaucracies. These new "managers" accordingly sought to refashion American schools in the pattern of American business organization. *Efficiency, centralization,* and *professionalism* were the movement's prominent slogans.

During the first forty years of this century, much of the rhetoric of American schooling became a curious mixture of community boosterism and almost evangelical advocacy of the virtues of business enterprise. Across the years, public schools, in fact, became increasingly bureaucratic. They also became more centralized. Policies and decision made about employment of teachers and daily schedules, about curriculum and textbooks, determined in earlier times by principals and/or teachers in individual schools were arrogated to central system-wide administration. The sizes of school district governance groups were reduced and these school boards began routinely to differentiate policy and administrative decisions. Many individual schools and school districts, although mainly those in large city districts, grew larger mainly as a result of the national shift in population from rural to urban centers. Many practices and the bulk of professional rhetoric constitute substantial evidence that the cult of efficiency and its centralized bureaucracy triumphed throughout American public education.

Upon closer examination of a number of school realities, however, a somewhat diminished view of this asserted victory becomes apparent. The bureaucracy that triumphed was mainly that in the school systems of the largest American cities. To be sure, organizational charts of schools in many small cities and some rural areas were redrawn to mimic those of their city cousins, but little serious organizational change seemed to occur in those districts. The professional "talk" may have stressed bureaucratic decisions, economic efficiency, and schools as producers of graduates. Reality, in most districts, seemed inconsistent with that rhetoric. Ordinarily overlooked, also, is that the documented changes were primarily *local* in nature. Not uncommonly, such shifts were led by local superintendents of schools who sought to emulate practices touted as "modern" or "innovative" by other superintendents, ones usually separated from them by considerable geographic distance.

Throughout most of this century, centralization almost *never* included *state* departments of education. These state agencies, in fact, led mainly by the exhortative influence of individual state superintendents of schools. They routinely were deprived of funds to expand regulatory and service functions until the 1960s. Even at that late date, the expansion was not prompted by an extension of the logic and rhetoric of centralization. Rather, that centralization was fueled by the necessity of state distribution and administration of federal government grants for targeted purposes (e.g., expansion of services to children whose native language was not English).

Consolidation of small and mainly rural schools, advocated consistently during the height of the efficiency movement, progressed by fits and spurts. It never truly succeeded until the 1960s. The economic efficiency of rural school consolidation, asserted passionately by its advocates for half a century, remains unproved.

In addition, the triumph of centralization *never* reached the federal level. Until the 1960s, at least, the federal Office of Education can only be described as a small, anemic, data-gathering organization. It had no power and very little voice and influence. Now, as a cabinet-level department, its anemia persists and its political capital is marginal.

The triumph of bureaucracy and efficiency was real—in some city school systems. Beyond those few still local but large systems, however, the victory appears rhetorical and illusory at best. Assertion and advocacy never sufficiently represented actual practice. This public rhetoric expanded into believed myth. Accurate historical understanding was contained in a very shallow vessel of memory (Davis, 1992).

In no case is this illusion more obvious than in the history of the American school curriculum. Standard accounts of the U. S. curriculum movement date its beginning with the technical and procedural outlines advocated by Franklin Bobbitt in the immediate post-World War I years. Without doubt, Bobbitt (1918) translated the time-management of manufacturing efficiency experts into a formulaic process for local curriculum making. His techniques led to adaptations advanced by W. W. Charters and other new curriculum "experts". Claims to the actual influence of these procedures on curriculum practice, however, appears tenuous. Not uncommonly, verbal assertion won bibliographic and unfortunate historical prominence. Even so, the beginning technical processes for curriculum making can be understood as crude approximations to the elegantly simple formulations advanced a generation later by Ralph W. Tyler.

A doctoral student of Charters and Bobbitt, Tyler entered the curriculum field through his leadership of the evaluation staff of the Eight Year Study. His understanding of local school curriculum development proceeded quickly. Especially with the assistance of Hilda Taba, he organized his ideas into a set of principles. Several years later, he issued them as an elaborated outline of his curriculum course at the University of Chicago (1949). His advice for curriculum planning, commonly known as the Tyler Rationale, enjoys the unlikely status as near secular canonization. Writers about curriculum ordinarily represent it as the classic statement about curriculum technical rationality. Clearly, it occupies pride of position on any bibliography and most discourse about curriculum. Its published text, not withstanding its exalted status, represents inadequately Tyler's experience in local curriculum development efforts. In addition, little substantial evidence supports its asserted influence on local school curriculum development. Likely, the Tyler Rationale's general usefulness has been exaggerated beyond any reasonable estimate. On the other hand, Tyler's modest course outline has served well the careers of a number of prominent advocates and critics and has been the intellectual foil for an entire school of curriculum reconceptualists.

Without regard to the Tyler Rationale's reputed errors, the most serious mistake is not its own or Tyler's. Rather, the error rests in the minds of practicing curriculum workers and scholars who simplisticly believe that this rationale represented and continues to represent *actual* and *practical* curriculum development in American schools. Stated differently, this all too common human condition substitutes wish for reality and confuses "should" with "is". Enough evidence is available to advance two reasonable conclusions. The technical rationality of the positions of Bobbitt, Charters, and Tyler represented neither properly nor adequately the rich variety of local, practical curriculum development initiatives undertaken in American schools. It also fails to reflect the contemporary scene. Assertion of and belief in the theoretic did not make the theoretic real. It still does not.

Dimensions of the Reality of the Practical in American Curriculum

Quite possibly, the local nature of American schools made possible their early attention to the practical. Separated within a vast geography, their teachers and administrators enjoyed independence from most control even by state governments. Their problems, consequently, were practical. For example, choice of textbooks, usually, was a decision of the teachers who would use them. Curriculum was a matter of action by necessity. Theories of that action only slowly developed and, even in these days, do not compete well for acceptance with formulations labeled as *scientific*. Still, the practical ordinarily demands and receives attention in American education.

Active involvement of teachers became an early feature of city schools' curriculum development activities. Chicago and Los Angeles school superintendents, for example, required inclusion of teachers on curriculum committees in the early years of this century. Charged with the production of a course of study, these committees considered the wisdom, merits, and nature of the suggestions in the document as well as details of goals, content selection and organization, and teaching materials and procedures. Slowly, increasing numbers of school districts, although surely never a majority, involved teachers in this type of curriculum work. To be sure, most of these committees also included principals, supervisors, and, in some cases, the school system's superintendent. The nature of this early practical curriculum work, likely a nascent form of deliberation, remains unknown. In all probability, it is lost to history because documentation of such activity was and continues to be less important than the action itself.

Local school curriculum revision efforts, by the early 1920s, constituted an educational cottage industry. They focused on quite different problems, took varying forms, and employed no standard procedure. Some of these local projects, for example, one in Denver, Colorado, yielded sustained, public, and highly visible curriculum reforms.

Other programs quickly faded away, their successes and/or failures unrecorded. Accounts from several of these inter-war efforts illustrate the importance and viability of the practical. They also reveal that the reality of school curriculum development was neither directed by nor reflected the prominent curriculum rhetoric, specifically that framed by the advocacies of Bobbitt and Charters and, later by Tyler.

In 1922, the Los Angeles' superintendent of schools invited Franklin Bobbitt to advise the city's secondary school teachers on a comprehensive revision of the system's high school curriculum. Bobbitt accepted the task. As part of his preparation, Bobbitt directed his University of Chicago curriculum students in the analysis of adult activities and, from them, the development of a set of objectives. In essence, he followed his own technical procedures. Bobbitt subsequently took these objectives with him to his meetings with Los Angeles high school teachers. At this point, the historical evidence thins. An individual reasonably close to the situation described the Los Angeles teachers' reactions to Bobbitt's procedures and objectives as a "revolt". Apparently, the teachers refused to write additional objectives called for by Bobbitt's procedure.

They also rejected the objectives that his students had helped prepare. Quickly, this Los Angeles curriculum revision sputtered to premature closure. Bobbitt, back in Chicago, published the objectives that were rejected in Los Angeles (Hopkins, 1978a). Curriculum techniques confronted the practical; the practical won.

During the same general time, Jesse Newlon became superintendent of schools in Denver, Colorado. As an early assertion of the legitimacy of his leadership, he persuaded the city's Board of Education to launch a number of highly visible initiatives. These included construction of several new schools. He also secured their agreement to finance a total revision of the Denver school curriculum. With a number of activities underway, Newlon invited a number of prominent educational scholars to come to Denver to advise the committees of teachers that he appointed. These individuals, each an authority in a curriculum subject (e.g., spelling, arithmetic), spent a period of time with local teachers and administrators. By the end of its first year, the project floundered in listless activity and unfulfilled expectations. Again, the practical overwhelmed the theoretic. In this case, however, a significant and rapid change in course rescued the operations.

Superintendent Newlon employed two nearby university professors of education to co-direct the local curriculum revision efforts. Within the following year, the committees of teachers became increasingly active and productive. Released part-time from class assignments, teachers on the committees conducted research. They developed agendas important to their perceptions of need and possibility. They gathered information, including that from visiting authorities, about the advances in scholarship related to their school subjects. They reported and listened to colleagues at their schools about topics that should be stressed and abandoned. They did much more. Slowly, but within another year, the first of a complete set of subject curriculum guides were produced, discussed with other teachers, and disseminated for trial use throughout the system. Teachers on the committees helped their colleagues to understand the rationale and newly selected content and next steps to classroom practice. The committees worked at different speeds, employed different procedures for their work, and produced different kinds of reports and courses of study. Some committees (e.g., home economics) employed task analysis as part of their inquiries; other groups never attempted this procedure. Subsequently, Newlon appointed an assistant superintendent and, later, a curriculum director to replace the part-time university consultants in an effort to institutionalize the continuous nature of curriculum revision in Denver's schools (Newlon, 1927; Hopkins, 1978a, 1978b). Throughout this experience of a system-wide change, the curriculum development operation accepted *partial* rather than *total* change. The practical was honored.

The popularity of local curriculum revision during the 1920s swelled. Many school superintendents and some of their teachers believed that a revitalized curriculum could benefit students in their schools. This belief in the efficacy of curriculum revision, approaching almost faddish intensity, was held by school leaders across the nation and in large systems as well as small towns and rural districts. In 1923, the professional association of the nation's superintendents called for the establishment of a National Commission on the Curriculum. Within only a few months, this Commission began operations, received major funding support from a foundation, and outlined an ambitious three-year program. The Commission subsequently developed four annual books which highlighted the current research related to the curriculum offerings at elementary, junior high school, and high school levels, and which described local school curriculum activities as an aid to superintendents and teachers in systems of all sizes and types. Also, it established a group of 100 school systems across the nation, each of which pledged to undertake a curriculum revision project and to assign local administrative leadership to the project. This effort clearly magnified the interest, activity, and variety of local school curriculum improvement in the United States. Of the extant reports of local efforts, only a very few reported the influence on their work of Bobbitt's or Charters' technical procedures. Almost all reports noted the involvement of local teachers. Most observed that the curriculum revisions were suggestive and tentative, not prescriptive nor final. Some projects called on out-of-system consultants; others did not (Davis, 1995a). Nationwide, the theoretic did not direct local efforts; the practical guided those developments.

Even during the economic depression of the 1930s, curriculum revision remained lively in a number of local settings. Clearly among the most enduring legacies was that of Hollis L. Caswell's pioneering series of state-level reforms. Indeed, Caswell's work lifted the term *curriculum development* to replace *curriculum making* (Caswell and Campbell, 1935). Several of Caswell's ideas, in retrospect, seem deceptively simple. They were sparked during his visit to schools in Mississippi, one of the nation's poorest states, a year after a statewide committee had written a new state course of study. Routinely, in school after school, he found copies of this curriculum document used as doorstops, unopened copies hidden away in cupboards and desks, and copies opened but unread. After reflecting on this and other experiences with teachers and administrators, he developed three notions that became features of his subsequent curriculum work.

Teachers, according to Caswell's notion, were not just included as members on committees; they were essential to the entire process. Their contributions emphasized a "bottom-up" procedure rather than the conventional administrative "top-down" process. Too, he concluded that the idea of curriculum revision itself was inadequate. For curriculum to be revitalized, i.e., made viable and to live, teachers must learn more about their subjects, must consider with one another the purposes of schooling and their subject's role in those goals, and more about advances in teaching practices. In his reconceptualization, Caswell understood that *curriculum development* involved teachers' development of *their own new and increased understanding about the curriculum*. Many years later, some scholars would advocate that teachers become their own "curriculum theorists". Such a notion likely would have been too grand an expectation for Caswell. He recognized that teachers must know more in order to act more appropriately and that their own curriculum development would begin with their awareness of their present actions. Caswell also advocated that teachers study together in groups for at least a year before they began to invent and to discuss possible changes in the local curriculum. He advanced a conception of curriculum that sought, most of all, that teachers understand that curriculum must attend both to substantive knowledge and to the nature of pupils' personal experiences (Burlbaw, 1989).

Another major contribution to understanding curriculum development as attention to the practical emerged from the Eight Year Study (1932-1942). Among several persisting ideas developed in that program, one feature was central. The project consultants, including Ralph Tyler and Hilda Taba, encouraged teachers, as their first and continuing activity in curriculum development to talk together about what they were doing. Their first questions to teachers were, "What are you now doing? Describe what you did yesterday in your class." Only later, sometimes much later, did teachers begin to wonder what they might do or what organization, emphases, and materials might help them do better what they wanted to do (Rice, 1978). In the real world of schooling, certainly, Tyler understood curriculum work properly to begin and to proceed with the practical. His landmark rationale, published some years later, unfortunately obscured the practical and seemed to emphasize a linear, means-ends, factory production model of curriculum work.

This series of episodes from the real scenes of curriculum development in local schools could be expanded to discuss a number of recent examples. This treatment could include, for example, most of the science and mathematics projects of the 1960s, several composition or "writing" projects, even Madeline Hunter's prescriptive teaching procedures. A common thread runs through explanations of failure and success. It is the recognized sense of the practical, local, and particular (Doyle and Ponder, 1977). Robust understanding of curriculum development in practice betrays the illusion of American curriculum development as procedural, only rational, and technical. The rhetoric of Bobbitt and Charters and Tyler and their followers simply does not accord with reality. Their rhetoric, in sum, was intended to be modern, scientific, and persuasive; it clearly was persuasive to many. Unfortunately, those persuaded understood the technical prescriptions as verifiable, tested recipes for action. They were neither. Additionally, they were not accurate predictors of practice. In fact, they never "worked" as they were portrayed. In the meantime, this persuasive rhetoric survived and continues to obscure the evidence of actual and reasonably successful curriculum development activities. Consequences of this persisting misunderstanding about American curriculum development are as real as they perniciously endure. Their errors blind or frustrate contemporary curriculum developments.

Prospects for Re-imaged Curriculum Development in the United States

As noted earlier, perhaps the most serious consequence of this unremembered curriculum history is the degree to which American educational and political leaders believe the myth of rationality. They actually believe that they can manage curriculum revision from state, federal, or local central offices, by fiat or directive, and by technical "training" of teachers. They believe that curriculum work is of the same order of problem as a malfunction of school plumbing. Not only can the problem be "fixed," that "fix" can be accomplished rapidly, inexpensively, and likely, can be accomplished best by calling on the services of an out-of-system maintenance person or consultant. Such grievous error is only compounded within the current political climate which emphasizes reduction of public expenditures and increased external controls.

The early prospects of serious, widespread, and refreshed curriculum development in U. S. schools, consequently, appear only faintly. Political manifestos, like Education 2000, and inflamed rhetoric about necessary "systemic change" and "world class educational standards" provide neither support nor guidance for solid, local curriculum development. All ignore the practical and its routine commonplaces. Note, for example, just three prominent current curriculum advocacies.

Systemic change of curriculum and schools appears to be the one best remedy for the perceived failure of American economic competitiveness. Altered international economic realities and changed patterns of American production and consumption magnify Americans' concern that something seriously is wrong with the nation. Massive restructuring of business represents a sober response to the perceived national need. Legislators who seek to reduce public spending easily target schooling, the major cost item in state budgets. In a call too reminiscent of President Lyndon B. Johnson's assertion during the Vietnam war that the nation could have both "guns and butter," legislators call for school staffs to be reduced (or "downsized"), for programs to be streamlined, for schools to be restructured, while promising the public that more pupils can be educated to higher standards at lower costs. Systemic change is the curative slogan of the moment. Political faith insists that the changes be accomplished promptly. Educational leaders, emboldened by their possession of procedural and technical guides, fall into ranks. Neither current politicians nor educational leaders recognize their uninformed actions. They remember the past incorrectly and act as if they really control situations and people. The price of exaggerated expectations continues to be excessive. Curriculum change, as Alice Miel (1946) reminded the field fifty years ago, is a social process. This change, similar to other public policy, must account for the practical, is almost never rapid, and almost always proceeds unevenly and partially. Appropriate public policy, in fact, reasonably can hope for only marginal results (Neustadt and May, 1986). This reminder can serve curriculum reform initiatives.

Proposals for *national curriculum standards* likely share the prospective failure of calls for systemic change. The standards movement is burdened by liabilities. Current political climate in the United States, for one example, opposes national guidance or control of almost all public efforts, except for the armed forces. This opposition is grounded in the belief that national guidelines and support for health care, welfare, and, certainly, education are unnecessarily invasive of local responsibility and control. This political situation all but assures that the proposed national curriculum standards are dead-on-arrival. Were the political climate favorable, adoption of proposed standards would proceed on a district by district basis, and, even, a school by school basis, absolutely an ineffective route to general changes in public policy and practice. Such adoption, again disregarding inherent political contentiousness, could be effective only by a massive re-education, not the technically unsophisticated notion of "retraining", of American teachers. The costs of such a reeducation enterprise, without attention to the expense of new materials and equipment, have not even been estimated.

Political demands for *curriculum accountability* extend the myth of rational curriculum reform. They are coupled, of course, with the political threats of retribution, embarrassment, and dismissal of teachers and administrators if pupils do not learn the politically determined curriculum. Again, the myth of a rational industrial production model is asserted. Supported by profound ignorance, the model assures an active role only for teachers and the curriculum; the myth assumes that pupils, their parents, and the context of community agency are passive only. Such misunderstanding misconstrues the nature of curriculum. Simply, the curriculum is intentional, not consequential (Davis, 1995b). Teachers and public education surely will endure a host of miseries until this flawed sense of accountability is withdrawn as it inevitably must be.

Important amidst these several flawed theoretic proposals for curriculum reform are other diversions and detours from the practical. Attention to thinking skills, multiple intelligence, brain-based teaching procedures, integrated curriculum, and authentic assessment name only a few of these diversions. Through commitment of time, "teacher training", and funds to these highly visible and assertedly innovative practices, American schools divert public concern from possible, practical actions to theoretic proposals that are unlikely to survive except as empty slogans.

Awareness of the political demands and attractive diversions, however, is not simply a matter of interest. It can constitute a ground of opportunity to restore robustness to the practical through deliberation (Reid, 1992, 1994). This possibility for right understanding derives from recent advances in political-cultural theory, or what some have called grid-group analysis (Thompson, Ellis, and Wildavsky, 1990). Schooling and curriculum development in the United States emphasize both hierarchy and external prescription. These features seem unlikely to disappear not withstanding a number of trenchant critiques. What *can* change, what *changed* during previous episodes of productive curriculum development, is the *relative influences* of external prescription and hierarchy.

Characteristics of several prominent curriculum proposals (e.g., systemic reform) include *high* external prescription and relatively *low group* involvement. In this kind of situation, teachers assume that they are powerless; moreover, these assumptions are shared by others. Teachers' actions are understood to be only capricious; their professional lives, in essence, are a kind of lottery. Administratively, this situation reasonably may be described as a *despotism*. The predictable consequences for teachers is much more than "deskilling"; it is the rapid growth of *fatalism*. Not dissimilar to slaves or prisoners, they seek only to survive. Essential to survival is an endless series of diversions, none that challenge external authority but some of which offer the prospect of sanity amidst personal despair or anguish. Understood in these terms, curriculum demands or requirements external to the school (e.g., state mandated curriculum assessment tests), at least within schools of a democratic society, approach the opprobrium of utter immorality.

Removal of external requirements in this type of situation, however superficially attractive, likely would change but not improve either the condition of teachers or of schools. On the other hand, the rigor and force of some external demands could be *reduced*. This decreased force, *coupled with* an *increased* and authentic group involvement, makes possible an increased sense of community (Macmurray, 1991). It also appears to *reduce* individual teacher isolation. As individual teachers increasingly connect with one another and as they recognize that their personal power within the hierarchical group has expanded, individual teachers once isolated are gripped by an exhilaration of surprise. As individuals, they matter. Although not free to act on individual whim or caprice, they recognize the potential of their contributions to communal deliberation and decisions. Indeed, decreased external requirements within a hierarchy of differential roles appears to move individuals closer to the margin that separates hierarchy and egalitarianism.

The Practical and Its Continuing Pursuit

Within this reasonable domain of lessened but not absent external requirements *and* the continuing construction of solid community relationships, deliberation of the practical in curriculum appears to be a fruitful prospect. That the theoretic has suffered loss tumbling over loss in previous times offers solid assurance that the practical will claim victory in subsequent confrontations. Recovery of belief in this probability, to be sure, is a political and social enterprise. It will not happen by wish. On the other hand, the necessary work for its achievement represents, without guarantees, the continued pursuit of curriculum possibility.

Notes

I acknowledge appreciation to Matthew D. Davis for his important contributions to this paper.

References

Bobbitt, F. (1918). *The Curriculum.* Boston: Houghton Mifflin.

Burlbaw, L.M. (1989). *Hollis Leland Caswell's Contributions to the Development of the Curriculum Field.* [Unpublished Ph.D. dissertation]. Austin: The University of Texas at Austin.

Callahan, R.E. (1962). *Education and the Cult of Efficiency: A Study of the Social Forces That Have Shaped the Administration of the Public Schools.* Chicago: University of Chicago Press.

Caswell, H. L. & Campbell, D.S (1935). *Curriculum Development.* New York: American Book Co.

Davis, O.L. Jr. (1977). The Nature and Boundaries of Curriculum History: A Contribution to Dialogue over a Yearbook and Its Review. *Curriculum Inquiry, 7,* 157–168.

Davis, O.L. Jr. (1991). Historical Inquiry: Telling Real Stories. In E. C. Short. (Ed.), *Forms of Curriculum Inquiry,* pp. 77–87. Albany: State University of New York Press.

Davis, O. L. Jr. (1992). Memory, Our Educational Practicc, and History. *The Educational Forum, 56,* 375–379.

Davis, O. L. Jr. (1995a). *Nationwide Cooperation to Revise Local Curricula: American Superintendents and their 1920s Commission on the Curriculum.* [Unpublished paper presented at the Society for the Study of Curriculum History, San Francisco, April 18].

Davis, O. L. Jr. (1995b). Schools and Teachers Offer; Pupils Take. *Journal of Curriculum and Supervision, 10,* 283–285.

Doyle, W. & Ponder Gerald. (1977/1978). The Practicality Ethic in Teacher Decision Making. *Interchange, 8,* 1–12.

Hopkins, L.T. (1978a). Oral History Interview, April 28–29, 1978. *Oral History in Education Collection.* The University of Texas at Austin: College of Education

Hopkins, L.T. (1978b). My Curriculum Viewpoint. [Unpublished paper, mimeo.]. August 1978. *Hopkins Papers, Oral*

History in Education Collection. The University of Texas at Austin: College of Education

Kliebard, H. M. (1986). *The Struggle for the American Curriculum.* New York: Routledge.

Macmurray, J (1991). *Persons in Relation.* Atlantic Highlands, NJ: Humanities Press International.

Miel, A. (1946). *Changing the Curriculum: A Social Process.* New York: D. Appleton-Century.

Neustadt, R. E. & May, E. R. (1986). *Thinking in Time; The Uses of History for Decision Makers.* New York: The Free Press.

Newlon, J.H (1927). *Review of Four-Year Period August, 1923 to July, 1927.* Denver: the Board of Education.

Reid, W.A. (1992). *The Pursuit of Curriculum; Schooling and the Public Interest.* Norwood, NJ: Ablex.

Reid, W.A. (1994). *Curriculum Planning as Deliberation.* Report No.11. 1994. University of Oslo: Institute for Educational Research.

Rice, C.R. (1978). Oral History Interview, October 5, 1978. *Oral History in Education Collection,* The University of Texas at Austin.

Tanner, D. & Tanner, L. N. (1990). *History of the School Curriculum.* New York: Macmillan.

Thompson, M., Ellis, R. & Wildavsky, A. (1990). *Cultural Theory.* Boulder: Westview Press.

Tyack, D.B. (1974). *The One Best System: A History of American Urban Education.* Cambridge, MA: Harvard University Press.

Tyler, R.W. (1949). *Basic Principles of Curriculum and Instruction.* Chicago: University of Chicago Press.

Chapter 6

Changing Concepts of Curriculum: From "Bildung" to "Learning" to "Experience"

Developments in (West)Germany from the 1960s to 1990

Ewald Terhart

Will curriculum research solve those problems . . . left over by traditional Lehrplantheorie? *(H.Blankertz, 1970)*

Curriculum research has not reached the goals its proponents formulated. *(H.Blankertz, 1980)*

Introduction

The title of my chapter, *Changing Concepts of Curriculum,* has two implications: one derived from an active meaning of *changing* (we changed the concepts) and the other from a passive or descriptive one (concepts have changed themselves—somehow—and thus have changed us). It is not easy to settle on one or another of these meanings because both make sense: The concept of curriculum has been changed by the users of the concept, and also—and in retrospect we can see this—the different concepts themselves changed as if they had some kind of autonomous inner life, some inner dynamic of their own. Of course we have to face that fact that, on the one hand, concepts cannot change themselves without people using and changing them but, on the other hand, we all know that concepts have an immanent power for organizing us and our view of a certain (uncertain?) object. The use of concepts is inevitable, and while we use concepts, especially when we use old concepts in new contexts or new concepts in old contexts, they do change us—their users.[1]

This intertwined threefold relation between *concept*, concept *users* and the *object* the concept is used for, is well-known as one of the fundamental problems of scientific knowledge and scientific development—be it in the "hard" or in the "soft" sciences. This theme is pervasive in all courses on research methods, on philosophy of science, etc. The reason I mention it here bears on what I want to do in this paper, to review the development of the leading concepts in the curriculum discourse in West Germany from the 1960s to the beginning of the 1990s. This sounds simple. But reconstructing concept development, especially in a field situated between educational research, school politics and classroom practice, is not simple.

To sketch some of the difficulties: in the philosophy and sociology of science there are several models available to describe scientific change, i.e. to explain the emergence of the new and the fading—and sometimes the return—of the old. What is the moving energy behind this—if there is something like an energy? Is there a rhythm in it? Is the process cumulative? Does it lead to a fixed end, a *telos*—or is it just dynamic but without a fixed end? Is it evolutionary? Does a concept of scientific change, or scientific change itself, emerge for rational reasons—or can it only be explained by mob-psychology?[2] And if we use the evolutionary principle of the survival of the fittest concept, what is the surrounding or ecological context operating as a pressing, selective force? And how does conceptual variation (as an equivalent to genetic variation) come in? This leads to further questions: How does the *inner*, cognitive-conceptual development of knowledge interact with the *external* organizational and societal context of science? Who is active, who is passive, who *believes* himself or herself active and believes that the other is passive, etc.? In other words, it is not possible just to describe how it was and how it all changed—in telling the story you have to show the principles, viewpoints or guidelines used while telling the story. And this additional duty somehow threatens the story itself. It is similar to telling a joke and, while telling it, explaining it.

First things first: Whenever one starts to describe developments in the German school system (including the development of curriculum concepts) it is necessary to remind non-
Germans of the fact that the educational system in Germany
has had a long and very strong tradition of separating schooling for the masses from schooling of a small "elite." Until the
end of the 19th century, and then fixed by the Weimar Republic and the National Socialist regime, the structure of the school
system separated three tracks: the *Volksschule* (until the 1960s
lasting eight years, now 9–10 years) for most children; the
Realschule, starting at grade 5 and lasting for six years; and the
Gymnasium, also starting with grade 5 and lasting for nine years.
In 1952 80% of 7th graders attended the Volksschule, 6% the
Realschule and 13% the Gymnasium. By 1965 the Volkschule's
portion had sunk to 64%, that of the Realschule increased to
14%, and the Gymnasium to 18%. Today we have the situation
of equal division between the three tracks; the Realschule and
Gymnasium still are slowly, but continuously growing. The
Gesamtschulen (Comprehensive Schools; initiated in the early
1970s) today are attended by up to 7% of 7th graders. This
picture of a three-tracked (with the Gesamtschule, a four-
tracked) system is a simplification, because each of our sixteen
Länder has established variations of this system (!).

In addition to a separation of tracks (streaming) we have the
tradition of separating general and vocational education.
Whereas the lower tracks included some preparation for vocational qualifications, the Gymnasium never integrated such
useful, utilitarian elements: *Allgemeine Bildung* (general, "pure"
education) was the aim and was strictly separated from *mere*
vocational education and training. The general education of
the masses was oriented towards their lower positions in the
hierarchy of occupations.

This separation of different school types has been defended
to the present day as official policy in most Länder. The decision about which school form to attend (at the end of the
Grundschule at grade 4) is dependent on the parent's decision:
Bildung ist Bürgerrecht (to strive for the highest degree of edu-
cation/qualification is the self-evident right of everyone). Thus
strict planning of the quality or quantity of formal school qualifications by the educational administration according to predictable necessities of the labor market is forbidden by the con-

stitution. Nevertheless the state controls the allocation/streaming of students by selection to the higher grades/tracks and by building or not building new Realschulen, Gymnasien or Gesamtschulen. And you know how life is: in some regions there are as many *Gymnasiasten* as there are students' chairs in the Gymnasien of that region. This leads to problems in a context of demographic decline because, despite a decrease in the total number of children/students, no Gymnasium will be closed, and thus the percentage of *Gymnasiasten* places grows rapidly.

The point to keep in mind is this: In Germany we have a strong tradition of separating different types of schooling, and this tradition is still alive. This is important because the concept of curriculum in the several school tracks is also different.

The Tradition: Curricula Aimed at Bildung

For curriculum these three tracks were separate worlds. They had separate *Bildungsideale*: they had their own sets of aims and functions said to fit different types of students' personality and intellectual potential and to match the three levels of qualification needed on the labor market. This division of tracks and separation of curricula was not interpreted as a (social) hierarchy—which it in fact was—but as a horizontal differentiation necessary to meet different types of pupils' capacities (*Begabungstypen*) and society's needs. So hierarchy and domination were established but ideologically denied. Each school type thus had its own *Bildungsideal*: *All* students had to participate in *Bildung—but in different ways!*[3]

The traditional curricula as *Lehrpläne* explicitly formulated this division of *Bildung*. For the Volksschule, the *volkstümliche Bildung* consisted of reading, writing, arithmetic, religion, a subject called *Heimatkunde* dealing with local topography, culture and folkways, very elementary forms of natural history, an introduction to the occupational sphere on the level of craftsmen and workers, and in the rural areas, farmers. And of course singing and sports (play). The *Lehrplan* of the *Realschule* was oriented towards the "modern" spheres of trade and administration on an intermediate level (including English language, economics and the sciences). The *Bildungsideal* of the Gymnasium was academically oriented and based on the long tradition of a liberal, non-specialized and non-utilitarian, "humanistic" educational philosophy of cultivating a person by bringing him or her into contact with the cultural standards of (western) mankind—thus preparing him or her for *self-cultivation* and for participation in the further *development of culture* itself. The ancient languages (Greek, Latin), history, and modern sciences and languages were and are the elements of this curriculum, with, of course, music and sports. The central concept of the three-fold curricula of the three school types was nevertheless *Bildung*. *Bildung* was the integrative *and* the separating element.

This is a brief and somewhat simplified summary of the *ideas* about curricula and schooling in the three tracks. Where did this lead on the level of the curricula themselves and especially at the level of the classroom? The abstract and official level of thinking and discussing education is an interesting object for a critical analysis investigating its ideological elements, its illusions and self-illusions, and the camouflage or covering of the powerful interests lying behind it. This critical work has all been done. But the critique of ideological elements is not an analysis of reality. There was little empirical work on curriculum realization and classroom interaction before the 1960s. Empirical research only appeared and developed at the end of the 1960s.

The traditional curricula first defined the *Bildungswert* of a special subject and thus legitimated the appearance of this subject in the *Lehrplan*. It then formulated general aims, and then presented lists of curriculum elements, i.e. *contents* and the *temporal sequencing of these contents*. This content orientation of the *Lehrpläne* was quite obvious—the teachers had the duty to reconstruct for themselves the special *Bildungsgehalt* (educational substance) of the listed content elements and then "combine" them with their students. This suggest the *relation between the concept of curriculum-as-Lehrplan and Didaktik*: *Lehrpläne* listed contents on a general level and, on the classroom level, Didaktik had to relate contents (objects of learning) to students (subjects of learning). *Bildung* had "to occur" where content and a student met. The teacher's role was to arrange this encounter (*Begegnung*) of subject matter and student(s).

The traditional *Lehrpläne* were in fact ordered content lists. In the official *Lehrpläne*, developed in state committees (with experts from school administration, scholars, representatives of the economic sphere, the churches, etc.) and published as official documents, there was no advice on teaching methods, classroom management, textbooks, tests, media, etc.. Nevertheless it all worked because the teachers were well-trained; they had been socialized into the tradition of their school type and their *Fach* (subject matter)—and they followed this tradition. The textbooks for the several school types, grades and *Fächer* were controlled/licensed by the school administration/the state; several textbooks were licensed and a school/a teacher could choose one. The curriculum pointed out *what* to do during a school year, the textbooks supplied the material, but the *how* to do it on classroom level belonged to the traditional and officially accepted "freedom of method" of teachers.

The *Lehrpläne* were not developed and evaluated by educational researchers. Until the late 1960s there was no systematic empirical research on schools, classrooms and curricula. The discipline of *Pädagogik* was a combination of philosophy and history of education/educational ideas combined with a practical introduction to the necessities of being a teacher. *Lehrpläne* were viewed as the result of the struggle for influence among the different societal interest- and powergroups (E. Weniger). According to the concept of curriculum as *Theorie des Lehrplans* in this struggle for influence the "State" had a double-role: it was itself an interest-group—and it was the referee. The role of educational reasoning and of educational scholars and philosophers was to influence the state-as-a-referee in a way that the influences of interest groups seeking to focus youth and their futures in their own particular interest were excluded or oughtweighted by other, contradictory or compensatory influences. All particular interests should be measured by/checked against the criterion "Does this lead to responsible *Bildung* or does it prevent *Bildung*?" This is an optimistic, even idealistic view of the state as a neutral agency striving for general and legitimate pedagogical aims—it is a German, maybe a Prussian-Protestant view of "the state."

Educational scholarship and wisdom in this first phase could only *reconstruct* the processes of curriculum formation by hermeneutical methods. This form of educational reasoning *could not* and *did not intend* to construct new curricula in the "modern" way; it could not even change the concept of curriculum as *Lehrplan*. It was only able to *react* to changes in the reality of the educational sphere, which was conceived as a "living" culture with a dignity of its own—a dignity which scientific rigor, normative prescriptions and technological interventions were not to be allowed to destroy: The event of *Bildung* cannot be explained (*Erklären*) and constructed—it has to be understood (*Verstehen*)—but as an educator/teacher could strive for it on the basis of practical pedagogical wisdom and the pedagogical ethos.

The Modernists: Curricula Aimed at "Learning"

This concept of curriculum changed in the late 1960s. This is a simple sentence—but the process this sentence relates to is very complicated. The changing (of the) concept of curriculum was only one part in a broader process of modernization of education and education-as-a-discipline in West Germany. We call this the era of the *Bildungsreform* ("Educational Reform Era," 1965-1975). And this *Bildungsreform* itself was again just one part of a very broad process of modernization West German society in economic, political and cultural respects. I can only mention a few elements. However, the most important thing to note is that there was a strong will to overcome the tradition of separating school forms and the division of their *Bildungsideale*. The tremendous social selectivity was now perceived as scandal; the economy was seen as needing a higher proportion of highly qualified persons; and the political sphere—a new social democratic-liberal government—placed the reform of the educational system on top of its agenda. The traditional pedagogy changed to become educational research, integrated empirical research methods, integrated modern (and that meant Anglo-American) learning theory, analytical philosophy of science, economic models relating investments in education to outputs, innovation/evaluation models, behaviorism, taxonomies of educational objectives, criterion-oriented testing . . . and *curriculum theory*.

The first milestone in the development was an article by Roth (1968) treating the question "Are the German *Lehrpläne* still appropriate?" and came—of course—to the conclusion they were not. Roth argued for a rearrangement of the curricula, text-books and teaching methods of *all* school forms and levels according to the principles of the modern sciences (*Wissenschaftsorientierung*). *Bildung* was now conceived as an ideological, uncontrollable, impractical, historically burdened overall aim of schooling and teaching. *"Learning"* seemed to be neutral, scientific, rational and controllable: it was more "modern." The double-thesis was: (1) In a modern civilization only an orientation towards modern science and its rationality can be accepted as a fixed point or a basis for legitimate decisions, and (2) life is more and more shaped by science and its results so it is necessary to integrate all citizens into the world views, the results and methods of science—to also enable people to develop critical insights. So in a functional and in a critical sense, curricula and classroom work had to be guided by the principles of modern (natural and social) sciences. All school levels and forms should be organized around this *one, unifying and integrative principle ("learning according to science")*—a thesis directly attacking the separatist implications of the different *Bildungsideale* of the three school forms.

A second milestone was a small booklet written by Saul B. Robinsohn, the director of the Max-Planck-Institute for Educational Research in Berlin in 1967. This book *Educational Reform as Revision of Curriculum* included (in its 3rd edition) a chapter entitled "A Conceptual Structure of Curriculum Development" (first published in German in 1969; published also in English in *Comparative Education*, 8/3 1969). This conceptual structure offered a rationale for constructing new curricula:

First Step: Prognosis of (future) life situations of the younger generation.

Second Step: Identifying the qualifications the members of the younger generation would need to handle these (future) life situations.

Third Step: Identifying the curriculum elements leading to these qualifications.[4]

For Robinsohn the traditional "Lehrplantheorie" and "Didaktik" were unable to modernize curricula and classrooms because of their hermeneutical, interpretive relation to the educational sphere. He thus pointed out the limits of the *Bildungs-Didaktik*. Robinsohn thought that his three steps could be performed on the basis of the modern social sciences and in a centralized manner. His group started the work—and lost itself in the complexities of the program. Nevertheless, in the following years "curriculum" was the most used word in German educational research. Several approaches/researcher groups were established and the theoretical and methodological elements they used were in a great part adopted from the Anglo-American discussion. Some examples:

— *Decision-oriented approaches*: analyzing the process of curriculum decisions and developing models for rational decision making (Flechsig, Haller)
— *Process- and/or structure oriented approaches*: adopting the Bruner approach, combining it with Ford and Pugno, and organizing curricula around the structure and processes of sciences (Tütken, Spreckelsen, D. Elbers)
— *Situation-oriented approaches* (in elementary education): taking into account the "life world" of children, and starting from "the child" to formulate curricula (J. Zimmer)
— *Taxonomy of Educational Objectives*: Bloom Taxonomy, specifying educational objectives and developing the appropriate test-material (Möller, Peterssen)
— *Middle-range, fachdidaktische approaches*: combining "structure of a discipline" (fields of learning) with concepts from Critical Theory, all directed to critical Didaktik (the Blankertz Group).
— *Participatory approaches* ("school-based curriculum development"): seeing curriculum development as a collaborative process among teachers and curriculum specialists in reform-oriented schools and integrating "action research" elements (the Klafki Group)
— Curriculum-development in reform-schools functioning as *curriculum laboratories* disseminating their results to the "normal" school culture (v. Hentig)

It is important to note that during this phase a curriculum was conceived as a thing that *can be and should be planned* in a rational and democratic manner, and that curricula should be modernized so that they accorded with a civilization fundamentally shaped by democracy, science and the principle of meritocracy. In this sense a curriculum was *more than just a structured content list*: it was a plan for teaching and learning in schools, including general aims, specific objectives, content lists, information about methods, media and controls accompanied by coordinated textbooks, material and media packages and control schedules.

Much was invested—and much money and much paper was used and misused. But the theoretical and methodological problems of curriculum research and development were spelled out—not solved. And below the level of academic discourse about these problems new curricula in fact were developed—again by committees, boards, groups of experts etc., often as "frame curricula" leaving room enough for schools/staffs/teachers to realize them in their own manner.

The main problem was that there was a coincidence of the *slow growth* of knowledge and experience necessary for the revision of curricula on the one hand and the *rapid growth* of two contraproductive elements on the other hand: (a) the decrease and—in the end—the fading away of the political consensus that there should be a broad and fundamental reform and modernization of schooling and (b) the growing financial problems of the state. Thus I mentioned Roth and Robinsohn as the initiators of curriculum-discourse in 1968/69. This opened up a tremendous, but short boom period of "curriculum." In 1975 a "Curriculum-Handbook" (in three volumes) was edited by K. Frey from the IPN: this was the peak *and* the turning point of the "curriculum" wave. After that point the interests of educational research and of educational politics changed and turned towards other themes. In the second half of the 1970s the topic *Bildungsreform* vanished from the agenda. In 1983 a voluminous *Handbook of Curriculum Research* was published, again by K. Frey and others (Hameyer, Frey and Haft 1983) and new editions of this *Handbook* were planned for the then-future. This has not happened.

Today the intensive phase of curriculum discussion (1968–1975) has become history. And those who were postgraduates and/or research assistants in those times and who now belong to the scientific establishment sometimes talk about "those wild days" in the same manner veterans of war talk about their long-gone experiences.

Of course, the revision of curricula went on—without an intense curriculum discourse on the scientific/research level. In fact the practical process of revising curricula has not changed its fundamental elements during the last thirty years: it was and is a matter of school administration, a matter for expert-commissions established by the school ministries/the school administration. But, reflecting the change of climate, the school ministries abbreviated and abandoned the contacts they had developed with *independent* educational research(ers) in the universities—this was the end of the curriculum-debate on this level—and founded new service, development and research institutions for curriculum development and in-service teacher training as *dependent* agencies that they controlled. The amount of genuine empirical research on this ongoing process of curriculum development performed by expert commissions, boards etc. is very low (cf. Haft et al. 1986; Menck 1986).[5]

The Reconstructionists: Curricula and "Experience"

The decline of the technocratic curriculum movement in the late 1970s was accompanied by a process of redefining or reconceptualizing[6] "curriculum": from *curriculum-as-a-plan-for-teaching-and-learning* to *curriculum-as-an-enacted-experience-in-situations*. If it is so complex, that means difficult and, because of the financial cuts, no longer possible to reform schools and teaching/learning in a centralized, macro-level manner, and if it is true that these plans are constantly changed when implemented (*if* implemented), and if the basis for the learning of students in the classroom is their *experience* of classroom work, than we have to climb down from the level of macro-structural planning (or the meta-level of planning the planning . . .) to the *level of enacting and experiencing the "curriculum" in classrooms*. In the early 1980s this was called the "didactical turn" *away* from curriculum *(back) to* Didaktik. This was embedded in a broader tendency to look at the social reality, the "everyday world" of education and teaching, to look at the micro-structure of schools and classrooms. And this also meant using qualitative, ethnographic methods for the study of the socially-constituted pedagogical life in classrooms (For the turn towards qualitative educational research in West Germany cf. Terhart 1982, 1985).

This was a conceptual change in several respects: from centralized top-down thinking to decentralized, "grass-roots"—or bottom-up—thinking; from psychometric and/or survey research (quantitative) to ethnographic, qualitative, hermeneutical strategies; and from a technological view of organizing and evaluation learning to a concept of "experiential" teaching and learning (*erfahrungsorientierter Unterricht*). "Curriculum" is what teachers and students do/experience in (and out of) classrooms. This leads to a new role definition of the teacher—which, in fact, is in a new rhetoric a return to the old tradition. This third concept of curriculum is basically *a re-invention of tradition*, the tradition we call *Reformpädagogik* (from the beginning of the century), and what is called "progressive education" in the English-speaking world.

This process of returning to a traditional reform movement and its curriculum concept—not that of the modernizers and technocrats of the early 1970s (a modern manifestation of *enlightenment*), but to that of the culture- and education-critics of the early years of this century (at that time and today also a manifestation of *romanticism*)—has its positive aspects, but there is some danger in it because it temporally coincides with a strong tendency to reduce expenditures for schooling, to deregulate the school system, to reform schooling by giving autonomy to the single school and, by empowering school staffs, to develop specific school profiles. In one respect this can be regarded as a positive tendency, to an increased "pedagogical autonomy" of schools that means the stripping off of administrative/bureaucratic chains. But on the other hand it is a strategy to integrate market mechanisms in the school system—an element which is very strange to the German school system and very problematic in my view.

Thus for a general overview on the changing concepts of curriculum in West Germany it is helpful to keep in mind two distinctions:

— First, a *temporal distinction*: In West Germany we had a *pre-curriculum phase*, a phase, in which the traditional

Lehrpläne were organized around the concept of *Bildung*. The intense *curriculum-phase* was a short one and lasted from 1968 to 1975. Then, a *post-curriculum-phase* in which "curriculum" as a concept vanished.[7]

— Second, *a distinction between levels:* These changes are developments at the level of the scientific discourse. But independent of this scholarly discourse and its ups and downs or "waves" the practical process of revising or reorganizing curricula maintained its traditional, administration-controlled structure, and arguments and ideas from the scientific level found and find their way to the expert groups and—in the end—to the reality in schools and classrooms only *if they are compatible* with this traditional structure. For school administrators the revision of old and the development of new curricula is a matter of school administration—and not a matter of educational research and theorizing (Haft and Hopmann 1987).

Conclusions: Five Theses for Discussion

1. The revision of curricula, of plans for teaching and learning in schools, is a *continuing challenge and duty for school administration, teachers and educational researchers.* A dogmatic clinging to *tradition* (but what is "the" tradition?) as well as a constant, immediate and uncritical *adaption* to new challenges resulting from cultural and societal changes, as well as declaring education as a motor for societal change *(pedagogical progressism)* would be wrong—there must be a balance between the modalities of tradition, adaption and progress.

2. There is *no archimedean point* which can legitimate decisions about what and how students should learn, how far schooling, curricula and teaching should be oriented towards universal or local, communal conditions and criteria etc. Legitimacy is always scarce and it is a constant challenge—it cannot be "produced" by politicians, administrations or researchers.

3. The process of curriculum enactment (that means *realizing and experiencing curricula in the classroom*) must be studied in a more intensive way—instead of investing energy

in and developing new normative or analytical models for curriculum revision (the ideas of the traditionalists concerning the "dignity of ongoing, living educational practice" are still alive !), we need more knowledge about what teachers do with (old and or new) curricula, how they use them, how they incorporate them into their professional culture and their everyday activities.

4. The process of changing curriculum concepts that I have sketched gains its energy, and its direction, from shifts in the general cultural and societal climate and attitude towards educational questions. I prefer an *"external" explanation of concept change* in this field because education as a discipline does not have strong boundaries against the "outer world." All moves and developments outside (in culture and society) lead more or less directly to reactions inside.

The ideas, concepts and models and the amount of energy invested in "curriculum" in West Germany followed the general cultural trend of our society:

— In the reconstruction period up to the 1960s, the view dominated that we should not break with traditions, let things slowly grow and not plan them because planning seemed to be inhuman and—last not least—connected to communism. H. Becker marked this period by the word *Planungsphobie* (plan-o-phobia; Becker 1975; 92).

— At the very end of the 1960s and in the 1970s there began a rapid modernization of the educational system and education as a discipline. This modernization process was based on a immense confidence in science, rationality, technical solutions and political planning (Becker: *Planungsmanie*, plan-o-mania).

— This optimism changed into skepticism when it was quite clear that reality is always more complex than even the most complex model, when the political consensus concerning "reform" faded away—and when money became scarce because it moved to other themes and places. So today a nostalgic, some say, a cynical attitude can be observed (Becker: *Planungsnostalgie):* letting things go, little hope in intervention, systems/cultures do regulate themselves—let's observe this! No planning and reforming of curricula—just learn and live together with your students and strive for conversation and collaborative experience. Obviously this is the attitude of an aesthetically interested indifference typical of post-modern thinking.

5. But independent of the comings and goings of (sometimes just fashionable) waves in curriculum discourse on the disciplinary, and scientific level, the reform and revision of curriculum as a practice must go on, and goes on. So, of course, curriculum revision has a future. It *must* have a future. A definitive end of curriculum revision would also be the end of schooling. Because schooling, compulsory schooling—and that means forcing our children and youngsters to go to school every day—can only be legitimated *by what they learn in this place and how they learn it.* ("Learning" is understood here in a broad sense). If they do not learn anything, or if they could learn it elsewhere in a better manner no one should be permitted to force children to go to school. The organization of teaching and learning is the necessary center of schooling—and curriculum and Didaktik are instruments for organizing teaching and learning in a responsible manner—in political *and* pedagogical respects. Keeping up this sense of responsibility is the constant challenge of *Bildungstheorie* to modern educational research.

Notes

1 For a full discussion of the conceptions of and perspectives on "curriculum" see Jackson (1992a). For a German reader it is remarkable that in the Jackson *Handbook* (1992b) the US traditions of curriculum research are reviewed in two separate articles: one article reconstructs "the scientific tradition" (Darling-Hammond and Snyder 1992), another "the humanistic tradition" (Lincoln 1992).

2 I found a paper by H.Y.W. Hodysh (1977) with the interesting title "The Kuhnian paradigm and its implications for the historiography of curriculum chance". Hodysh uses Kuhn's model to analyze changes in medieval scholasticism.

3 For the English-speaking world there is a remarkable source of data on the reality of West German schools in the 1960s: Warren (1967) on *Rebhausen*; Spindler (1970; 1973); and Spindler and Spindler 1978 on *Schönhausen* and *Burgbach*).

4 This was—in 1969—the German equivalent to the American "Tyler rationale". Tyler's *Basic Principles of Curriculum and Instruction* (1949; 3rd. edition 1971) was also translated and appeared in Germany—in 1973. It is interesting that a prominent German educational reformer in the era of Enlightenment, *J.H.Campe (1748-1881)*, had developed a quite similar rationale: *Es gehört . . . ganz vorzüglich zu der Pflicht des Erziehers, über diejenige Lage, worin sein Zögling wahrscheinlicher Weise künftig kommen wird, nachzudenken, und reiflich zu erwägen, welche Körper- und Seelenfertigkeiten ihm in dieser Lage unentbehrlich . . . seyn würden, um danach die Gegenstände auszuwählen, an denen die auszubildenden Kräfte desselben geübt werden müssen.* Cited from Ballauf/Schaller: Pädagogik II. Eine Geschichte der Bildung und Erziehung, Bd.II, Freiburg 1970, p. 351.

5 For a review summarizing this second phase of curriculum discourse in West Germany see Becker (1980) and Knab (1983). A comprehensive picture of the American discussion is presented in the *Handbook of Resesearch on Curriculum*, edited by P. W. Jackson (1992).

6 There are some similarities between our reconstructionists and the "reconceptualists" in the USA (Pinar, Grumet, Macdonald *et al.*, and also the critics like Apple, Giroux, and McLaren): The critique of technocracy and psychometry, the broader scope of thought including culture and society, the political impetus criticizing oppression, power and ideology, etc. But the position of our reconstructionists also is different: What Pinar and others call "the traditionalists" (Tyler, Taba and others) in Germany were regarded as the Anglo-American "modern"

technocrats, and when their concepts were adopted (1968–1975) they were *at the same time* criticized by German educationalists inspired by the Critical Theory of the "Frankfurter Schule". So in fact during the "boom"- period from 1968 to 1975 we had all approaches simultanously, all perspectives at the same time: technocrats and critics. But their discourse was situated high above the levels of developing and implementing new curricula in the schools.

It is interesting to see that the US reconceptualists, in their wish to develop a theoretical basis of their position, read European and even German educational philosophers (Buber, Bollnow, Schleiermacher, Langeveld) who are *our* traditionalists!! Thus the proposal of the Jackson *Handbook* is appropriate: probably there have always been two constant traditions of curriculum thinking: the *scientific* one and the *humanistic* one. Sometimes the first stands in the forefront, sometimes the other. But none of them completely and definitively vanishes, and none of them can win absolute hegemony.

7 The differentiation between these three phases, and the terms I use, are adopted from Erik Wallin

References

Becker, E. (1980). *Curriculare Sackgassen*. Frankfurt: Scriptor.

Becker, H. (1975). Rede anläßlich der Einweihung des Neubaus des Max-Planck-Instituts für Bildungsforschung. *Neue Sammlung*, 15, 82–94.

Blankertz, H. (1970). Lehrplantheorie und Curriculumforschung. *Der Deutschunterricht*, 22 (2), 7–32.

Blankertz, H. (1982). Rekonstruktion geisteswissenschaftlicher Lehrplantheorie nach dem Ende der Curriculumeuphorie. *Siegener Hochschulblätter*, 18–29.

Darling-Hammond, L. & Snyder, J. (1992). Curriculum Studies and the Traditions of Inquiry: The Scientific Tradition. In P. W. Jackson (Ed.), *Handbook of Research on Curriculum* (41-78). New York: MacMillan.

Frey, K. (Ed.). (1975). *Curriculum-Handbuch*. 3 vol. München: Piper.

Haft, H. et al. (1980). *Lehrplanarbeit in Kommissionen. Ergebnisse einer Untersuchung*. Kiel: IPN.

Haft, H. & Hopmann, S. (1987). Lehrplanarbeit in der Bundesrepublik Deutschland. Veränderungen zwischen 1970 und heute. *Die deutsche Schule*, 79, 506–518.

Hodysh, H.W. (1977). The Kuhnian Paradigm and its implications for the Historiography of Curriculum Change. *Paedagogica Historica*, 17 (1), 75–87.

Jackson, P.W. (1992a). Conceptions of Curriculum and Curriculum Specialists. In P. W. Jackson (Ed.), *Handbook of Research on Curriculum* (3-40). New York: MacMillan.

Jackson, P. W. (Ed.) (1992b). *Handbook of Research on Curriculum*. New York: MacMillan.

Knab, D. (1983). Der Beitrag der Curriculumforschung zu Erziehungswissenschaft und Bildungstheorie. Versuch einer Zwischenbilanz. In U. Hameyer, K. Frey and H. Haft.

(Ed.), *Handbuch der Curriculum-forschung* (697–711). Weinheim: Beltz Verlag.

Lincoln, Y. S. (1992). Curriculum Studies and the Traditions of Inquiry: The Humanistic Tradition. In P. W. Jackson (Ed.), *Handbook of Research on Curriculum* (79–97). New York: Macmillan.

Robinsohn, S. B. (1973). *Bildungsreform als Revision des Curriculum (1967) und ein Strukturkonzept für Curriculumentwicklung (1969)*. Darmstadt: Luchterhand.

Roth, H. (1963). Stimmen die deutschen Lehrpläne noch? *Die deutsche Schule*, 55 (2), 69–76.

Spindler, G. (1970). Studying Schooling in Schönhausen. *Council on Anthropology and Education Newsletter*, 1 (1), 1–6.

Spindler, G. (1973). *Burgbach: Urbanization and Identity in an German Village*. New York: Holt, Rinehart & Winston.

Spindler, G. & Spindler, L. (1978). Schooling in Schönhausen Revisited. *Anthropology and Education Quarterly*, 9, 181–182.

Terhart, E. (1982). Interpretative Approaches in Educational Research: A consideration of some theoretical issues—with particular reference to recent developments in West Germany. *Cambridge Journal of Education* 12 (3), 141–160.

Terhart, E. (1985). The Adventures of Education: Approaches to Validity. *Curriculum Inquiry*, 16 (3), 451–464.

Warren, R. L. (1967). *Education in Rebhausen: A German Village*. New York: Holt, Rinehart & Winston.

Chapter 7

Changing Paradigms
of Curriculum and/or Didaktik?[1]

Erik Wallin

The title of this book is "Didaktik and/or Curriculum: An International Dialogue". At present, this is a most debated issue from a Swedish perspective, the more so in the light of the subtitle: "Didaktik and Curriculum of the 1960s into the 1990s." In my paper I will reflect on this theme from a Swedish viewpoint and with the Swedish development as a case.

During the last two decades, we have had an intensive discussion in Sweden about the need for reviving the concept of Didaktik on the national education scene and, as a result, a discussion of how Didaktik should be conceptualized. One aspect of the discussion has focused on Didaktik as a social fact—in terms of disciplinary characteristics such as chairs, journals and special university departments. This discussion has different origins but two main roots can be seen. One is disappointment with educational research as it has been represented in university departments of education. This disappointment has been voiced from departments of teacher education in terms of a dissatisfaction with the relevance for practical purposes of the outcomes of educational research. It should be noted here that, in the organization of the Swedish university and university college system, teacher training departments have had no permanent resources for research in terms of, for instance, professorships. However over the last few years there have been measures taken to change this state of affairs.

A second focus is to be found in the changes in the (political) conception of both education and governance of the educational system that have taken place over the last decade. These changes will be at the center in this chapter. I should also remark that I have consciously chosen to address the emergence of a renewed interest in Didaktik as connected to teaching and instruction. One reason for this is that it allows me to relate the issues I will be discussing to educational technology as it appeared on the Swedish educational scene during the 1960s. The development of a changed conception of education and/ or teaching that I will be describing could, however, also be discussed in terms of curriculum work as the development of *Lehrpläne*. My concern is the rationalities associated with both curriculum work and Didaktik that have developed since the 1960s.

A Conceptual Excursion

To Continental and Nordic Europeans the title of this book with its phrase "curriculum and/or Didaktik" presents both conceptual and terminological problems. To them it is more satisfying to talk of the *Lehrplan* and Didaktik that they are born into as covering the concept of curriculum in an Anglo-Saxon sense. The entry into the educational vocabulary, in the 1960s, of the word "curriculum"—but not the concept—created bewilderment of a kind and degree that led to what could be termed "epistemic drift." This taking over of a term, and its effects, is a nice example of the character of concepts as artifacts within the field of education as a humanistic field of endeavors—its concepts are culturally determined. From this perspective, the theme of the chapters of this book is important as an attempt to clear up the conceptual and terminological field. At the same time it does seem, because of the cultural definition of concepts, that a continuing dialogue is needed: the issue cannot be settled once and for ever.

The Swedish Case

The development of Swedish education during this century has, as in the other Nordic countries, been part of the "modern project," the modernization of the whole society. In education, with the turn of the century, the emergence of a "classical and moral code" (Lundgren, 1979) determining the conception of education and its goals was being replaced by a "rational/scientific code" concurrent with the needs of the emerging industrial society with strong popular movements resulting in demands for a more democratic society. This had some effects for upper secondary education and vocational training but the first most telling and important example was seen in the *Lehrplan,* (i.e., the national curriculum guide for primary public education of 1919). It stressed progressive and democratic values, propagating active teaching/learning in classroom work and, e.g., introduced civics as a subject for all.

The reforms of the 1960s, beginning with committee work after the second world war, were extensions of what had started in 1919 but also marked the peak of the modern project. This, again, can be seen not only in Nordic but also in other Western European countries. Sweden, however, has had a reputation for being a sort of laboratory for testing the ambitions of the modern project, not the least in education. To understand Swedish educational development, however, this project has, as is always the case, to be related to developments of the total public sector.

In Sweden after the war the modern project consisted of the building of the modern welfare state as the creation of the "folkhemmet;" the state (or, as it was said, the society) should be legitimated by solidarity and community and should intervene to guarantee the welfare of and security to individuals. The Swedish Labor party was dominant, creating a sort of hegemony that consolidated the welfare state concept. However, it is worth noting the changes in the Labor party program from the early to the late 1960s—from stressing the need to create the conditions for the good life to the ambition to create the good life.

As I have already suggested, the development of Swedish society was founded on the concurrent formation of industrialization and democratization. Two new power elites emerged in this process—major employers and entrepreneurs on one side and the labor movement on the other side. A historical compromise between these two elites created the conditions for a development whereby the Labor party—the Social Democrats—was the political power in an economy based on private ownership. The result was the "Swedish Model" with an expansive public sector and a number of reforms in different sectors of society. In retrospect, these reforms might be codified using concepts such as consensus, centralism, and social engineering.

In the present context, centralism and social engineering are the most interesting of these notions. The "Swedish Model" has been a model of governance with decisions passed by the parliament and government being implemented through a hierarchical system from central authorities to the local level. The model has been, to a considerable extent, rule-based. Social engineering was the other side of the rationalism seen in the modern project that had great confidence in science. The scientific optimism of the 1960s has, probably, never been greater and no era has seen such hopes placed in the fruits of science in terms of technology and technological products. The spirit of the time, and very much so in Sweden, also set the stage for education and educational endeavors. The arena was ready for ideas about rational planning and technology in education.

Education and Educational R&D

There was another respect in which the arena was prepared for the reception of rational decision making and technological approaches in education. From the early 1900s onwards Herbart had a strong influence on educational thinking. His division of ends as an ethical issue directed by philosophy and means as an issue for psychology was misunderstood as a partition and not as a whole. Contributing to this was the rapid development of psychology and its ambition to reflect natural science. With its German roots American psychology came to exert great influence also in Sweden—and in education. The chairs of education were primarily devoted to psychology. When in 1948 education as a university subject was divided into education and psychology, and the professors could choose which they preferred, all of them opted for psychology.

Psychology at that time meant, in Sweden as elsewhere, an often-behaviorist psychology of learning and psychometrics. Thus, the arena was prepared for the signals of a technology of education that were flagged during the 1950s from Skinner with his behavioral technology and Glaser with his experiences from military training during the war, and Bobbitt and Charter as forerunners. It should be added that education as a university discipline was not particularly strong. An interpretative orientation considering personal values and individual mental idiosyncrasies was almost non-existent. The scientific ideal was that of natural science and a value-free positivism.

The Educational 1960s and Technology

In education, the rationalism of the "Swedish model" and its accompanying social engineering received its clearest expression in the educational technology of the 1960s as this movement was conceptualized and applied in Sweden. The Tyler Rationale was influential but the behavioral impact via Skinner and Glaser was more influential. Educational technology represented the high point of rationalism within public sector education and is thus illustrative of the conception of education and teaching that held at that time. As Bunge (1967, p. 139) writes, "For technology knowledge is chiefly a means to the achievement of certain practical ends. The goal of technology is successful action rather than pure knowledge." Technology is the application of scientific knowledge for practical purposes in the form of equipment and/or rules for action. The concept "successful" implies criteria external to science, i.e., criteria of practical success as opposed to criteria which are internal to science, i.e., "truth" and "validity." The quotation from Bunge sums up the total problem of technology in its philosophical as well as practical aspects. In terms of knowledge, ends and successful action Bunge, thus, sums up the problems of educational technology.

In the 1960s two understandings of educational technology were predominant. The first defined educational technology in terms of apparatus, equipment, teaching/learning aids, audio-visual aids, etc.. This conception referred to the use of products of technologies outside education in education. This tools concept of educational technology was unthinkingly applied to buttressing the *status quo* in education. Teachers' aims and intentions were not challenged; the tools were advocated on the premise that teachers could teach the same things more effectively and to larger numbers of pupils. This illusion of "change the tools and all else can stay the same" was not to last. The technology had built-in tensions which resulted in the negotiation of a new concept of educational technology.

The second definition described educational technology as a systems (or in Sweden often as a systematic) approach to problems within education in order to develop successful courses of action. In this view educational technology was defined in terms of planning for educational action, which could also include planning for the use of the products of other technologies. The emphasis of the systems technology was on "software"—the teaching/learning materials accompanying the tool—and the learning milieu (or system) in which it was to be used. The tools were taken for granted. This systems technology was much influenced by the systems analysis which was in vogue at that time, especially in the USA. Many of those who worked as educational technologists adopted the jargon of input and output, feedback and cost-benefit, trade-off and network analysis in their ambition to also establish a rational vocabulary.

The key idea adopted from systems analysis (which the Skinnerian background also cleared the way for) was that what should be put in a learning system should not be decided until it had been determined what should be gotten out of it. Having decided on an output a clear indication of the inputs necessary in order to achieve it will emerge. Educational technology began to ask the basic question: "What are your objectives"? By this was meant: "Tell me exactly what you want the learner to be able to *do*". Once the end was clear, the means could be selected. This was the fundamental tenet of the systems approach—but also of rational planning. It should also—once more—be added that this was completely in line with a behaviorist technology.

As an indication of its scientific approach, educational technology attached great significance to evaluation. That is, having identified goals and the best means of achieving them, and having implemented those means, the outcomes were evaluated. If the desired results were not achieved, the means, the teaching methods, had to be modified until they were. The approach was sometimes described as hypothesis-testing but it was, at bottom, a symbol of the empirical (not to say empiricist) base of educational technology which was, in turn, consequence of the character of education/teaching and of the existing knowledge of teaching and learning as processes.

At the turn of the century William James (1899) made his famous statements to teachers:

> we make a great mistake if we believe it possible to derive from psychology definitive curricula, plans and methods which can, without more ado, be used in classrooms. Psychology is a science and teaching an art, and science never create art forms directly. An inventive mind must mediate the applications by use of original thought.

James seems to deny the possibility of an educational technology as a direct application of scientific knowledge to education. It has to be mediated by an inventive mind. This, of course, is a major problem for educational technology and calls into question the legitimacy of it very existence. Another problem, related to the empiricist nature of educational technology, is that the state of scientific educational knowledge does not seem to provide a sufficient base for technology. The scientific base has to be supplemented by experiential knowledge, i.e., knowledge generated by current practice and an inventive mind.

Skinner (1969) referred to James but believed that his statements no longer applied once a behavioral technology had emerged from a his branch of psychology, namely, experimental behavioral analysis. With Skinner as the main proponent, educational technology was built around the concept of learning. The products of this technology were instructional programs in their original forms. But based on principles of analysis of behavior the Skinnerian approach contained what further developed into the systematic of educational technology. In terms of planning the systems orientation became important. However the demarcation of the use of "systems" in terms of planning and in terms of the products of systematic planning was not always clear. One example of this is the use of "system" in multi-media system.

Thus in the systems approach to planning we find that "systems" refers more to operative knowledge, i.e., knowledge of how to proceed when planning, than to an integrated knowledge about the educational phenomena themselves, i.e., substantive knowledge. When operative knowledge is better developed than substantive knowledge, it will dominate. When this happened educational technology was characterized more by elaborate operative models for planning than by substantive knowledge on which to base decisions *within* these models—thus the emphasis on evaluation as trying out selected means for achieving the objectives.

Without an integrated base of substantive knowledge, educational technology also became eclectic. Eclecticism may be useful when applied within a conscious value system. But educational technology was characterized by a lack of value-base, or a philosophical consciousness. In educational technology there was thus freedom to use, within the limits of the accepted procedures, any means to achieve success. In this situation, means, interacting with other unanticipated features of the educational situation, would sometimes lead to outcomes that ran counter to the intended ends.

For the present purpose, the educational technology of the 1960s might be summarized in three points: First, the importance of the detailed specification of the objectives that formed both the starting points for planning and criteria of achievement; second, eclecticism which depended on both the lack of an integrated base of substantive knowledge and lack of a conscious value-base; third, empiricism expressed in the emphasis on both formative and summative evaluation.

It should be noted that the rationalism and instrumentalism of the educational technology of the 1960s also implied a conception of teaching as applying techniques and the teacher as a technician. This conception, in a further step, also implied a conception of how to achieve change.

The empirical character of educational technology and its neglect of values led to, on one hand, a world view in which there were no inherent relations between ends and means and, on the other hand, to an exclusive interest in methods. Part of the neglect of values was a neglect also of a selection of content as value-based. Both goals (objectives) and content were taken for granted and problematized only in method terms. There was no need for a didactic asking "What?" and "How?"— and "Why?".

The educational technology of the 1960s is a very significant illustration of rational educational planning as part of
the social engineering model of that time. In Sweden, strongly
influenced by US trends, there was no counter-discussion in
terms of Didaktik. The word Didaktik was seldom used, method
had taken over. As indicated earlier, instrumentalism was, in
different sense, a starting point for the development of the
national curriculum guides.

The 1970s into . . .

One aspect of the prevalent planning model (as well as the
conception of education/schooling) during the 1960s, was the
absence of a view of school as societal institution. Although it
was intended to realize political intentions the instrumental
perception of the school did not pay attention to the school as
being determined by the surrounding society in terms of, e.g.,
traditions and norms with known and unknown effects on the
pupils. In 1968 educational technology was being criticized as
the "extended arm of the state". This was one indication of a
changing perception of the school, and education, that can be
embedded in a view of the school as an institution or in terms
of critical theory but it was, more so, a reflection of more general developments in Swedish society.

The Swedish Study of Power and Democracy discusses this
development and points out that, since the 1960s, the Swedish
model has been transformed in different ways and the public
sector has been increasingly discussed as a problem rather than
a solution. The authority of experts in societal decision has
been questioned as well as the use of science as a basis for
social engineering. According to the commission, this transformation is explained by internal and external causes of
change. The internal causes reflect tensions between different
elements in the model, e.g., between political bargaining and
the role of experts and between equity as a social value and
efficiency. The external causes of change are outside the model
as such and reflect, e.g., shifts from an industrial to a post-
industrial and international society, cultural diversity resulting from to increased immigration, and better articulated interest groups.

The main conclusions from the studies performed by the commission are summarized by Petersson (1991, p 190) as follows:

> The era characterized by strong public sector expansion, centralized collective bargaining based on a historic compromise between labor and capital, social engineering and centrally planned standard solutions has come to an end. The present period is characterized by individualization and internationalization.

The fundamental problem of democracy, i.e., how to reconstruct individual freedom is now re-emerging in a partly new constellation. The old institutions linked to industrialization as well as the democratization of the Swedish society have, according to the commission, become weaker as citizens have become better educated, independent, and autonomous.

The transformation of the Swedish model also indicates changes in the conditions for and demands on education. It is obvious that the era of standard solutions and social engineering is reaching its end. The authority of teachers as well as the content of teaching is questioned not only by pupils but also by citizens who often have more extensive education and training than teachers and greater access to other sources of information and knowledge than earlier generations.

In Swedish education, the transformations have taken place along two main lines. One concerns increased freedom of choice. This has, e.g., implied increased freedom for individual schools to develop their own profiles along with the right of parents to choose schools for their children. What are called free schools, i.e., schools approved by state authorities and with public financial support from the municipalities, have been introduced. This development has introduced a (quasi-) market concept in the educational arena and, more than before, shown the political and value implications of education. In the public discourse private good has been contrasted with the public good; equality and equal rights are discussed in terms of the education system; justice in a philosophical sense has been given due consideration; and "voice" and "exit" have been given an enlarged and deepened meaning in terms of pluralism and participation in the public discourse on education.

The second line of transformation centers on changes in the model of steering of the educational system. A decentralization has taken place in terms of a change of distribution of power between the center and periphery together with a deregulation of the system. Goal-steering is said to have replaced steering by rules and this has been accompanied by demand for evaluation. In terms of evaluation there has been a change from *ex-ante*, the testing out of rules and directives in a centralizing and social engineering model, to *ex-post* the control of results.

Decentralization does not, however, mean abdication by the center. Instead it brings into focus the issue of balance between center and periphery. This issue may also be expressed as an issue of the control over the enlarged scope for action that on a local level is opened up by decentralization and, crucially, by steering by goals.

The changes are described in Table 1.

The left side of the table illustrates the older centralized and rule-governed system and the right side the present system. The same levels are present in both systems the main difference being the horizontal bars to the right. These illustrate that each level has its responsibility within the system; the municipal and school level within the frames of the goals decided upon by parliament and government. The bars are hori-

Centralistic, rulegoverned system   Decentralised, deregulated system

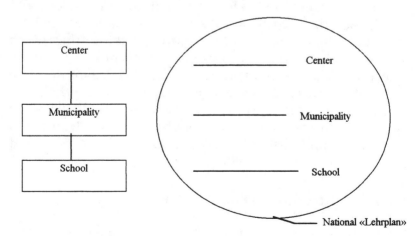

Table 1

Wallin

zontal to emphasis the responsibility of the different levels to arrange for conditions in schools and the educational/teaching activities in schools, engaging different interests (and interest groups) on the same level.

On both the municipal and school level this responsibility can be defined as local curriculum work within frames set by the national curriculum. This responsibility engages the local school administration as school leaders and teachers. For school leaders, and more so teachers as responsible for the activities in classrooms, this means that considerations and decisions defining Didaktik and didactical planning become more important than they were in a system steered by rules and directives: the issues of "What?", "How?", and "Why, what, and how?" of teaching become centrally important. These questions open up consideration of the relation between objectives as ends, and content and method as means. It also opens up questions of the meaning of teaching over and above what seems to happen in classrooms; e.g., reading instruction methods are not neutral to those engaged as pupils or teachers either in terms of reading outcomes or of reading instruction as a social situation.

The purpose of this fragmentary description of Swedish developments over two decades has been to show both the new setting and the need to discuss value issues, and how this discussion must center on the local levels of the municipality and schools—and their teachers and school leaders. A changed political and administrative culture has created a setting where the need for Didaktik as a value-laden conception of and approach to education and teaching has emerged. This development and its consequences seem more significant for the growing importance of Didaktik as theory and practice than a mere distrust in educational research. One telling example of this is seen in Englund (1990), who emphasizes both value issues and content. (cf also Wallin, 1988.)

Revisiting Educational Technology

During the second half of the 1970s the Council of Europe established a series of workshops to undertake a critical reappraisal of educational technology. The outcomes reported reflected, to a considerable extent, a reaction to the tools and systems technology on the part of the technologists themselves. The report advocated a reflective approach to educational technology. It was reflective in the sense that it made it possible for educational technology to consider, in a perspective of values and integrated substantive knowledge, the field itself seen the as products of its planning and for the student to do the same.

This approach will be treated here not to show that some broke with the rationality of the 1960s in education but as an example within education itself that was part of and reflected the general developments described above. In this sense it reflected the rediscovery of Didaktik (at least in Sweden), but the conception of a reflective technology also points not only to the emergence of Didaktik but also into what is at stake on the educational arena today.

As Bunge (1969) wrote, educational technology is the application of (scientific) knowledge to problems of education. Knowledge is transformed into rules for action. But one major issue for educational technology is, as I suggested above, the relation between ends and means. One point of criticism of educational technology relates to how it has treated questions concerning ends and objectives. Within the Skinnerian model, intended outcomes were formulated in terms of behavioral objectives. This might well have been acceptable as long as it was spelled out how objectives were related to or derived from ends. The mistake of educational technology, or rather that of many technologists, was to consider the objectives, and even the formulation of the objectives, as the intended ends. Another side of the criticism focuses on the unwillingness of educational technologists to discuss and evaluate the ideology or value assumptions of the educational situation within which they were working, i.e., to discuss the rationality of ends, and ask how these might be justified. Educational technology was instead more concerned with the rationality of means.

But, in order to fulfill its mission as *educational*, technology has to consider the rationality of both ends and means. The objection has been raised that this would mean that educational technology encompasses the whole domain of education. This should not be the case. The emphasis is still on means in the relation ends-means but it emphasizes the fact that at least a partial analysis of ends is necessary in order to find means consistent with ends.

This relation of ends to means might be discussed in terms of the demand on educational technology to contribute to the solution of problems within education. In the process of, e.g., planning a course or producing a package of teaching/learning materials, educational technology should have as a starting point *some* kind of description of a problem *and* its context *and* the intended outcomes. A first task for educational technology is to analyze the problem in relation to its context and thus find a basis for elaborating the ends and transforming them into means. Thus, it is not a search for means to achieve ends but the transformation of ends. This is the very essence of the relation between ends and means.

This brings into focus another central term within the reflective approach to educational technology. In the systems technology the relation of means to ends was predominantly an instrumental one, resulting in *rules for action* with theoretically few degrees of freedom in their application (i.e. "teacher-proof learning packages"). However, the relation is a *strategic* one. Ends are to be transformed into strategies for action rather than into rules for action. The use of the term "strategy" indicates that action is not directed by specific rules which can be followed more or less automatically independent of the actual context. Hence the practitioner has to understand more general principles for action in order to interpret rules and transform them into action. This gives the user of a "strategy" greater freedom in action and consequently makes him or her less liable to outside control. On the other hand, the practitioner must have a thorough understanding of the knowledge underlying the chosen strategies in order to justify an action both on theoretical grounds and as far as its values are concerned.

To sum up the previous argument, a reflective educational technology should

- explicitly declare it value premises as well as its metatheoretical premises, and its relation to the societal context for which it claims to be valid;
- be able to demonstrate (a) an internal consistency of the knowledge base within the technology, (b) the justifica-

tion for (the rationality of) the ends, (c) the rational connection between ends and means;
- be able to evaluate its effectiveness upon reality;
- be able to help the learners relate their consciousness to the basis (value/knowledge) of the technology.

This makes possible different technologies that can and should develop their own self-understanding and open themselves to reflections and criticism from different stake-holders—including students. This approach also opens up the need to focus on the content side of education and educational planning.

Educational technology in its reflective version and Didaktik thus come close to each other. Educational technology's development can be perceived as parallel to trends in society at large as it reflects values and demands from a changed political and administrative culture.

Curriculum and/or Didaktik . . .?

I have chosen to discuss the emergence since the 1960s of Didaktik on the Swedish educational scene. My choice could be seen to imply that I would prefer *and* as the answer to the question "Curriculum and/or Didaktik?", meaning that curriculum and Didaktik should be seen as completely different. But the issue at stake is not that simple and I could instead have chosen to focus on curriculum making and curriculum theory. More or less the same changes would have been discovered: from a Tyler Rationale to a reflective rationality. Or from psychology in a simplistic sense to psychology chosen in a conscious context of values. The common thread has been the increasing importance of bases in social (and cultural) sciences as a development from functionalism to critical theory, from curriculum as an ordered series of intended learning outcomes to curriculum as an offering to create meaning. In broader terms this might be conceptualized as a change from structure to content as meaning.

Thus, it seems that the "and/or" question is, on one hand, a matter of political and scientific context but, on the other hand—and in different terms—a matter of definition. If curriculum is defined as "What students have the opportunity to learn" (cf Englund), we delineate a broad field as well as a professional arena or a body of knowledge and a field of research. If curriculum is defined as "Lehrplan" (curriculum guide) in the German-Scandinavian sense we have again both a professional field and a field of research.

But it is, of course, also dependent on the definition of Didaktik. If Didaktik is defined as reflection on teaching, this has its implications for the answer. This is true both if Didaktik is action-oriented (reflection on teaching as basis for practice) or cognitively- (knowledge-) oriented (with the purpose to increase the understanding of teaching). Furthermore if Didaktik is conceptualized as a discourse on teaching as action, this will have its own implications. This last definition comes close to both "curriculum as offerings for learning" and a reflective technology and could delineate curriculum and/or Didaktik as aspects of the discourse.

Changing Paradigms . . .?

The developments described, with Sweden as an example, seems, in their principal aspects, to be a phenomenon found in many other countries. Whether it should be considered a shift of paradigms is, to some extent, a matter of taste. Whether it is a shift in a Kuhnian sense is a question that demands further analysis both of the meaning of what has happened and of the development taking place now and in the future. The changes in conceptions of education and teaching, of the meaning of curriculum and Didaktik are, anyhow, profound and far-reaching enough to warrant serious consideration.

What, then, is indicated as present and future trends? I believe there are different parallel developments depending on national context but still with common international denominators. Reflection on education and teaching as action and its premises seems to be one way of describing them. These trends seem to apply to *both* curriculum and Didaktik as both fields of practice and as fields of research.

To offer some illustrations, from a Nordic perspective, it would be possible to refer to Lindblad who has been addressing issues of teachers' practical reasoning and teachers' thinking (Lindblad, 1990, Carlgren & Lindblad, 1991) and Handal who addressed somewhat the same problem area in terms of "teachers practical theories" (Handal & Lauvås, 1982)—for both are extensions of their initial engagement in the establishment of a concept of a reflective educational technology. Another reference could be to Englund and his chapter in this volume on both content as meaning and also teaching as an offer of discursive meaning. All three reflect the move towards reflection on value issues in philosophic terms. These reflections concern not only Didaktik in whatever sense but also general curriculum (*Lehrplan*) work as, e.g. historic/philosophical analyses of basic terms like justice, autonomy, citizenship and democracy. What, not the least, bring them together is that education in whatever sense always, for good and/or for bad, is under the compulsion to act.

Notes

1   In this chapter I have drawn heavily on earlier papers along with work by Gunnar Berg, Gunnar Handal and Sverker Lindblad. Together with the two last-mentioned I prepared a background paper for the "reflective technology" prepared workshops that are referred to in the text. Misunderstandings and misuse of these texts fall on me.

2   It could be said that one other root is the situation for education (and training) in the economic recession in the early 1970s. School's legitimacy was questioned and demands on greater efficiency were voiced. This cleared the ground for "Fachdidaktik". I consider, however, this situation as part of the trend I refer to .

References

Bunge, M. (1967). *Scientific Research II. The Search for Truth.* Berlin: Springer Verlag.

Carlgren, I. & Lindblad, S. (1991). On Teachers' Practical Reasoning and Professional Knowledge: Considering Conceptions of Context in Teachers' Thinking. *Teaching and Teacher Education,* 7 (3), 507–516.

Council of Europe: Council for Cultural Cooperation. (1980). *Educational Technology for Permanent Education. A Critical Reappraisal.* DECS-EES/TE (78) 4 Final. Strasbourg.

Englund, T. (1990). På väg mot en pedagogisk dynamisk analys av inneholdet [Towards a pedagogical dynamic analysis of content], *Forskning om utbildning* 17 (1), 19–35.

Handal, G & Lauvås, P (1982). *På egna villkor.*[On Their own Premises.] Lund: Studentlitteratur.

James, W. (1899). *Talks to Teachers on Psychology and to Students on Some of Life's Ideals.* London: Longmans Green & Company

Lindblad, S. (1990). From Technology to Craft: On teachers' experimental adoption of technology as a new subject in the Swedish Primary School. *Journal of Curriculum Studies,* 22 (2), 165–175.

Lundgren, U.P. (1979). *Att organisera omvärlden. Introduktion till läroplansteori.* [Organizing the World Around Us. An Introduction to Curriculum Theory.] Stockholm: Liber.

Petersson, O. (1991). Democracy and Power in Sweden. *Scandinavian Political Studies.* 14 (2), 173–191.

Skinner, B.F. (1969). *The Technology of Teaching.* New York: Appleton, Century Croft.

Tyler, R.W. (1949). *Basic Principles of Curriculum and Instruction.* Chicago & London: University of Chicago Press.

Wallin, E. (1988). Notes on Didactics as a Field of Research. *Scandinavian Journal of Educational Research,* 32, 1–7.

Wallin, E., Lindblad, S. & Berg, G. (1992). The Swedish School -to Where is it Heading? In Johan van Bruggen (Ed). *Case studies: Strategies for and Organization of Curriculum Development in Some European Countries.* CEDRE. Mim.

PART 2

DEALING WITH CHANGE

The Making of Curriculum Making

Chapter 8

The Making of Curriculum Making: Reflections on Educational Research and the Use of Educational Research

Ulf P. Lundgren

In Sweden, as in most of the nations of Northern Europe, education as a university discipline—or pedagogy—was formed within philosophy and came to follow a specific philosophical tradition, mainly Herbartianism. As a result, education as a discipline was divided into two main parts: moral philosophy, the determination of the goals and content of education based on ethics; and principles of instruction with psychology as the necessary base. We have to be reminded here that, for Herbart, psychology was constructed on apperception theory which he claimed could be refined into a logico-mathematical structure.

Within this tradition pedagogy had two main tasks and purposes. One task was normative in character, and treated pedagogy as a part of the cultural reproduction of society. The other task was to explain the limits and possibilities of pedagogy as a transmission process. It is in this pattern of thinking that we see the emergence of a distinction between a theoretical side of pedagogy—including the two aspects—and a practical side. These two sides were, according to Herbart, two sides of the same thing. By mastering the science as discipline, correct observations of the child can be undertaken and, in turn, the practice of education mastered. Or to use his own words:

> Of those responsible for upbringing I demanded science and intellect. For others, science serves merely as spectacles; for me it is an eye

... The first, but far from the complete, science for the educator is psychology. ... But never could it replace the observation of a pupil; an individual can only be discovered, never deduced. (Herbart, 1806: my translation)

This linkage between the theoretical side and the practical one was not a simple one. The practice of education was an activity to reflect on, with the aid of science. Reflection is a complex process of linking abstract thinking to concrete activities.

As early as 1780 lectures in pedagogy were offered at the University of Uppsala and the Academy of Åbo (Turku) in Finland. (At that time Finland was a part of Sweden.) The lectures covered "Foundations for systems of private and public education" and were an amalgamation of ancient pedagogic ideals with ideas of the Enlightenment. It is interesting to note that there is a thematic similarity between these lectures and the German discussion on the concept of *Bildung*. Four years later, in 1784, Kant published his article in *Berliner Monatsschrift* in which he talks about *Bildung* as the exit from the human self-made liberty, to translate roughly.

But it was in 1910 that the first chair in Pedagogy was established at Uppsala University. The first professor—Bertil Hammer—expressed in his inaugural lecture ideas about the relation between the theoretical side and the practical side of education that came close to the pattern of thinking formed in the Herbartian tradition. But Hammer also argued for an empirical foundation for educational research. It is by empirically-based knowledge that the practice of education can be changed. To use his words: "the more we know the powers of educational activity the more we will be able to intervene in it."[1]

There is a point to be made here. There is an inbuilt pattern of thinking in education as a discipline that can be seen from the beginning of this century, an assumption that there can be a relation between theoretical studies of education and the practice of education. This bridge can be built by enlightening teachers: by knowing more about education and, mainly, psychology the teacher will practice better. The other linkage is between science and educational systems: with the aid of science it is possible to intervene to reform and develop education as a system.

The Birth of Modern Pedagogy

By the end of the 19th century the roles of education had drastically changed. Societal changes, demographic changes, and changes in production structures, reflected in labor markets and the increasing domination of salaried work, had created new forms of social and cultural reproduction. Schooling, i.e., formal education, was more and more defined as an instrument to re-establish lost links between production and reproduction and to establish links between qualification and the new types of work which were emerging. Demands for vocational training were expressed.

In these changes new ideas about education were formulated. A pragmatic conception of curricula emerged. A new empirically-based psychology gave the promise of and reinforced the idea of psychology as a basis for improving instruction. And with the new psychology the individual child came into focus. The publication in 1900 of the book *Barnets århundrade*—"The Century of The Child"—by the Swedish author Ellen Key, indicates in its very title the change in focus of educational thinking and debate. A rational and pragmatic code was established by which education was looked upon as an instrument for change. The rise of democracy called for the education of a new democratic citizen: a democratic citizen to be furnished with objective knowledge and skills, to be educated in an educational system that gave equal opportunities; a citizen who was able to make rational choices in a modern world.

In these changes there is an inbuilt paradox which is important to identify in order to understand the role that was ascribed to education as a science. In creating a school system that gives the same opportunities for all, educational processes have to be independent of the very same society they are a part of. At the same time a pragmatically oriented system must depend on and be related to the society. The teaching of a dead language like Latin gives few rewards to the individual child. To teach a modern language gives rewards to children living in a social context where such languages have an orientation to meaning. To make the point: the traditional school system was unfair due to selection; the modern school system is unfair due to content.

One solution to this dilemma is to separate intellectually the content of education from the methods of instruction. Basically this distinction is there already in the Herbartian pedagogy. And this pattern of thinking was reinforced by modern pedagogy—the progressive pedagogy. In Herbartian pedagogy questions of content had to be answered using ethics and by a basic classification of human interests. Methods of instruction were based on apperception psychology. In the pedagogy that was formed with modernism goals and content were to be formulated in the political arena and methods of instruction formulated by the use of modern psychology. The science of pedagogy thus strengthened the idea of two bridges between theory and practice and thereby formed two lines of research. One line linked to political decision-making, giving a basis for decisions, for planning, implementation and evaluation. The other line linked to the practice of teaching and, thereby, to teacher education. The two sides of pedagogy—the theoretical and the practical—are present in both lines, but the relation between theory and practice is different. In the first line researchers provide decision-makers with facts. *They* have to value and decide. In the other line research brings insight that can be used.

The political skirmishes, fights, victories and losses during this century illustrates this dilemma from another perspective. From a political point of view it is perhaps not a dilemma but rather is a question of relating values to how change and development is defined. To illustrate this the best example is seen in political standpoints on the question of a differentiated school system or a common school system. This question—the issue of differentiation—has been central for most European nations in the years since the Second World War. It was the central political issue in Sweden during the great reforms from 1940 to 1962.

If the school system is to be used as an instrument for changing society it is important that each child has the same opportunity for education and the same opportunity to choose further education. If the school system is also given the task of creating a society in which children learn to work together, not only to be taught democracy but also to practice democracy, the school system must be undifferentiated. From this point of view there must be a political control over goals and content, the organization must be comprehensive and the process of teaching built on a scientific ground. The distinctions between politicians and professionals, i.e., teachers and school leaders, must be clear. The teachers have to follow a given curriculum. The evaluation of education is a control related to the implementation of political governance.

From the other point of view societal changes have to follow changes in production and markets—where the state should intervene as little as possible. The opportunities offered for all lie in what they produce. A school system that is as independent as possible will best adjust to changes and at the same time give students opportunities of choice. Evaluation of education will give an objective and scientific basis for choice. Selection, if necessary, can be fair if scientifically developed instruments are used.

I have described these two ways of thinking solely to pinpoint the main elements of the issue. In reality various combinations are possible. *But the consequences mean quite different school systems with quite different tasks.*

The Swedish School Reforms

The work of reforming the Swedish school system, which led to the establishment of the nine-year comprehensive school, was begun by the 1940 Parliament. An expert committee was set up. The committee was unable to form a viewpoint on the question of the organization of the new compulsory school. The dividing issue was the question of differentiation. The committee was replaced by a parliamentary commission—the School Commission of 1946.[2] A politically acceptable answer to the question of differentiation was not found. The Commission moved the question over to administration and research. Thus the question was moved from the political arena to the academic arena and a program of research and development was undertaken. It is in this context that a tradition of educational research related to policy-making and decision making was formed, and it is in this context Swedish curriculum research was formed.

The first curriculum studies were carried out by Urban Dahllöf and two of his colleagues (Dahllöf, 1960), as empirical studies of the actual content taught. Later Dahllöf (1963) conducted a study of curriculum demands on the upper secondary school system. An empirical study was also carried out—the Stockholm Study (Svensson, 1962)—of the effects of ability grouping, i.e., the question of differentiation. These early studies were pure empirical studies. The Stockholm study illustrates the type of problem that was specified and the type of research called for. From the politicians the demand was for answers to broad questions. They were not satisfied by theoretical explanations. The value system was there; the task was to produce what Comte (1844) calls "social facts." And these demands were well calibrated to the self-understanding of social scientists: science was the use of appropriate methods; the questions were formulated in the political and public debate; the role of science was to deliver facts. Educational science did that with its use of objective methods.

Subsequently Dahllöf (1967, 1971) undertook a reanalysis of the Stockholm study using data on the time used on content covered by the test in the Stockholm study. He used the results of this reanalysis to formulate a theoretical model—the Frame Factor Theory—about the relations between organizational frames, teaching processes and outcome. This model, or theory, opened up a new line of thinking about curriculum research. It took off from the purely empirical studies and opened up research seeking relations between concepts in order to explain how educational processes were formed and how decisions on organization and content framed possible teaching process. The type of questions that the Stockholm study tried to answer were in fact not possible to answer by comparing outcomes. As I pointed out earlier, the question about differentiation was a much deeper issue centering on the role and purposes of a compulsory school system. To ascribe to a school system the role of changing society implies a different school system than one that should adjust to changes in production and markets. What is the best school system is not an empirical question!

On the way research questions about education were moved from the political arena to the academic arena. With curriculum research inspired by the frame factor theory curriculum research changed its purpose from serving decision-makers to analyzing the consequences of decision making and, later, to critical studies of the conditions and values behind decision making.

The Forming of Curriculum Theory

The development of the frame factor theory emerged from an empirical study of the teaching process (Lundgren 1972, 1974; Gustafsson, 1977) directed towards finding relations between organizational frames, the rules of the language in classrooms, and the pedagogical roles of the students. These studies of classroom teaching were deepened by focusing on the relation between frames, language rules and use and content taught (Lundgren, 1977). These studies in their turn produced patterns of results that made it possible to see how various frames, on the one hand, formed the role of the actors and rules for when and how to act and, on the other hand, how teachers built up strategies to survive.

There were two areas for inquiry that these results pointed to. One was to link studies of classroom or teaching language to studies in sociolinguistics in order to explore social differentiation. To return to my earlier observation on the dilemma of modern education, this arena for inquiry concerned the question of how a specific content and instruction carried out within a given organization will give different orientations to meaning. The other arena for inquiry was to explore how schools as institutions were formed, i.e., to explore how content was selected, organized and how thinking patterns in and around education were constituted.

Much of this research was carried out at the Stockholm Institute of Education within a research group for studies in Curriculum Theory and Cultural Reproduction (Lundgren & Pettersson, 1979),[3] which I had the privilege to direct for 15 years. Early on a cooperation was established between the research group in Stockholm and the Sociological Research Unit at the University of London headed by Basil Bernstein (Bernstein & Lundgren, 1983), The concept of "code" became central in the work of the group. Gerhard Arfwedson (1985) used the code concept in studies of how schools developed specific orientations to meaning and Lundgren (1979, 1983,

1991, 1992) used the concept of curriculum code in an historical analyses of how curricula had been formed. Tomas Englund (1986) has made an important contribution to the curriculum code model. Later a cooperation was established with a research group in Paris headed by Pierre Bourdieu which resulted in several studies of the use of cultural capital (see Broady, 1990).

I will not try to summarize and elaborate the research carried out at Stockholm Institute of Education within the research group for Curriculum Theory and Cultural Reproduction—I am not the person to do it—but what I do want to point to is the change in educational research that came about during this time. Curriculum Theory was established as a research field. The research became independent in one sense of the political arena. But in another sense it was related to decision making.

Let me now return to my distinction between two lines of educational research, one line linked to decision-making and reforms, the other related to the practice of teaching.

After the main reforms of the 1960s the Swedish educational system expanded and the changes made in the educational system were merely adjustments, not comprehensive reforms. In 1970 the 1962 national curriculum for the comprehensive school was changed. In 1980 a further change was implemented. The administration of a school system which includes around 1.5 million people produces different types of questions than those formulated when changing the system. The questions given researchers were question that demanded theoretical answers, not only "facts." The relation between researchers and decision-makers changed in character. The role of the researcher was more of a consultant than one of carrying out a specific study to answer a specific question. Critical studies were called for. Curriculum research was used, but in a more sophisticated and personal way than before.

The Decentralization Reform and
the New National Curriculum

The educational system in Sweden has always been centralized and, after the postwar reform, became still more centralized. The state has governed in the main by financial means—state subsidies—and regulations but also by a national curriculum.

This steering or governing by state subsidies has followed a model in which the state pays for teacher costs and the municipalities for buildings, etc.. The costs for the schools were rather evenly divided between the state and the municipalities. Because the state subsidies were linked to teacher salaries there were regulations covering the school organization, e.g., number of pupils per class, etc..

The national curriculum contained the Education Act, the national goals, the syllabi for each school subject, and the number of lessons to be taught each year for each subject. The number of lessons was thus related to the regulation of teacher work and were thus the object for negotiations with teacher unions. For each category of teacher the work load was defined as a maximum number of lessons. Thus there was a "steel chain"; state subsidies—number of lessons in each subject—teachers responsibilities.

In July 1991 the division of responsibilities between state and municipalities changed. Each municipality [4] was now given the total responsibility for running the schools. They can decide matters of organization, teacher salaries and teaching time. There is still a regulation concerning the number of lessons for each subject taught, but it is now a time frame (one for the nine-year compulsory school and one for the three-year upper secondary school) giving the minimum number of lessons that each student is guaranteed during his or her 12 years of schooling.

The national curriculum as well as the national syllabi for each subject has changed in character. They are now short documents giving goals and objectives but saying nothing about teaching methods. The goals and objectives are expressed on two levels. On one level there are goals "to strive for," which means long-term goals indicating the quality the school must seek to attain. On the other level there are the goals that the school must achieve. For the compulsory school these latter goals are expressed for the end of the last grade (grade 9) and for the end of grade 5. The latter in order to provide the municipalities with a basis for comparison, and thus provide a base for resource allocation. This political governing, or steering, of the educational system can be characterized as a system built on management by goals, results and quality control, with clear rules concerning the division of political and professional responsibility.

In addition, with the reform of 1991 the central state administration changed. The former National Board of Education and the Regional Boards of Education were replaced by one agency—The National Agency for Education (NEA). The NEA has the national responsibility for following and evaluating the system. Basically the NEA has to contribute to the national development of education. The municipalities are responsible for the schools and thus for the development of the schools. At the same time there must be a national equity, meaning that each child will have an equal education irrespective of municipality. The national development supports schools with comparisons, with examples, with networks, etc., that makes them able to compare, to develop and evaluate their own education.

The NEA is organized from one perspective into five programs and within the programs, various projects. From another perspective the NEA is organized in two division; one central division situated in Stockholm and a regional division with eleven regional offices.

The five programs are:

- development
- follow-up and national statistics
- evaluation
- research
- inspection.

Within the program for follow-up and statistics, data are collected concerning number of students, teachers costs, etc.—and also outcome data. For Swedish, mathematics and English there are centrally administered tests related to the goals for achievement.

Educational research has played a role in these changes, but the role not one of a simple relation between decisions and results from research. But the construction of the national curriculum, where goals are specified in terms of outcomes and not, as before, in terms of content, is a consequence of research around how curricula are articulated and the role of pedagogical text. This just to indicate one example. However, the relationship between policy-making, decision-making and educational research is subtle. It is easy over-emphasize, to see influence due to similarities. This is a field for research.

My point has been that we can see two lines of educational research and two sides. One line is research linked to changes of educational systems, the other is research linked to teaching. One side is theoretical and one side practical.

In this chapter I have discussed educational research linked to educational systems. My point has been to show how the link between research and decision-making has changed from a simple relation between specific question and delivery of social facts, to a set of complex relations where questions formulated in both the political and the academic arena create much more elaborated conceptual answers than before.

Finally, as a personal remark, research linked to educational change has seemed to fade away in this period. At the same time dramatic changes are taking place, changes that need be understood from outside the reformers' own self-understanding. As part of these changes I need help to see new perspectives, new ways to understand what consequences various decisions can have. But research into these areas seems to be moving away from education as a science to political studies, sociology and economies.

At the same time research on teaching, or didactics, has grown significantly in scale. But, going back to the dilemma of modern education, without research on the system—how it is established? how it is constituted? how content is selected? and how frames are decided?—we will never understand what teaching is about. And the improvement of teaching must be founded in some form of understanding of teaching as social phenomena. Otherwise we are returning back to the construction of "social facts" and our lost Comtian world.

Notes

1 Quotation from Lindberg, G. & Lindberg, L.: *Pedagogisk forskning i Sverige 1948-1971*. Umeå: Institutionen för pedagogik, Umeå universitet. 1983. p. 20. (My translation).

2 A description of the work of the various committees is given in: Lundgren, U.P.: *Model Analysis of Pedagogical Processes*. Lund: Liber. 1977. Revised edition 1981.

3 Many of the reports from the research group have been published within the monograph series: *Studies in Curriculum Theory and Cultural Reproduction* by Liber Läromedel in Lund.

4 There are 288 municipalities; the median population is around 14.000 inhabitants.

References

Arfwedson, G. (1985). *School Codes and Teachers' Work*. Lund: Liber Läromedel.

Bernstein, B. & Lundgren, U.P. (1983). *Makt, kontroll och pedagogik*. [Power, Control and Education.] Lund: Liber.

Broady, D. (1990). *Sociologi och epistemologi. Om Pierre Bourdieus författarskap och den historiska epistemologi*. [Sociology and Epistomology. On the authorship of Pierre Bordieu and the historical epistomology.]Stockholm: HLS förlag.

Comte, A. (1844). *Discourse préliminaire sur l'esprit positif*. 1844.

Dahllöf, U. (1960). *Kursplanundersökningar i matematik och modersmålet. Empiriska studier över kursinnehållet i den grundläggande skolan*. [Empirical Studies on the Content in Basic Schooling.] Stockholm: SOU 1960:15.

Dahllöf, U. (1963). *Kraven på gymnasiet*. [The Demands on Upper Secondary Schooling.] Stockholm: SOU 1963:22.

Dahllöf, U. (1967). *Skoldifferentiering och undervisningsförlopp*. [Ability Grouping and the Curriculum Process.] Stockholm: Almqvist & Wiksell.

Dahllöf, U. (1971). *Ability Grouping, Content Validity and Curriculum Process Analysis*. New York: Teachers College Press.

Englund, T. (1986). *Curriculum as a Political Problem*. Lund: Studentlitteratur.

Gustafsson, C. (1977). *Classroom Interaction: A Study of Pedagogical Roles in the Teaching Process*. Lund: Liber.

Hammer, B. (1910). Om pedagogikens problem och forskningsmetoder. [On the Problems of Education and Research Methodology.] *Svensk Lärartidning*, 1910 (42), 940–943.

Herbart, J.F. (1806). *Allgemeine Pädagogik*. Bochum.

Lindberg, G. & Lindberg, L. (1983). *Pedagogisk forskning i Sverige 1948–1971*. [Educational Research in Sweden 1948-1971.] Umeå: Institutionen för pedagogik, Umeå universitet.

Lundgren, U.P. (1972). *Frame Factors and the Teaching Process. A Contribution to Curriculum Theory and Theory on Teaching.* Stockholm: Almqvist & Wiksell.

Lundgren, U.P. (1974). "Pedagogical Roles in the Classroom." In Eggleston, J.: *Contemporary Research in the Sociology of Education.* London: Methuen.

Lundgren, U.P. (1977). *Model Analysis of Pedagogical Processes.* Lund: Liber. [Revised edition 1981].

Lundgren, U.P. & Pettersson, S. (1979). *Code, Context and Curriculum Processes.* Lund: Liber Läromedel.

Lundgren, U.P. (1979). *Att organisera omvärlden. En introduktion till läroplansteori.* [Organizing the World Around Us. An Introduction to Curriculum Theory.] Stockholm: Liber Förlag. (5th edition 1995).

Lundgren, U.P. (1983). *Between Hope and Happening.* Geelong, Australia: Deakin University Press.

Lundgren, U.P. (1991). *Between Education and Schooling: Outlines of a Diachronic Curriculum Theory.* Geelong, Australia: Deakin University Press. 1991.

Lundgren, U.P. (1992). *Teoria del curriculum y escolarización.* Madrid: Morata.

Svensson, N-E. (1962). *Ability Grouping and Scholastic Achievement.* Stockholm: Almqvist & Wiksell.

Chapter 9

Approaches to Curriculum Development in the United States

M. Frances Klein

Talk of curriculum reform in the United States is not a new phenomenon. Efforts to improve curriculum and instruction have been documented in educational history since the early days of the country. Perhaps the most intense and varied period of curriculum change, however, has been since the late 1950s and 1960s. This period began with unprecedented federal support for curriculum reform in the public schools when the U. S. was perceived as losing the space race to the then-Soviet Union (Goodlad; 1964, 1966). More rigorous standards for student learning; reorganized, up-dated, and new content and processes; improved instructional techniques; more detailed curriculum guides; challenging new learning materials; availability of teacher-proof curricula; increased teacher-student planning; and other such innovative, and often opposing, ideas are only some of the changes proposed during these past 40 years.

Curriculum change has been included as a part of broader educational reforms, and it has been the sole target of many efforts. It has been advocated because of political agendas; it has had stimuli from educational research; it has had impetus and support from prestigious university scholars; and it has even been developed occasionally by practitioners. Parents demand better educational practices to help prepare their children for the future. Politicians abandon programs which do not seem to work in favor of some new approach guaranteed to deliver "more bang for the buck." Scholars in the universities decry present practices which ignore or shortchange the contributions of their disciplines, and they propose needed changes. Researchers tout their latest findings and try to convince practitioners how significant they are in improving the processes of teaching and learning. Publishers advertise their newest materials, including those using the latest technology as well as traditional print, which are guaranteed to help students learn whatever content or process is representative of the latest trends in curriculum reform in the U. S. Attempted reform of some aspect of the educational system, often including the curriculum, has become a way of life in the United States. One attempt to improve the curriculum seems to phase into another with increasing rapidity, sometimes moving from one fundamental value position to another with little time and help for teachers and students to make the necessary conceptual and practical shifts in their thinking and practices.

At first glance this period of attempted curriculum reform appears to be full of confusion and contradictions about alternative ideas, proposed practices, and opportunities to reform the curriculum of the public schools. Although there are clearly some contradictions among the ideas, some trends and similarities become apparent after careful consideration. It is these similarities of many of the major attempts to improve the curriculum which is the topic of this paper. The paper is composed of three parts. First, some criteria are identified for classifying the attempts at curriculum reform. These are helpful in understanding why some curriculum changes had considerable success while others of equal or greater merit failed in their attempts to reform the curriculum. Then some of the approaches to curriculum development are analyzed for their common characteristics, and the final section is a discussion of some important factors which could have a very significant impact in the U. S. regarding the future of curriculum reform.

Curriculum Reform or Revision?

The many, varied, and often conflicting proposals for improving the curriculum have been described as curriculum reform, curriculum innovation, or curriculum change, each one heralding the promise of significant improvement in what is taught and learned in the public schools if only teachers and students would heed and practice whatever is being proposed. As each new wave of proposed curriculum reform finds its way into the public domain and educational practice, both the lay public and educational practitioners are led to believe that profound changes will occur. The success of these varied projects in affecting practice, however, has been less impressive than the sheer numbers of them.

From the early beginnings of this period, efforts were made to document the success of the projects, especially upon student learning. The literature is very disappointing regarding the impact upon student learning (Cuban, 1993). Increases in student achievement were modest at best even for some of the most heavily funded projects (see, for example, Gibboney, 1994). Some research indicated that curriculum changes and projects carefully supported in many ways by school districts never were actually implemented in classrooms (Goodlad and Klein, 1974). In spite of the sometimes great fanfares and public announcements about basic changes in what teachers teach and students learn; in spite of extensive funding of curriculum changes at the federal, state, and local levels; in spite of massive inservice education programs to retrain teachers; in spite of bold, innovative learning materials available for classroom use; and in spite of great enthusiasm of teachers and administrators for specific projects; the success of all the attempts has been far less than that expected and desired. Many ideas have been offered as to why the promising changes never found their way into sustained practice, and some answers to this failure are now available, particularly in the change literature (Fullan and Miles, 1992).

The work of Rich (1988) is very helpful in understanding conceptually why some of the proposals had great difficulty in finding their way into sustained practice. Rich identifies fundamental differences between an educational reform and an educational innovation. An educational reform represents an attempt to make basic changes in the underlying structure of the educational enterprise. A reform, by definition, cannot fit into the existing structure and practices; for it to become operative, the structure and practices must be permanently changed.

By contrast, an educational innovation demands no underlying change in the structure of education; it requires changes in thought and practice but they continue to be based upon existing assumptions and structures. An innovation is an attempt to make the system better than it is now with no attempt to alter it.

As the preceding definitions suggest, there have been only a few attempts to actually reform American education. Such reforms as open education, alternative schools, and community schools have been proposed, and, as might be anticipated, they were met with considerable resistance and had very limited success within the mainstream of American education. To change the entire system of schooling is a very daunting task, and any reform encounters formidable obstacles, opponents, and costs. Other changes such as moving to site-based management, establishing effective schools, and adopting goals emanating from political agendas would be classified as innovations since the intent is to improve the existing system, not change the underlying structures and assumptions. These innovations should have (and often do have) a much better chance of success than reforms.

Applying Rich's (1988) criteria to attempts to "reform" the public school curriculum since the 1960s, it becomes clear that many of the so-called curriculum reforms were not reforms at all. They were attempts to renovate a curriculum with little change in its existing structure, and with all its renovations, the curriculum continued to fit comfortably within the entire educational system. Little wonder, then, that the U. S. continues to experience wave after wave of so-called curriculum reform with only limited changes in what and how students learn in school. That is not to say that improvements have not been made; in some cases great strides have been made. Content of some curricula has been significantly up-dated and restructured from what had been previously taught; teachers have increased clarity and skill in methodology correlating with student achievement; and achievement tests have been revised to include more higher-order thinking skills, for example. These are no small improvements—in the system as it now exists. In Rich's terminology, however, they should not be considered reforms, just important curriculum improvements which fit more or less comfortably into the current system of American education.But even some of the innovations lasted for only limited periods of time. The concentrated effort required by some of the projects on the part of teachers faded away over time, and the enthusiastic support of administrators to keep classroom changes in place disappeared as administrators transferred to other schools and as funds were substantially reduced yet again at the district level. It was not long before classroom practices returned to comfortable tradition. (See also the work of Gibboney (1994) which examines many specific curriculum projects based upon Dewey's criteria of intellectual engagement and democratic processes.)

It should not be surprising that curriculum reforms which required fundamental changes in the educational system did not last long nor have much of an impact on classrooms. Open education with open-access curricula; alternative schools and free schools with much student control over the curriculum and, thus, much unpredictability in what would be learned; community based schools with investigative or problem-solving curricula are currently not active concepts currently except in isolated instances. They exist primarily in the historical literature, perhaps to rekindle the imagination and excitement of future reformers. This is not a value judgment regarding their worth, however. Many of the projects intended to change the system seem to some educators to be of more inherent worth than others which were far more successful within the system. Reforms, it could be said, require too much of the system, especially since one of the major purposes of the system is to maintain itself as any good bureaucracy always attempts to do. It has been proposed that the toll for curriculum reform is simply too high to ever occur in the United States; we are not prepared to pay the essential costs (Klein, 1994). By contrast, some of the innovations had at least some success in affecting what teachers teach and what students learn, even though some may have been replaced not too much later by yet another innovation.

The innovations which had some success in finding their way into the system had some fundamental similarities which were probably a major reason why they survived within the educational system—they were basically compatible with the structure and basic assumptions of the American educational system. Although these characteristics are considered to be significant strengths by some curriculum theorists, others view them as major limitations and even having erroneous assumptions about how to improve the education of young people. These fundamental characteristics of the more successful curriculum innovations reflect what curriculum theorists refer to as the subject matter curriculum (Klein, 1985). The next section identifies some of the most basic, shared characteristics of these attempts to improve the curriculum.

Analysis of Recent Curriculum Innovations

With the great variety of curriculum projects available since the 1960s, it is very difficult to generalize regarding all of them. With the use of Rich's (1988) framework, however, the focus can be rather easily narrowed to those projects—still the great majority of them, however—that did not attempt to change the system. This focus would include all those innovations intended to fit into the existing structure of American education, and, thus, had at least some degree of success—as these projects defined success. Virtually all of these curriculum innovations shared some common assumptions and characteristics about curriculum development.

First, the approach to planning assumed that any curriculum was a predetermined entity; a set of facts or other content, processes, or skills; to be specified in careful detail prior to engaging classroom teachers and students in the implementation phase of curriculum development. Along with this specification, prescribed ways of teaching, either implicitly or explicitly, were set forth for classroom practice. The specification was usually in the form of a curriculum guide or a teacher's guide often containing detailed behavioral objectives, an extensive outline of content, or comprehensive lesson plans which gave much structure and guidance to the teacher as the curriculum (content) was implemented. Some of the guides gave very specific instructions to teachers, including what questions the teacher should ask at every step of the lesson and what acceptable responses were to be elicited from the students. Curriculum was considered the same thing as content or the "what" of the process of schooling with instruction as the "how". Even when some flexibility presumably existed as in the 1960s approaches using inquiry learning or discovery learning, the body of content for teachers and students was clearly defined.

This approach to curriculum development assumes that curriculum is a monolithic entity which can be rigorously and systematically planned before students and teachers engage in the curriculum. It further assumes that there is agreement on how various participants in planning and implementing the curriculum view, interpret, and experience it. It reflects nothing regarding the work of some curriculum theorists who propose that there may be, and usually are, differing views of the same curriculum which may not be in congruence and about which there could be conflicting views and expectations of "the curriculum" (Cuban, 1993 and Klein, 1991). It also overlooks the interactive nature of curriculum and instruction by separating them into two distinct and separate components in both the planning and implementation phase of curriculum development.

A second assumption was that student learning is predictable and would be an assured outcome if teachers did what they were expected and trained to do. Nothing about the curriculum was to be left to chance or considered flexible enough for spontaneous classroom opportunities which would encourage other learnings; what was in the curriculum plan determined precisely what and how teachers teach and students learn. Carried to the extreme, some projects even developed teacher-proof curricula, trying to minimize the possibility of teachers interfering with student learning. This approach to learning draws heavily on the works of psychologists such as Skinner, Bloom, and Berliner.

This view of learning has been criticized as placing students in very passive roles—a process controlled and reinforced by the teacher designed to assure that students provide "correct" answers. A further limitation is that the passive view is most compatible with factual learning so that the end result for students is largely a body of facts which they have memorized and which often is not useful in their daily lives. Higher cognitive thinking skills, problem solving, and creative thinking are sorely neglected in this approach. Other views of learning such as those advocated by scholars such as Duckworth, Eisner, Piaget, and Vygotsky reject this controlled, hierarchical approach, and advocate that curriculum development be based on the assumption that students have a much more active role in learning and constructing their knowledge.

Third, most of the approaches utilized a traditional set of learning materials, most often a textbook with accompanying materials for students. One exception to this was a deliberate rejection of the textbook by some of the disciplines-based projects in the 1960s in favor of much more creative materials. These projects, however, were very much in the minority; even some of the best funded projects of the 1960s were centered around a textbook for student use.

These learning materials were, and still are, usually produced by national publishing firms who must secure the business of the most populous states in the country in order to show a profit from their texts and related materials. Thus, publishers work closely with only a few state departments of education as they develop new texts and accompanying learning materials or revise currently popular ones. In spite of the apparent choices from which local practitioners might choose (when authorized to do so by the state agencies), the choices are in reality quite limited and circumscribed by the similarities to be found in the curricula of the largest states and by the traditional format of a textbook.

This developmental process of learning materials imposes at least two serious limitations upon what students have available to learn from in the classroom. First, the continued reliance upon textbooks for teaching and learning does more, perhaps, than any other single factor to create a "national" curriculum in the U. S. This is something that the U. S. has carefully avoided in theory but in practice, the curricula of most public schools across the country is depressingly similar. Second, these learning materials much too often are very poor in quality. Analyses of textbooks by scholars who have examined their content and the types of learning activities included within them document this poor quality (see, for example, *Educational Leadership*, April 1985 for a special section on this topic and Farr and Tulley, 1985). Clearly, the format of teaching and learning as structured by textbooks severely limits the type of curricula which are to be found in practice.

Fourth, success of the projects was defined in terms of student achievement and linked closely to achievement tests, some more carefully developed than others. Most of the innovative projects of the 1960s developed their own achievement tests while the success of the recent approaches has been tied to nationally used standardized achievement tests. The assumption that achievement tests can determine the success of curriculum plans has a significant and limiting effect upon what ultimately is developed and the kinds of classroom practices which are sanctioned for the practitioners. As with the view of learning held by most of the developers of these projects, the nature of achievement tests overemphasizes factual knowledge in spite of more recent attempts to include conceptual thinking and complex thinking skills. The power of achievement tests over the curriculum must not be minimized. Teachers will teach and students will learn what they know will be tested, especially when the test has considerable power over the future of both groups in the educational system.

Finally, the curriculum innovations shared a common position regarding who should make curriculum decisions. With very few exceptions, curriculum decisions during the past 40 years have been removed from the school and classroom levels. Decision makers about how teachers teach, how students learn and what they will teach and learn have been those who least knew the students; who only knew about students in general with no personal knowledge of or experience with any specific group of students in their recent careers. Legislators at the federal and state level, scholars at the universities, researchers at institutes and universities, and influential professionals at foundations and institutes have unhesitatingly made decisions about what students should learn in very prescriptive terms which defined the curriculum. Some curriculum theorists have objected to this and have stated their belief that those closest to the student (Connelly and Clandinin, 1988), and even the students themselves (Kohn, 1993) ought to have considerable control over what is to be learned.

This approach to curriculum development—a cycle of distinct and sequential phases of curriculum planning, implementation, and evaluation—reflects a time-honored concept of curriculum called the subject matter curriculum in the literature of curriculum theory (Klein, 1985). The subject matter cur-

riculum uses a model of learning adapted from the industrial/
technological world and behavioristic psychology in which complex learning tasks are analyzed and broken into small components for students to master. It has extensive support from most
people who have any degree of power over the schools from
curriculum theorists to researchers to commercial publishers
to politicians to practitioners, and it does some things exceedingly well. It organizes and imparts the knowledge accumulated
by humankind over the centuries; it teaches specific sets of
skills thought to be needed by students in their daily lives; it is
easily measured and reported to the public for educational
accountability; it has the weight of tradition behind it—the way
things have always been done. Those are powerful factors which
help maintain this approach to curriculum development and
preclude other approaches which would challenge the existing
structure—reforms, in Rich's (1988) terms—and keep them from
finding their way into mainstream schooling.

This approach, at the same time, has been severely criticized
as offering an inappropriate education for the current and future needs of students, one that is passive and stagnant, and
one in which students only memorize factual knowledge and
learn isolated skills removed from any context requiring their
use. Some curriculum theorists have proposed alternative ways
of curriculum planning (see Eisner, 1985; Doll, 1993; and Pinar,
1988) which they believe are more in keeping with the kind of
education which students need in their complex world of today and are likely to need in their future.

And What of the Future?

The question of whether curriculum reforms will ever have a
chance for a lasting impact upon the American educational
system is a sobering one to consider. After much thought, I
have concluded that it is highly unlikely unless some very powerful forces have a direct impact on the schools. To reform an
entrenched, fundamental structure of education in any country, including the dominant, traditional approach to curriculum design and development, is no easy matter. It will require
many components of the process working together: a clear vision of what the curriculum should be and how it will be

changed (not all details, however, have to be developed before attempting a reform); allocation of adequate resources needed to support the change, including time, money, and space for the support of teachers and administrators; dedication to the hard work of changing perceptions and practice; education of the public to be knowledgeable and supportive of the proposed changes; and close monitoring of the process of change and the impact of it upon all those involved.

There are undoubtedly other important components in such a radical change that could be named, and others essential to the process which will become known only as the path of reform is undertaken. Such a complex undertaking in the U. S. can succeed only if a number of highly influential factors come to bear upon the educational system in close proximity to each other. These factors include: (1) the revision of professional education, (2) the widespread use of technology in the schools, (3) the establishment of government sponsored alternative schools such as charter schools or the school voucher system to provide for choice in schooling, (4) changes in the fundamental nature of schools and classrooms, and (5) changes in the views held by the public regarding educational accountability and desirable classroom practices.

Curriculum Studies in Professional Education

Curriculum as a field of study has not been a featured part of professional education in the past. An introduction to the richness of curriculum literature traditionally occurs only in graduate school, and then only in superficial treatment except for majors in the field. In preservice teacher education, curriculum is a given; it is what is included in the adopted textbook or what is spelled out in a state or local curriculum guide. Beginning teachers are given no alternative to the curriculum as a given, albeit they are often admonished to individualize it for their students but with little to no concrete help as to how to do that. Regardless of their creativity in developing alternative learning activities or in individualizing instruction for their students, future teachers are not likely to deviate much in their classrooms from the given curriculum when they have no knowledge of alternatives and when the achievement tests by which they and their students will be judged are either based directly upon that curriculum or are, at least, compatible with it.

Curriculum alignment as reflected in the concept of curriculum mapping, popularized by English (1980), has not been taken lightly in the U.S. Much effort in many districts has been made to assure that all components of the curriculum such as objectives, materials, teaching strategies, and tests support each other in the planning, implementation, and evaluation phases of curriculum development, and that administrators and teachers are, indeed, making every effort to implement the curriculum in expected, predictable ways. Although many creative teachers engage in alternative practices and think about curriculum in different ways, they often do not have the language or theory to communicate adequately why they engage in different types of classroom practices. Neither do they have the power to negotiate the adoption of new ways of organizing curriculum or to legitimatize alternative classroom practices. They remain apart from traditional practice and are sometimes even suspect because of their different way of doing things. A study of curriculum theory and design would greatly assist even these creative teachers and provide choices for other teachers who seem now to have no choice but to be bound to a given, imposed, and, often, sterile curriculum and traditional practices.

The richness of the curriculum literature in proposing alternative ways to think about and plan curricula rarely is reflected in even graduate education. In my doctoral level courses many very capable leaders in the schools of southern California were totally unaware that there were alternative ways of planning and organizing the curriculum. They knew of no way but through the assumptions of the subject matter curriculum (Klein, 1985). The work of scholars such as Eisner (1985), Doll (1993), and Pinar (1988), for example, remain out of the purview of far too many educators. Their work is being given increasing recognition but the mainstream of American education continues to function with curricula much as described in the preceding section. If real curriculum reform is to occur, teachers and administrators must study the richness of the curriculum literature and learn how to create and engage in curriculum practices based upon alternative ways of thinking about and designing curricula.

Technology and Education

The availability and use of technology in American classrooms is, in most places, limited in quantity and quality while in the rest of our culture the computer has transformed the way in which businesses and governments at all levels conduct their affairs. The information highway is a reality in the United States—with all its problems and promises. Further, the technological gap between what many students have access to outside of school and inside of school is alarmingly great. While strides have been made to upgrade the schools, the technology made available is rarely up to date. In addition, far too many students have the opportunity to learn only with the limited technology available in their schools since their homes offer no opportunity to augment their learning with technology outside of school. Other students who have access to computer networks at home are still expected to continue much of their learning from a textbook and worksheets at school. The technological gap between what could be and what is available in schools and between students who have much or little access to technology outside of school must be resolved if the schools are to remain a viable social institution.

It is through the promise of up-to-date technology in the schools that some hope for real curriculum reform exists—IF enough of it can find its way into schools. The quality of computer software will continue to improve from the drill and grill format of the earliest versions to user-friendly data banks instantly available to assist students in solving real-life problems in geography or science, for example, and in connecting with scholars in universities regardless of their locations for their latest knowledge and beliefs about the perplexing problems in their fields. This shift in learning could easily emerge into a problem solving curriculum design over time—curricula in which ideas and problems are identified and studied where students help select what they will study, where answers are not predetermined or predictable, where teachers become managers of learning rather than fountains of wisdom, and where achievement tests cannot adequately assess what students learn though their studies. The objections and improbable nature of a learner-centered curriculum design which many teachers currently perceive will be less and less overwhelming and more and more possible as individual students design their own unique curriculum based upon ideas and topics that intrigue them and where they can customtailor any requirements of a common curriculum (Klein, 1985).

Technology has the capacity to replace many of the assumptions of the subject-matter curriculum design and push educators, perhaps unwillingly and probably not well-prepared, into alternative designs. In fact, Lewis (1995) believes that technology will completely change the current educational system and that educators will lose control over the scope and sequence of curricula, a fundamental aspect of the subject matter curriculum. Such drastic changes will not occur soon nor easily just as they have not occurred in any significant way in the past within mainstream American education. The possibilities of technology as they become a reality in classrooms, however, increase the probability that alternative options to the entrenched assumptions and practices of the subject matter curriculum design will eventually become a reality in the schools.

Choice in Schooling

There is much activity in the U. S. regarding choice in schooling and how to provide for this with public funds. The interest is being generated primarily by politicians at the federal and state levels, church leaders and private school faculties with vested interests in increasing the funding available to their schools, some professional educators and researchers, and some lay citizens. Although it is a hotly debated topic, many people believe it is only a matter of time before some degree of choice becomes widespread in what schools students may attend. Several options are being advocated: to provide choices only among the existing public schools; to provide for charter schools—publicly-funded schools freed from existing state regulations in order for different groups to develop a different approach to schooling; and to provide all students with a voucher who can then use it wherever they and their family choose, either in the public or private domain.

It is difficult not to express a value position on such a fundamental issue in a democratic society. In my view, the role of the public schools has been a critical one in helping to shape and nurture our democratic system. At the same time, fundamental changes do not seem likely to occur unless some powerful outside forces act with unmistakable direction to force reform upon public schools. It is my hope that real choices will develop within the public arena, enough to provide significant options to parents and students in the type of school and type of curriculum they wish to experience. If public funding for alternative public schools becomes a reality, creating such new schools which hopefully will incorporate alternative curriculum designs may well turn out to be easier than reforming existing ones. Such unprecedented measures may be necessary to insure the survival of the public schools as a viable institution.

Transforming Organizational Structure
of Schools and Classrooms

The self-contained, graded, egg-crate structure of the public schools is a significant barrier to change. It is a structure which reinforces every aspect of the subject matter curriculum and helps to maintain it in very significant ways. If fundamental reform is to occur in the curriculum offered to students, changes in the organizational structure of schools and classrooms must also take place. Two alternative ways to organize schools and classrooms have been identified and used in some schools: nongraded schools and team teaching. Neither of these is a new idea; each has been tried during the recent period of educational change (Goodlad, 1963).

There is renewed interest in the concept of nongraded schools (Goodlad and Anderson, 1987). A national organization has been formed recently by Robert Anderson to encourage networking among nongraded schools, and the literature on the topic continues to grow. It, like many curriculum projects, was a concept which was popular during the 1950s and 1960s; was implemented in some schools (Goodlad, 1958); and all too often was abandoned when the existing system could not support the necessary changes. Also, it was a concept which had many forms of implementation, some of which only substituted very specific levels of reading or math achievement as a structure for the curriculum instead of other more open forms of curriculum planning which were envisioned by many proponents. No curriculum reform will have occurred when smaller levels of "gradedness" are substituted for traditional grade-level expectations inherent in the subject matter curriculum. The nongraded structure can provide for considerable openness and flexibility in curriculum design, encouraging much student-teacher planning of the curriculum if such an opportunity is seized and nurtured within the schools. When this occurs, curriculum reform will have a much greater opportunity for success.

The organization of teachers into self-contained classrooms with students moving from teacher to teacher as specialists in different subjects is an organizational pattern common to nearly all high schools and many elementary schools. It supports the subject matter design to a very large degree, and, thus, acts as a major barrier to reform. It fosters the separation of the subject areas (based upon the disciplines) as well as the separation and isolation of teachers from each other.

Team teaching is an alternative organizational arrangement to the self-contained classroom. It is also an idea which has been around for a while in American education (Goodlad, 1963). The concept has taken different forms in practice, been used at different levels of schooling, and offers many benefits not to be found in self-contained classrooms. In it several teachers work together, along with larger numbers of students, as a basic group. Instead of only one teacher every 50 minutes, groups of students have several teachers during an extended period of time. With this arrangement, teachers are encouraged to maximize their differing and particular talents and students have opportunities to learn from several teachers during a broadly focused study. The blocking of students, teachers, and time in such a broader organizational pattern encourages more unified teaching and learning with less artificial separation of content in the curriculum.

Team teaching not only has the potential of enhancing student learning, it also can contribute significantly to the induction of new teachers to the profession, to continuing teacher education, and to specialization in planning and teaching skills. Just as with all other promising ideas, however, if it is modified to adjust to the system rather than allowed to change the system, the promise of team teaching will never be realized.

Nongrading and team teaching as alternative ways of organizing schools and classrooms, accompanied by new ways of thinking about and designing curricula, would do much to encourage curriculum reform in American education. They help challenge the existing structure of education and the dominant curriculum design, and can help to legitimatize and support new classroom practices which must be an inherent part of any curriculum reform.

Visions of Public Accountability and Educational Practices

All of the above factors will have a greater probability of supporting fundamental curriculum reform only if the different publics interested in American education are helped to significantly alter their views of public accountability for educational expenditures and practices. As long as behavioral objectives, textbooks, achievement tests, report cards, and grade level expectations are the bases of forming and maintaining expectations about what schools should do and as the bases for communication with the publics, educators will have powerful reasons for maintaining the current structure and allowing no significant change to penetrate the system. Much creative effort must be made, for example, to help the publics change their perceptions of "good" classroom practices currently supporting quiet, teacher-dominated classrooms to more noisy, active classrooms; to support changes in ways of assessing and reporting student progress from achievement tests to alternative forms such as more realistic assessment situations (Wiggins, 1993); to support changes in ways of communicating with parents and the general public about student progress from the traditional report cards to such forms as written narratives, student portfolios, and parent-teacher-student conferences. As long as the publics maintain their traditional expectations about how schools ought to be organized and conducted, about what good classroom practices are, and what their general expectations are regarding what schools should do, curriculum reform has little chance in American education. Only as their expectations change through whatever means are available to professional educators to work with their publics can educational reform, including curriculum reform, become a reality.

Such forces as those discussed above are likely to be the only hope for fundamental reform in the structure and curriculum of American schools. If American schools are ever to get beyond the stage of shifting aimlessly from one innovation to the next, the impact of these forces will have to be very powerful, indeed. It is only through real reform of the system that the type of education so desperately needed to help students in living their daily lives now and to be prepared for living in the 21st century can be developed. It will be no easy task; it may well be an impossible one. The need, however, is so great that we dare not but try.

References

Connelly, E. M. & Clandinin, D. J. (1988). *Teachers as Curriculum Planners*. New York: Teachers College Press.

Cuban, L. (1993). The Lure of Curriculum Reform and Its Pitiful History. *Phi Delta Kappan* 75 (2), 182–185.

Doll, Jr., W. E. (1993). *A Post-Modern Perspective on Curriculum*. New York: Teachers College Press.

Educational Leadership. (1985, April). Washington, DC: The Association for Supervision and Curriculum Development.

Eisner, E. W. (1985). *The Educational Imagination: On the Design and Evaluation of School Programs*. New York: Macmillan.

English, F. W. (1980). Curriculum Development Within the School System. In *Considered Action for Curriculum Improvement. Yearbook of The Association for Supervision and Curriculum Development*. (pp. 145–157). Washington, DC: Association for Supervision and Curriculum Development.

Farr, R. & Tulley, M. A. (1985, March). Do Adoption Committees Perpetuate Mediocre Textbooks? *Phi Delta Kappan*, 66(7), 467–471.

Fullan, M. G. & Miles, M. B. (1992). Getting Reform Right: What Works and What Doesn't. *Phi Delta Kappan* 73 (10), 744–752.

Gibboney, R. A. (1994). *The Stone Trumpet: A Story of Practical School Reform 1960–1990*. Albany. New York: State University of New York.

Goodlad, J. I. (1958). Illustrative Programs and Procedures in Elementary Schools. In *The Integration of Educational Experiences*, Fifty-seventh Yearbook. Part II, Chapter 9. The National Society for the Study of Education.

Goodlad, J. I. (1963). *Planning and Organizing for Teaching*. Washington, D C: National Education Association of the United States.

Goodlad, J. I. (1964). *School Curriculum Reform*. New York: The Fund for the Advancement of Education.

Goodlad, J. I. (1966). *The Changing School Curriculum*. New York: The Fund for the Advancement of Education.

Goodlad, J. I. & Anderson, R. M.(1987). *The Nongraded Elementary School*. New York: Harcourt Brace, and World.

Goodlad, J. I., Klein, M. F. and Associates. (1974*). Looking Behind the Classroom Door*. Belmont, California: Wadsworth Publishing Company.

Klein, M. F. (1991). A Conceptual Framework for Curriculum Decision Making. In M. F. Klein (Ed.). *The Politics of Curriculum Decision-Making: Issues in Centralizing the Curriculum*. Chapter Two. Albany, New York: State University of New York Press.

Klein, M. F. (1985). Curriculum Design. *International Encyclopedia of Education* (1163-1170). Oxford, England: Pergamon Press.

Klein, M. F. (1994). The Toll for Curriculum Reform. *Peabody Journal of Education*. 69 (3), 19-34.

Kohn, A. (1993). Choices for Children: Why and How to Let Students Decide. *Phi Delta Kappan,* 75 (1), 8-20.

Lewis, A. C. (1995). An Overview of the Standards Movement. *Phi Delta Kappan*. 76 (10), 744-750.

Pinar, W. P.(Ed.). (1988). *Contemporary Curriculum Discourses. Scottsdale*. Arizona: Gorsuch Scarisbrick.

Rich, J. M. (1988). *Innovations in Education: Reformers and Their Critics* [Fifth edition]. Boston: Allyn and Bacon.

Wiggins, G. (1993). Assessment: Authenticity, Context, and Validity. *Phi Delta Kappan*. 75 (3), 200-214.

Chapter 10

Dealing with Change:
The Making of Curriculum Making

Carlo Jenzer

When I suggested in the mid-seventies an analysis of the curriculum, the plans d'études, the programs of the 26 cantons of Switzerland to the Swiss Conference of Cantonal Education Ministers, there was not only an immediate agreement, but I was also given the leadership of the corresponding study-group. When I also suggested to our cantonal Minister of Education, two years later, the development of a new curriculum for the nine years of compulsory school, he not only agreed but also charged me with the leadership of the revision of the whole curriculum (as it often happens to people who suggest something).

In Switzerland in the mid-1970s, the time was right for revision of the curriculum because

— the situation around the curriculum which was being used at that time was rather chaotic;
— the then-new discussions about curriculum theory were creating insecurity and controversy;
— there was a confusing abundance of curricular and instructional innovations.

Let me explain each of these conditions.

Chaos in the Curriculum

In my canton (Solothurn), in the 1970s, we had ten official curricula: one for elementary school, one or two for each section of the secondary school, as well as special curricula for several subjects. All these curricula originated from different periods. The oldest one, the one for elementary school, dated from 1944. These curricula were very different in appearance (i.e., size, etc.) and very different in their content and ideology. They did not harmonize with each other. Additionally, we had copied documents developed by inspectors and workgroups, which filled in the gaps in the official documents, clarified obscure paragraphs, and gave good advice to teachers.

Next to the official and working curriculum documents there were unofficial documents as well, developed by teacher associations as instruments for self-assistance. Last but not least there was a so called hidden curriculum.This exciting term was used in a very broad sense and it was, and still is, quite obscure. This is the reason, I think, why it was so exciting.

In a preliminary survey with about 200 teachers we realized that many of them knew of a curriculum only by hearing about it and did not possess any curriculum documents themselves. One of the reasons was that the curriculum had been out of print for many years. Some teachers had an official curriculum but did not use it at all or only rarely—when, for example, a new teacher started, or at the end of a school year to check if they had covered all topics.

In other words, the situation of the curriculum was, in a way, irresponsible. We could find the same situation in most cantons, outside the French-speaking part of Switzerland. One can imagine how difficult it was to describe the curriculum situation in those chaotic circumstances.

In 1977 we devoted the Yearbook of the Swiss Conference of the Cantonal Education Ministers to the curriculum. In this book not only the incredible diversity of curricula became obvious, but also the diversity of schools themselves. Just one example: The total instructional time ranged from 6860 (Zug) to 10.230 hours (Valais), during the nine years of compulsory school, a 40 percent difference. We could confirm what Werner Lustenberger (1957) had written 20 years earlier: the differences in curriculum between the cantons of Switzerland are greater than the differences between the European countries.

I used the terms "chaotic" and "irresponsible" to describe the situation. But this does not mean that teaching was bad or that co-ordination between schools was lacking. Examination standards, teaching itself, and teacher training managed what curricula did not manage. The patrimony of practice was strong and assured a good quality of teaching.

It was the curriculum that did not cope with the situation. Many teachers told us that curriculum did not matter; all that matters, they said, is the quality of teaching, not the quality of the curriculum. And for that reason the revision of the curriculum did not have priority.

We disagreed with this conclusion. We believed that traditional teaching might serve for the moment to direct the schools, but it would not cope with the needs of the future. We felt that innovations in traditional teaching and curricula were to come and that it was the task of my generation to realize this new world. One task was to bring innovation by renewing the curriculum.

The Idea of a New Curriculum

Compared to Germany and the northern states of Europe, curriculum revision started late in the German-speaking cantons. However the then-new idea of a scientifically-constructed curriculum, which Robinsohn had brought to Germany from the U.S. in 1967, had found its way to Freiburg. In 1970 Freiburg published a first version of a curriculum for the German-speaking part of the canton, a pioneer curriculum constructed according to the principles of American curriculum making. This curriculum, created by the Freiburger Arbeitsgruppe für Lehrplanforschung (FAL), a project group for curriculum research, was considered everywhere, causing in some places heated discussion. In fact, it could be argued that the mixed reception given to the FAL curriculum was one of the reasons why the revision of cantonal curricula was once more postponed.

Many teachers rejected this new style of curriculum construction: it was too technical, too centralized and it placed them in the role of employees, of executive civil servants, without the freedom they were accustomed to. Nevertheless, the FAL undoubtedly already had some effect. In many teacher-training colleges and training-courses young teachers were trained in

the art of formulating learning objectives according to Robert
F. Mager. Bruner and Bloom were read as well as Wolfgang
Klafki and Wolfgang Schulz in courses on pedagogy. Readiness for the curriculum development of the 1980s was being
developed among teachers.

Informal Education

The curriculum idea picked up in the FAL. The curriculum
was based on an extreme conception of planned teaching with
the curriculum tending to program everything to the level of
lessons in all their details. One example of this, which we discussed, was a science curriculum (SUS) that Spreckelsen had
imported from the USA and had adapted to the German context. This curriculum suggested even the words which should
be used in class teaching!

In the early 1970s, a radical movement against curriculum
grew with the theoretical support in two pedagogic bestsellers,
Neill's *Summerhill* (translated into German in 1969) and Illich's
Deschooling Society (translated into German 1972). This anti-in-
stitutional and anti-curricular movement found great support
among teachers as well as among non-teachers. The central
point in this philosophy was not the subject, but the child: the
interest of the child only should direct teaching, and not an
abstract government-prescribed curriculum. I will not emphasize this point further; all of us are aware of this trend during
the years after 1968. But in the discussions about the curriculum this trend did have an impact on our task in a fruitful way.

In summary, in the German part of Switzerland in the 1960s
and 1970s:

— there we had complicated and obsolete curricula;
— there were opposed views (an American curriculum vs.
  Informal education) in educational theory—and these differences repeatedly delayed a radical revision of cantonal
  curricula.

The 1980s: the Curriculum Decade

At the end of the 1970s, as I pointed out earlier, the situation
changed. The revision of curriculum became now an issue for

the school administration and for teachers. Why did this change happen? I think it was because the administration and the teachers identified interesting functions for the curriculum.

The administration wanted:	*The teachers wanted:*
Job directives	Support for planning programs
Legitimation	Explanation
Instruction	Information
Co-ordination	Co-operation
Control	Verification
Stabilization	Innovation

Thus, the administration hoped for clearer and less equivocal directions for schools—which could be useful for the organization of schools. The administration wanted the curricula to be an instrument for the continuing education of teachers. It wanted mechanisms for the coordination of schools of different levels and sections. Many members of the administration also wanted new curricula because they hoped they would lead to better control of the quality of teaching, for more calmness, for stabilization; in particular, they wanted new curricula in order to bring some measure of order to the numerous innovations which had swept through the schools in the 1970s, for a creation of a situation which would be more under control.

Teachers had the same concerns as the administration but with some slight differences. Their main interest in a new curriculum was that they could use it to justify and legitimate their classroom practices to parents and to the administration.

The coordination function of the curriculum was not a major issue. Indeed, the only discussion was about the extent to which the curriculum should be a tool to control teaching. Teachers wanted to develop such coordination themselves on their local level and that is why they preferred to speak about cooperation rather than about coordination. Thus, while the teachers did not like the control function of a curriculum, they supported the idea of a curriculum as a parameter or a tool that they could use to measure and judge their daily work (verification). Finally, some teachers wanted curricula which could function as inputs for innovative movements.

In other words, the administration wanted more order. Teachers wanted more protection and help for independent and self-responsible teaching.

This was the situation in the early 1980s. The discussions became more complicated in 1983/84 when politicians like Ronald Reagan in the USA and Jean Pierre Chevènement in France began to discuss the decline of the school and the school's role in preparing labor forces for international economic competition—"back to the basics." This neo-conservative movement had an influence in Switzerland but there was also a counter-movement which saw the school as a place which should allow, and support the development of the whole child.

The 1980s saw the creation of more than thirty curricula in the German part of Switzerland. Each canton had its own workgroups and the government of each canton implemented its own curriculum. This was an expensive way to proceed and in fact a curriculum could have emerged faster and with less costs if the cantons had opted for a common curriculum development. But they did not and, as a result, many teachers and politicians were involved in the curriculum adventure. Their engagement and their competence were crucial for success.

What we Learned in the Curriculum Decade

In the decade of curriculum of the 1980s we learned many things. I will highlight four major lessons:

— the importance of the discussion of main objectives;
— the curriculum as an element of a living system;
— the participation of teachers;
— the dynamism of school as an aim of curriculum.

The importance of the discussion of main objectives. The development of curricula brought up many basic questions about the role and the aims of school and of teaching:

— what is the school for?
— what should pupils basically learn at school ?
— what does the society expect from school ?
— what can the school actually achieve?
— what is the role of the parents?

— what can the school actually achieve?
— what is the role of the parents?
— how do the answers to these questions affect the construction of a curriculum? the methods? the selection of contents?

These central questions were widely discussed in many cantons. In my canton not only teacher organizations, but also political parties, labor unions, parent associations and churches participated in formal consultations and discussions.

At the conclusion of the consultations the drafted documents were further developed by experts and then ratified and published by the administration as now-definitive main objectives. They became the Magna Carta of all the further curriculum development so that when the curriculum was finally completed, the main objectives became the first chapter, replacing the rhetorical introductions found in the former curricula. At the end of the 1970s and at the beginning of the 1980s, these objectives became a frequent topic in inter-cantonal meetings of experts. We valued the outcomes of this democratic process for working through main objectives:

— The notion of "Leitideen" (main objectives) offered an incentive for people to talk about schools and they stimulated an interest in innovation.
— These guidelines created a common basis for the work of curriculum construction: a common vocabulary and a common Credo.
— Today, these guidelines are still a political and didactic reference often cited by teachers and by politicians.

The Curriculum as an Element of a Living System. A second experience, which has become more and more evident over the years, is that curricula are documents and documents cannot change schools. Curricula can only obtain significance:

— if they are used in teacher-training and in continuation courses;
— if exams are related to the curriculum;
— if teachers work together with the curriculum as a basis;
— etc. etc..

Curriculum makers who only focus on a curriculum do not get anywhere. In the whole field of school (teacher-training, school-books, methods of teaching, the interests of teachers, the interests of parents, etc.), the curriculum is only one part of the whole system. But if this is recognized, then curriculum may become very powerful. I often think that school reforms are like a living system and curriculum is just like an element in the system: an important element, like many others, without the system could not survive.

Participation of Teachers

The third experience emerging from the decade of curriculum is that curriculum becomes powerful if the teachers see it as their own and not as a political order coming from the outside or from higher institutions. Only teachers can make the curriculum an important instrument in the school reform. Because of this experience, we have given teachers a key role in development of the curriculum. The steering group and the working groups in curriculum projects consisted mostly of teachers. The first drafts of the work were presented and discussed by teachers at curriculum conferences. For some of the curriculum sketches, consultations were organized. The global designs of the curriculum were tested and evaluated—and here again teachers had the final say.

The new curricula were neither child-centered nor subject-centered, but, in a sense, "teacher-centered." The active participation of teachers during the curriculum project was a good experience for us. It forced us to develop and assert a convincing leadership in order to avoid too much freedom. On the other hand, the curriculum needed the professionalism of teachers. The new curricula require that teachers are aware of a wide range of teaching possibilities, that they are able to make decisions, and take responsibility for those decisions.

The democratic procedure of curriculum development was expensive. Our projects usually went on for ten years or even more.

The Dynamism of School as an Aim of the Curriculum

Curricula can provoke very special dynamism in a school. The most creative teachers we knew were the ones who participated in the curriculum revision projects. A good example is the north-west project, ELF, in which 1,200 teachers in seven cantons were involved. ELF means Erweiterte Lernformen (diversifying learning methods). The original idea was to use the new curricula as instruments to move away from traditional teacher-centered teaching to find space for more individual learning. The key words were Werkstattunterricht (workshop classes), Wochenplanunterricht (independently determined weekly plan where the student has to turn certain assignments in within a week), project-method, etc..

This aim was not very exciting. but a new idea overlapped the original concept: teachers wanted to manage their local school as employers manage an enterprise, that is to say in a rather autonomous way. From now on, they said, teachers should not work in semi-isolation in their classroom. A new innovation program is emerging: development of the school, we say, local development of the school. We do not know where the new movement is heading but we do know that many teams of local- schools are now creating their own local curricula, which (we are glad to be re-assured!) will be based on the cantonal curriculum- frameworks.

Outlook

In summary, I think that we now have a very interesting generation of Swiss curricula. They may have some defects—but teachers use them and they have inaugurated a new, as we say, school culture, a new understanding of school. The new curricula have also introduced some fundamental changes in the schools: equal teaching for boys and girls, early French teaching, etc.

But the new curricula will not be in force for 233 years, like the Ratio studiorum of the Jesuits and I assume that soon a need for new generation of curricula will be pressed on us!:

— Financial problems will bring about larger classes and force a shortening of numbers of lessons in some subjects.
— The new overall structure of the school system which gives the compulsory school a new role.
— Social demands, which forced us, e. g., to reduce the work week to five days.

- The increasing number of foreign children (20%) in our schools which requires us to question some of our aims and our methods
- The increasing number of children, who do not profit at home from a traditional education and parental care.
- Postindustrialization and other changes in our social life, which will force us one day to formulate new main objectives and accordingly to develop new curricula. If we will not, one can be sure that our school landscape will turn into steppe.

In future many changes in the forms of curriculum making will be necessary. Nevertheless I think, that in a democratic and federal state like Switzerland, the four experiences of our curriculum-decade should be valid for the next generation of curriculum as well:

- begin with main objectives;
- see the school as a living system;
- give a central role to teachers; and
- see the dynamism of school as an aim of curriculum revision.

And, fundamentally, encourage the participation of teachers! I have observed that teachers, who feel that they are taken seriously and who are allowed to play a central part in the school, are far more inclined and are more able to put the child at the center of teaching. Confidence in teachers is required: a person in whom we have confidence, whom we trust, is able to have confidence in others. I think that this point is the clue to and the secret of curriculum success.

References

Bloom, B. S. (1972). *Taxonomie von Lernzielen im kognitiven Bereich*. Weinheim: Beltz Verlag. [Orig. 1956]

Chèvenement, J.- P. (1985). *Apprendre pour entreprendre*. Paris: Librarie Générale Française.

Croci, A.; Imgrüth, P.; Landwehr N. & String, K. (1995). ELF, ein Projekt macht Schule. *Magazin zum Thema Erweiterte Lernformen*. Aarau/Luzern: Kant Lehrmittelverlage.

Hopmann, S. & Künzli R. (1994). Topik der Lehrplanung. Das Aarauer Lehrplanungsmanual. *Bildungsforschung und Bildungspraxis* 2, 161–184.

Illich, I. (1972). *Entschulung der Gesellschaft*. Muenchen: Kösel Verlag.

Jenzer, C.; Strittmatter, A. & Weiss, J. (Eds.). (1978). *Schulkoordination über Lehrplanreform/ Une coordination scolaire par la réforme des plans d' études/ Dalla riforma dei programmi si realizza una coordinazione scolastica*. Bildungspolitik. Jahrbuch der Schweizerischen Konferenz der kantonalen Erziehungsdirektoren. Frauenfeld: Huber Verlag.

Klafki, W.; Otto, G. & Schulz W. (1977). *Didaktik und Praxis*. Weinheim/Basel: Beltz Verlag.

Künzli, R. & Riquarts K. (1983). *Leitideen im Vergleich. Eine Gegenueberstellung von Leitideen in 14 Kantonen der Schweiz*. SIPRI. Werkstattbericht 4. Genf.: EDK.

Lehrerin/Lehrer sein. LCH-Berufsleitbild (1993). *Lernprofis im Schulteam–das neue Berufsverständnis*. Zürich: LCH.

Lustenberger, W. (1956). *Wochenstundenpläene und Probleme der Stoffverteilung in den ersten sechs Primarschuljahren*. Archiv für das Schweizerische Unterrichtswesen, 42

Mager, R. F. (1977). *Lernziele und Unterricht*. Weinheim/Basel: Beltz Verlag.

Neill, A. S. (1969). *Theorie und Praxis der anti-autoritären Erziehung. Das Beispiel Summerhill.* Reinbek bei Hamburg: Rowohlt Verlag.

Oswald, F. (1995). Zielansatz der Lehrplanreform—Anspruch und Wirklichkeit. Referat am OECD/CERI- Seminar 1983 In: *Innovationen im Bildungswesen als übernationale Aufgabe.* Die OECD/CERI—Regionalseminare der Bundesrepublik Deutschland, Österreichs und der Schweiz, 1977–1993. Bonn-Buschdorf (Köllen).

Reagan, R. (September 1984). Excellence and Opportunity: A Programm of Support for American Education. In: *Kappan Journal*

Robinsohn, S. B. (1971). *Bildungsreform als Revision des Curriculums und Strukturkonzept fuer Curriculumentwicklung.* Darmstadt: Hermann Luchterhand Verlag.

Chapter 11

Paradoxes of Educational Reform: The Case of Norway in the 1990s

Lars Løvlie

Introduction

It is a general observation that the aims of education are expressed by political and professional élites which also have the
knowledge and the power to determine the course of the
nation's schools. Only specific analyses, however, can reveal
the conflicts and contradictions which make up the undercur-
rent of reform. This paper is a critique[1] of a guiding idea of
the current curriculum reform in Norway which is part of a
major organizational overhaul of the entire national educational
system from pre-school through secondary school to teachers'
colleges launched in the early 1990s and to be finished by the
end of the decade. It is, by implication, a critique of the general educational rationale of the reform as well. The guiding
idea of this reform is a traditional individualism which—I would
suggest—has made a significant postmodern turn.

What is meant by individualism in a modern educational
setting? First, it is the Rousseauian view that the pupil's needs,
capacities and interests are the uncontested points of depar-
ture for schooling. This is "weak" individualism. Weak individualism is bolstered by a century of psychological research
on children's development and learning. The idea that education should take the learner's point of view is uncontroversial
and will not be discussed here. Second, individualism is the
idea that schools should educate for moral life—for a common

culture of norms, values and habits—by recourse to the individual and her ability to feel, think and act. This is "strong" individualism, which will be the topic of the following pages.

For many of us strong individualism is as natural as breathing the fresh morning air. Strong individualism is powerful, both because there seems to be no viable alternative to it and because it does not necessarily exclude the making of a national curriculum and a strong state intervention. It is not threatened by the idea of a specific "canon" of knowledge, which emphasizes the importance of the subject matter in teaching rather than the pupil's psychological and social needs. The reason is, of course, that education in general and the knowledge of the canon in particular is taken by individualism to be the individual's most important means of self-enhancement and progress in society. Yet I would suggest that this individualism, in its specific Norwegian version, makes for problems in educational thinking which cannot be solved within its own vocabulary. In fact, the thesis pursued in this paper is that the modernization of our schools according to individualism is characterized by paradox rather than prediction and progress, and that the vocabulary of the educational guidelines for the 1990s is unable to account for that problem in self-critical and productive terms.

The guidelines for the curriculum reform are set out in a programmatic document of 40 pages which presents the rationale of the reform (*Læreplan for grunnskole, videregående opplæring, voksenopplæring. Generell del* 1993). The document has a very attractive layout and is richly illustrated with paintings, drawings and photos from the modern European and Norwegian cultural past, and so breaks fresh ground in its self-presentation. The text was published in Norwegian in 1993 as the official Introduction[2] to the reform and is the political document in which the Ministry of Education sets forth the leading principles for the entire curriculum reform. On its appearance it was generally hailed by the reading public as a well written text, free from the cluttered and dull style of commissioned professionals. The document got a favorable reception in the press, too, as a well-rounded expression of an enlightened opinion on education. [3] The English version carries the title *Core Curriculum for Primary, Secondary and Adult Education in Nor-*

way (1994). The title is a misnomer. The document does not present a core curriculum in the traditional sense, but is a preamble to the specific curricular plans.

Individualism Old and New

It is of some interest to see the Introduction on the background of its possible historical inspirations. One of them seems to be the practical realism of the German philanthropinism of the late 18th century; the other the marriage of individuality and utility in the great British utilitarian tradition of the last century. In the Introduction there is, of course, a smack of Marx on the realization of man through work; and of John Dewey on the importance of joining the pupil's interests and the demands of the subject matter in practical problem-solving. But there is a considerable step from the idea of the practical in Marx and Dewey and the suspended individualism of the Introduction. Two citations suggest the close relationship between utilitarianism and the main idea of the Introduction. The first is:

> The aim of education is to furnish children, young people and adults with the tools they need to face the tasks of life and surmount its challenges together with others. (p. 5) [4]

The second is:

> The end of Education is to render the individual, as much as possible, an instrument of happiness, first to himself, and next to other beings.

There is a time span of about 170 years between the appearance of these two sentences. The first is the opening sentence of the Introduction of 1993. The second was the opening sentence of James Mills' essay "Education," originally published in the *Supplement to the Encyclopedia Britannica* in London (1819–23).[5] I will bring us too far afield to track the influence of utilitarian thinking in Norwegian educational thought. It must suffice to point out the paradoxes which the metamorphosis of Mill's individualism gives rise to as a postmodern educational project.

The one-page introduction to the Introduction is shot through with imperative "musts" which are to be realized by the independent pupils and teachers. The first page of the Introduction has not less than a dozen sentences with the imperative "must," of which the following one appears particularly paradoxical: "It [education] must accustom them [the young] to taking responsibility—to assess the effects of their actions on others and evaluate them in terms of ethical principles" (p. 5). This is a version of the familiar paradox that the individual ought to act both independently and on the authority of another person or institution. But if "taking responsibility" implies autonomous decision on the basis of a moral persuasion it cannot be taken on the authority of others. It has to be taken on the authority of the moral reasons of an independent person. It seems, indeed, that the idea of an independent person is—in a significant respect—at odds with the individualism of the Introduction.

To appreciate the extend to which the Introduction is steeped in its particular brand of individualism, an overview of its content is required. The text consists of seven sections with the following captions:

The spiritual human being
The creative human being
The working human being
The liberally-educated human being
The social human being
The environmentally aware human being

The integrated human being

The captions attest to the thesis of strong individualism by describing nature, culture and society in terms of a view of man. Even if these realms of education are primarily treated *within* a view of man and not *reduced* to that view, the text as a whole bears out the thesis of a strong individualism. The seventh and concluding section is crucial in this respect. The reader expects it to round off the discussion by offering either a summing up of the document or a sketch of an integrated concept of man and education. I have suggested this expectation by a space between the sixth and the seventh section. But this is not what she gets. The final sentence of the document reiterates elliptically the opening sentence of the introduction, by saying that "The ultimate aim of education is to inspire individuals to realize their potential in ways that serve the com-

mon good; to nurture humanness in a society in development."
(p. 40). The last section, then, just gives us more of the same
and strengthens the impression that the document offers a
menu of items, all presented on the same level of description.

Generally the final section speaks of integration of skills
and moral qualities, of individual character and commitment
to society etc., and so has the paradoxical effect of confirming
the disparities and oppositions which the word "integration"
promises to overcome. Here the imperative "musts," which on
the introductory page signal the will and power to educate for
integration, make their reappearance in a context which leaves
man and culture as fragmented as ever. The confident individualism of a James Mill is replaced by repeated appeals to curiosity, dedication and enthusiasm etc., words which now speak
their opposite and remind us not of the power but, rather, of
the impotence of the individual. Mill, as a one of the pioneers
of modernity, could speak from the moral person's point of
view, a person who had a "moral sense" and was directed by a
moral "ought" which promised the realization of his moral
potential as a social and political being. For the individual of
the Introduction, on the other hand, the world offers a steady
stream of individual challenges and tasks. When descriptions
are not individual, they are dyadic. For example, the paragraph
on "Teaching Ability and Active Learning" on page 21 lists the
virtues of the good teacher in dyadic terms, in this case in her
relationship to the learner. The next paragraph, on "Learning
and Teamwork," likewise has no qualitative or "deep" descriptions of togetherness, solidarity or culture as a setting for individual action. Collectivity is consistently presented and kept
within individual or dyadic descriptions.

Spurious Opposites

The failure of the Introduction to live up to its promise, the
assurances about the values of common tradition, signals the
impotence of a rhetoric which postpones infinitely its professed
aim of saying something substantial about integration, harmony
and solidarity. Thus the concluding chapter starts, quite surprisingly for a section on integration, by listing seventeen "seemingly contradictory aims" of education (p. 39). (The Norwe-

gian original says *motstridende*, which in this context favors the translation "opposite" rather than "contradictory.") The fact is that most—if not all—of the items on the list are not necessary opposites. The opposed items might be reshuffled into other sets of opposites, with much the same spurious effect. The first item, for example, which opposes "culture's moral commonality" (p. 39) and the ability to follow one's own course in life, leaves out of consideration that it is precisely the resources of the culture which makes the individual able to strike out on her own. The problems for education lie not with the opposites but with a rhetoric which constructs these dualisms in the first place. The practical conclusion is that "Education must balance these dual aims" (p. 39). Again, the need for balancing these aims is felt only within a kind of thinking that conceives of the world in terms of dualisms. But the problem of dualism in education is, as Dewey argued 100 years ago, a creation of an individualist epistemology which cannot logically account for a moral education in terms of participation and communication. The moral aims invoked in the last section amounts to no more than another string of "musts" which undercuts the Introduction's position as an authoritative text for a substantial reform in education.

There are striking parallels in intent and structure between James Mill's essay on education and the Introduction. But the historical context is as strikingly different. Mill wrote on the threshold of modernity while the Introduction bears witness to its demise. The demise of the modern tradition appears in the idea of the teacher, but extends to the idea of education itself. I shall invoke the theme of "the critique of the subject" on the assumption that the text of the Introduction implies a postmodern deflection of the teacher as an autonomous person, and so illustrates the problem of transition from a modern to a postmodern view of individuality. This means the transition from an individualism based on the idea of authentic moral qualities to a postmodern fragmented "surface" person or *persona* (*persona* being the word for the masks carried by the actors in the Greek theater).

The teacher of the Introduction shoulders an infinite burden of responsibilities. She ought to act according to the canon of enlightened and relevant teaching and in the interest of pupils, parents and principals. This may support the prejudice that when things go wrong in our schools, the teachers are to blame. But if the relevance of paradoxes in curriculum making is acknowledged, we should be more wary of blaming persons and rather take a closer look at the inconsistencies of an individualist rhetoric. Then the analysis is shifted from persons to paradoxes, that is, to conflicts which are internal to the curricular reform itself. Our interest is then less in the implementation of reform and more in the rhetoric of reform. This is where *critical* curriculum theory comes in. If it is shown that reform practices are caught up in typical paradoxes, curriculum theory can live up to its best intentions only by renewing its critical analysis of the traditional order of things curricular, partly as an analysis of the rhetoric of reform.

So far I have argued that the Introduction describes the school in terms of individual agency and not by substantial descriptions of a common lifeworld, of historical embeddedness and of educational institutions. In the next part of the paper I shall pursue the theme of strong individualism and show how it neglects the traditional core notion of the morally autonomous individual. The thesis is that by making individual autonomy a matter of self-management for the satisfaction of professional and institutional goals, autonomy in the traditional sense is lost. Let me go on with a brief historical sketch. We are used to thinking of the past 250 years—what is called modernity—in terms of Enlightenment rationality: as the proud realization of a scientific spirit which shattered superstition and prejudice, of a humanity which tolerated differences in religion and ethnic background, and of an idea of justice which makes all individuals equal under the law. Today the reaffirmation of the European tradition and of national identity is caught in the opposition between culture and civilization. To culture belongs the sense of local tradition, language and nation; to civilization a liberal and universalistic tradition referring to rights and duties under abstract law. This opposition, which for the past 15 years have lead to a heated discussion between "communitarians" on the one hand and "liberals" or "universalists" on the other, is bypassed by the Introduction.[6]

The Critique of the Subject

On the institutional level the opposition between culture and civilization is now resolved by recourse to economy (in the original Greek sense of *oikos* or household) and by outcome-oriented strategies. On the individual level it is dominated by the postmodern practice which Michel Foucault once called "technologies of self."[7] This postmodern stance contradicts a notion of autonomy which sees the individual as committed to her actions as an independent or self-determined agent. Morality is no longer a matter of what kind of person one is but of how one represents and stages oneself, so that performance overrides authenticity. The fully-functioning individual typically does not impose moral rules on herself but is determined by a system of social and legal constraints. In the words of Vincent Descombes (1990:131):

> Now the "critique of the subject" gives various philosophical reasons that tend to withdraw our right to seriously attribute an action to someone. According to this critique, actions are never *attributed*, in the manner of an ontological attribution, to persons. They are in fact *assigned*, in the manner of a purely "performative" attribution, to people who will henceforth be *held responsible*, with all the legal and social consequences that this implies, for what is done.

In this scheme the person cannot be responsible unto herself and others in any significant sense because responsibly is now defined primarily in terms of objective legal rights and duties. In the case of the teacher her self-interpretation is henceforth that of a person who manages and succeeds in the professional tasks she is expected to fulfill. Self-interpretation is sought in terms of self-management under institutional authority.

Let us avoid simple and misleading conclusions at this point. There is, of course, nothing untoward in defining a job in terms of functions. It is routinely done for industrial workers, janitors and doctors as well as for teachers—and necessarily so. The ability to understand educational aims, to enter into means-ends relations and to strive for effective teaching is a primary task for professional teachers.

Why, then, this talk about the "critique of the subject," which verges on the rejection of performance and on the infatuation with "authenticity" and the "pure" moral interests of persons satisfying self-imposed duties? Let us start to answer this question on a sober note and inquire into the Introduction's idea of performance. What problem would education have with the idea of performance and with the stress on individual virtues like "a *zest* for life, the *courage* to tackle it, and a *desire* to use and extend what they [the pupils] learn" (p. 11; my emphasis)? It is first of all because—as Descombes suggests—performance attributions like these cannot justify a philosophy of action because the *subject of action* is, a certain sense, dispensed with. This is more than a trifling loss since dispensing with the subject is to take leave of the idea of a individual who can serve as a moral example for the young and as a representative of the moral tradition which the Introduction wants to transmit.

Again let me sketch a general background. The critical voice of the Enlightenment is epitomized in the *Encyclopedia* of D'Alembert and Diderot, a monumental work which realized the idea of everybody's knowledge of everything. That idea, backed up by the English coffee house, the French *salon* and the German lecture hall, inaugurated a critical public or what today is called citizenship. Citizenship may be defined as the informed and reasonable commitment of public man to justifiable values, of which humanity, freedom and justice are the most important. But those liberal values were to be realized on one basic condition: that of an autonomous moral subject who judges according to her own independent reasons. In his famous 1784 essay *An Answer to the Question: "What is Enlightenment"?* Kant uses the metaphor of leaving the land of bondage about acquiring personal independence. His answer to the question in the title is the "deliverance of humanity from its self-imposed immaturity" or *Unmündigkeit*. Let us keep Kant's answer as a backdrop for the analysis of a key sentence in the text of the Introduction.

Means of Teaching

The sentence is taken from the middle of a section which describes the functions of the teacher. The full paragraph runs like this:

> *The teachers' most important means of teaching is themselves.* For this reason they must dare to acknowledge their own personality and charac-

ter, and to stand forth as robust and mature adults in relation to young people who are in a process of emotional and social development. Because teachers are among the adult persons children interact most closely with, they must venture to project themselves clearly, alert and assured in relation to the knowledge, values and skills to be transmitted." (p 22; my emphasis).

In the English version of the first sentence the Norwegian word *læremiddel*—literally "means of teaching"—is rendered by the word tool, which is slightly misleading. "Means" suggests both a tool and a "mean" in the sense of middle or between, thus suggesting the uneasy balance in self-interpretation between being a tool and being in a mutual relation, personal or moral, to others. The equivocality of the sentence points to the critique-of-the-subject problem by suggesting a postmodern "technology of self," that is, the practice of fulfilling one's duties by making oneself into a means.

About technologies of self Foucault (Martin *et al.* 1988: 18) says that they

> . . . permit individuals to effect by their own means or with the help of others a certain number of operations on their own bodies and souls, thoughts, conduct, and way of being, so as to transform themselves in order to attain a certain state of happiness, purity, wisdom, perfection, or immortality.

Such technologies seem to bid farewell to the subject as the independent source of its own actions, as being *auto nomos* or literally self-law-giving. They invoke the problem which is raised in the second version of Kant's Categorical Imperative, that man cannot be only a means for an end but must also be an end in itself. What is it to be an end in itself? For Kant it was to be free in the sense of being governed by an autonomous moral will and thus to be self-determined. In our context it would mean that the moral act basically refers to self-imposed "laws" or maxims rather than to institutional, professional or personal needs and pressures. The Kantian point is suggested by the difference between a bad teacher, in the sense of performing badly in the classroom, and a bad person, in the sense of acting immorally.

On the other hand in the modern rhetoric autonomous will figures, in the name of individual freedom, as the motive or interest to choose between alternative preferences or goods. Self-determination is described as the capacity to define one's professional intentions, set one's goals and to realize them within the constraints of institutional responsibilities. Now it may seem a bit far-fetched to see the paragraph just cited as a postmodern description of the teacher subject as a point of transition in a system of means. Is it not simply a description of personal autonomy and self-determination which the Kantian also would ascribe to? For the sentence "Teachers are their own best means of teaching" gives every person the freedom to turn the message into the self-directed imperative "In order to be a good teacher I ought to regard myself as a means of teaching." But let us have a closer look at the rhetoric at work in the Introduction.

First of all, who is the subject of the text? On the face of the text invokes the ideal teacher whose virtues are offered to the actual teacher to be taken over as her own property, that is, what is properly hers, the meaning of the word derived from the Latin *proprius*, literally that which belongs to the person. But it is actually the voice of the author as the *auctor*–literally origin–which governs the text. The authority of the text dwells in the origin of its rhetoric rather than in those who receive its message. In fact, the Introduction reads more like an instruction to the professional teacher than a dialogue with her. The authority of the text is to be accepted by the teacher as that of her own will, which makes for the be-independent-on-my-authority paradox mentioned at the beginning of this paper. It is the success of a rhetoric of subtle persuasion that it establishes the teacher as means of another's authority by insinuating it as the freedom to use her capacities and talents. It seems to me that here we have got a case of Kant's self-incurred immaturity: the text's power of definition is insinuated as authentically the teacher's by a subtle authority.

This authority is partly concealed by the text's anonymity. The Introduction names no author, which suggests it represents the voice of all and a general ideal which is now personified and honored in the teacher. So there is no obvious origin of power in this rhetoric, no-one to point an accusing finger at, no tyrants or impostors to topple, and consequently no victims to save or wrongs to be rectified. The rhetoric of the postmodern *oikos* does not urge into action like the rhetoric against classical repression, like in Freire's *Pedagogy of the Oppressed*. The transition from the rhetoric of emancipation to the rhetoric of performance connects with the system of external restraints and rewards. Confronted by the marriage between the rhetoric of performance and the political control by management, two main strategies point themselves out for critical curriculum theory. The first is to analyze the rhetoric of the reform, the second to show how a technology of self for autonomy is a contradiction in terms.

Authentic Acts

The sentence "Teachers are their own best means of teaching" not only contradicts the traditional "deep" notions of morality. It seems to contradict the moral (and quasi-moral) attributions which fill out the text itself, such as being self-reliant, robust, daring, spirited, etc.. I have argued that attributions like the ones mentioned above cannot serve as personal virtues under an instrumentalist description. Let me clarify by distinguishing between "non-authentic" and "authentic" attributions in the following citation.

> Teachers must show the way to skills that are reachable and to material that is manageable. And not least, they must be role models for their pupils: by their *dedication* and *enthusiasm* they must inspire their pupils to follow suit and dare to be challenged. (p 21; my emphasis).

Now skills as mentioned in the first sentence I hold to be non-authentic attributions, as when we say of a person that she is a good mathematics teacher. Dedication and enthusiasm, in the next sentence, I would say are authentic attributions. But the two are run together in the citation above, so that authentic attributions are treated on par with skills. The Introduction collapses the distinction between skills, which may be trained, managed and imitated, and personal qualities which are formed, nurtured and transmitted.

Authentic attributions, especially the clearly moral ones, come under the distinction between private and public, between what I keep to myself and what I disclose to others. In the case of telling a lie this distinction obviously takes on a moral dimension in the strict sense. There is the lesser moral evil of a sham, as when somebody pretends to know or be something she is not. Then there is the white lie or the cheerful face of one who is really rather discouraged, which more often than not belong to the social graces rather than to morality. The masking of one's views, feelings or intentions may also take place in cases where qualities like sincerity, compassion and commitment are required. But moral attributions like these cannot survive the pretension which is often allowed in the case of white lies.

Attributions are not themselves moral. They take on a moral quality only when the relation between inner and outer, me and the other, private and public is established and becomes transparent. The moral phenomenon of compassion is not particular: it is not just the compassion attributed to me nor only the compassion I feel towards the other, but the compassion which encompasses both of us in a relation. Just as important is the observation that compassion has an all-or-none quality that does not allow for degrees, a point to which I shall return below. The authentic relation is transparent, in the concrete sense of being without pretense or deception. Compassion is thus in the same class with love, trust and benevolence. These phenomena include the private and the public in the idea of an integrated person. They are also intersubjective phenomena, which means they are confirmed and sustained in the openness for the other, in the ability to take the other's point of view, and in mutual recognition.

Authentic qualities cannot be pretended without losing some of their natural immediacy. Consider the case of sincerity or honesty. Making oneself sincere by way of technologies of self often means that one loses the ease and self-confidence that goes with being sincere. This is because the person who separates inner and outer runs the risk of being found out and accused of insincerity. One acts from an artificiality in one's life, which in the sociopath is no longer reflected and so rightly is referred to the pathological. But there is also the case where technologies of self may be used as a supplement in relation to others, or as techniques of pretense, like for instance in the dancer who smiles during her performance despite the pains in her body. If she succeeds in these techniques she has made herself into a means for the good of art, for an enhanced self-respect and maybe for earning a living. This is what we hold to be good and acceptable in professionals, whether they are dancers or teachers—and rightly so.

But consider the case of honesty. Feigned honesty is a contradiction in terms because honesty cannot be pretended, that is, it cannot endure the split between inside and outside. Honesty is sustained only in transparency. Honesty is a property of honest acts. Pretended honesty is an outright contradiction in terms, that is, an act of dishonesty. You can of course feign compassion, commitment and enthusiasm, but that, too, it is like counterfeit money—in the end it buys you disrespect rather than respect, shame rather than sympathy. It seems that moral qualities like friendship, responsibility and honesty; "aesthetic" qualities like perceptiveness, enthusiasm and empathy; and even cognitive ones like being inquisitive, interested and fair-minded, cannot as qualities of personal relationships endure being only a means to an end. Authentic acts do of course have consequences which points beyond themselves. For example, being consistently honest makes a person trustworthy and so makes social relations more reliable and predicable. They may bring the benefits of goodwill if they succeed or the suffering of disappointment if they do not. But these consequences are not intrinsic to the act itself.

In general, from the moment a person's interest is revealed as a sham, she is simply seen as the person who feigns interest, and is not believed really to participate emotionally. The disclosure of pretense points back to the all-or-none character of these qualities, in the way a betrayed friendship heightens the consciousness of what friendship is. The Danish philosopher Knud E. Løgstrup makes a point of this "indirect" character of moral qualities. He stresses the ontological character of phenomena like love, trust, compassion and the "openness of speech," which means he sees them as unavoidable realities of the human world. That they make our world does not mean that they reign in the world, but that we measure the evil of hate, mistrust and callousness on the basis of their opposites. They are "spontaneous life-expressions" which ground our life with others and make the formulation of moral norms possible. Løgstrup (1983: 108; my translation) says:

To sum up: The spontaneous life-expressions live their life in the hidden. Situations of crisis, conflicting duties and clashes of interest are required to plow them up in consciousness, so that they are given to description. Ethical norms are formulations of spontaneous life-expressions, caused by crises, collisions and conflicts.

Løgstrup goes beyond Kant's grounding of morality in reason. In the process he strengthens Kant's idea of humanity as an end in itself, and as a fundamental concern for educational thought and practice. In his pre-Kantian way, Rousseau the moralist made no bones about authenticity. In *Émile* he warns us that the teacher caught in only one trifling lie will ruin the relationship to his pupil beyond repair. For all practical purposes "deep" authentic acts—those involving love, trust, sympathy and hope—cannot be feigned by everyone all the time without dissolving social life.

Teachers cannot consistently be their own best means of teaching. Any teacher who uses honesty, compassion and love as a *means* of teaching is a fake and a dissembler, and fakes and dissemblers cannot be models for moral and social life. The same holds for humanism, patriotism and the fight for justice. It seems, then, that most of the cherished ideals and aims of education cannot be a means to an end, however noble that end is. That is why the Introduction speaks paradoxes when it wants the teacher both to be her own best means of teaching and an authentic model person or an example for the young. In education the force of the example depends on authentic acts, that is, acts which are ends in themselves. This is what we can learn from the tradition, and that is what the notion of tradition demands of education. The great paradox of the Introduction is that in the name of the cultural heritage, one of the core element of that heritage is ignored. The way tradition is "traded" on to the next generation is emptied not only of its personal significance, but its moral and cultural significance as well. The teachers are urged to be representatives of the tradition—without portfolio.

On this background the Introduction's call for the teacher as models and examples again seems particularly inadequate. On page 24 we find that teachers should "function not only as instructors, counselors and role models for children. They must also work with parents, other professionals and the authorities, who together form essential elements of the school's broad educational environment." Again the critique of the notion of education in the Introduction rests its case on the lack of distinction between skills as means of teaching and moral qualities as aims in themselves. The teacher embodies the realization of values on the insight that an adequate idea of moral education (in contrast to instruction) distinguishes between skills and moral qualities; and on the parallel insight that moral education is a matter of bridging the gap between inner and outer, me and the other, in a mutual relation. Teachers who see themselves as a means for transmitting moral qualities are defeated in the very act of their realization. On the same token the educational concept which informs the Introduction defies its own aims. What is needed is a reconceptualization, not only of what we should expect and demand from teachers, but of what we can demand from education in the first place.

Authentic Acts are Social Acts

The Introduction describes acts in terms of the individual, that is, as belonging to individual persons and having their ground in personal dispositions or character traits. This easily leads to the mistaken conclusion that moral teaching is a matter of establishing individual virtues. But, as already suggested, attribution is the act of attributing something to someone. In attributing honesty, integrity or generosity to the pupils the teacher is herself recognized as honest, dependable and generous. Ascriptions are embedded in social practices and realized in a moral vocabulary which is specific for a given culture. On the same token authentic acts are communicative acts, involving two or more persons and generally embedded in what Wittgenstein used to call "forms of life." This marks the transition from the "egological" descriptions of the Introduction to communicative descriptions.

Jürgen Habermas makes the transition from an egological to a communicative description of authentic acts by replacing the self-supported moral subject with the subject-in-communication. He tries to establish the notion of a rational life as based in everyday language and speech. In Habermas'—admittedly too formal—scheme acts are authentic in the sense that whenever I mean what I say (and cannot all the time *not* mean what I say), I raise the claim that what I say is true, or right or truthful.[8] The important point here is that to discuss a proposition as to its truth presupposes the common ground of language and personal interrelatedness. Saying something and meaning what I say may be a means to something else, but only contingently so. More important is the fact that everyday speech reproduces its own practice as reasonable. In this sense saying something and meaning it, too, is circular and as such an end in itself. This clearly goes beyond the idea of personal technologies of self as the cement of society and replaces it by a common ground of communicative action and criticism. Teachers cannot, in any straightforward sense, be treated only as means or even models or examples in moral education. This is because moral education means both an initiation into a lifeworld or *ethos* and the questioning of that ethos. A moral education which reproduces not only itself, but also the conditions for its own progress, goes beyond performance and becomes creative or poetic. But the voice of a poetic education remains silent in the Introduction's rhetoric of performance.

Talk of commitment, enthusiasm and so on in terms of performance adds to the mistaken belief that cultural qualities can be taught in teacher's college courses and be managed in the classroom. *But commitment requires education by initiation*; it is what we learn by taking part in the life and practices of committed persons and by commitment to such practices. Personal qualities now enjoy a wider range: we do not look for them within persons but in the interactions between persons. Authentic acts are, of course, individual acts, but they are not within the skin but take place between teachers and pupils and the subject matter, as part of joint problem-solvings. Words like dialogue, communication, tradition and culture are the stock in trade of the Introduction. But teachers cannot just represent tradition. They have to live it according to their enlightened persuasions. In the western tradition teachers have acted as intermediaries between the family and the state, between the personal and the public. For teachers to be examples for the young, they must share a background or lifeworld with the pupils. As embedded in the lifeworld teachers can only express their more or less reflective and more or less self-critical positions as participants in a culture. As Charles Taylor (1989: 27) writes:

> To know who I am is a species of knowing where I stand. My identity is defined by the commitments and identifications which provide the frame or horizon within which I can try to determine from case to case what is good, or valuable, or what ought to be done, or what endorse or oppose. In other words, it is the horizon within which I am capable of taking a stand.

This view urges us to stop thinking in terms of facts, functions and technologies of self in the area of education and to approach the question of culture in the context of education. The promise of the Introduction is, apart from its positive merits, to point beyond its own paradoxes. This cannot, in postmodernity, be done without more substantial educational analyses of persons, traditions and the culture of education.

Notes

1. In the literary and philosophical tradition "critique" refers to the analysis and elucidation of a text or an argument. In our context a critique is the disclosure of the rhetoric of a text, that is, the way a text talks or keeps silent about (educational) issues. A rhetorical reading will be specifically sensitive to oppositions, paradoxes, and contradictions which occur in the text. It is more interested in what is said in the text than the author's possible intentions. It has given up the hopeless quest for what the text really says, and leaves to the reader the—often difficult—task of offering a plausible interpretation of it.

2. The Introduction will be referred to throughout this paper with a capital in order to distinguish it from its introductory page.

3. The text was in fact written personally by the present Minister of Education, by profession a university professor of sociology, who dared to break with a long tradition of curriculum making by appointed commissions, which left him to put his individual mark on the program of the Introduction.

4. The translation is not true to the Norwegian text, which does not use the equivalent to the English "tool." The translation "The aim of education is to prepare . . . for the tasks of life" would in fact be better.

5. Cited from Mill (1992: 139). James Mill (1773-1836), the father of the illustrious John Stuart Mill, was of Scottish descent. His ambitious mother changed the family name from "Milne" to the more English-sounding "Mill." As an intellectual of the early 19th century Mill made a point of belonging, not to the "middle class" but to the emergent "middle rank." Members of the middle rank did not owe their position to birth but to "the present state of education and the diffusion of knowledge." His "middle rank" wanted to replace birthright by knowledge, class by merit.

6. For some recent publications in this debate, see Rasmussen (1990), Mulhall and Swift, (1992) and Benhabib (1992).

7. The fact that the business of education figures within this economy moves the current Norwegian educational reform closely to the postmodern position which is expressed in the "critique of the subject."

8. See Habermas (1994). The interview "What theories can accomplish," is a straightforward presentation of this view.

References

Benhabib, S. (1992). *Situating the Self.* Cambridge: Polity Press.

Descombes, Vincent: Apropos of the 'Critique of the Subject' and the Critique of this Critique. In Cadava. E. Connor, P. Nancy, J-L, eds. (1991): *Who Comes After the Subject?* New York: Routledge.

Habermas, J. (1994). *The Past as Future.* Interviewed by Michael Haller Cambridge: Polity Press.

Kant, I. (1964). Beantwortung auf der Frage: Was ist Aufklärung? In *Theorie-Werkausgabe, Band 11.* Frankfurt.a.M.: Suhrkamp, 53–65.

Det kongelige Kirke-, utdannings- og forskningsdepartement (1993). *Læreplan for grunnskole, videregående opplæring, voksenopplæring. Generell del.* Oslo: Det kongelige Kirke-utdannings- og forskningsdepartement.

Royal Ministry of Church, Education and Research (1994). *Core Curriculum for Primary, Secondary and Adult Education in Norway.* Oslo: Royal Ministry of Church, Education and Research.

Løgstrup, K.E. (1983). *System og Symbol. Essays.* København: Gyldendal.

Martin, L.H., Gutman, H. and Hutton, P.H. (eds) (1988). *Technologies of the Self: A Seminar with Michel Foucault.* London: University of Massachusetts Press.

Mill, J. (1992). *Political Writings.* ed. T. Ball. Cambridge and New York: Cambridge University Press.

Mulhall, S. and Swift, A. (eds). (1992). *Liberals and Communitarians.* Oxford: Blackwell.

Rasmussen, D. (1990). *Universalism vs. Communitarianism.* Cambridge, MA: MIT Press.

Taylor, C. (1989). *Sources of the Self: The Making of Modern Identity.* Cambridge, MA: Harvard University Press.

Chapter 12

Teaching as an Offer of (Discursive?) Meaning

Tomas Englund

Introduction

In this essay I would like to briefly describe a perspective on teaching which sees teaching as an offer of (discursive?) meaning. This view of teaching is one of the principal themes in the work of a Swedish research group concerned with the content of socialization and dimensions of citizenship with which I am involved. Our intention is *to analyze the discursive meanings offered and created in institutionalized processes*. Our approach can be seen as part of and as one interpretation of a more general *critical curriculum theory*—which I think many of us writing in this book relate to—which breaks with a long-standing tendency within curriculum research to see the curriculum as a technological or scientific-rational problem. In another context I have labeled our research program as a third stage within Swedish curriculum theory: the development of a citizenship sociology of education and curriculum. Our approach can also be seen as one specific interpretation of a the recently-aroused *didaktik* concept in Sweden (cf. Englund, 1990,1995, 1996a)

First, I would like to outline the background to the perspective that has evolved in our group and also try to relate it to the themes of this book. Second, I would like to say a few words of the research implications of our perspective.

Background

I see our perspective, and my own contribution to it, as related both to the themes presented in the earlier chapters of this book on curriculum and curriculum making in historical perspective and the later chapters on reconceptualization, in the sense that I (and we) have tried to develop an approach which looks at teaching, education and curriculum as ethical and political enterprises (cf. Schilling, 1986).

Concerning *curriculum theory and history*, I was inspired in particular by the work of Ulf Lundgren who, in his development of the frame factor theory, distinguished a structure in the outwardly observable sense and a structure carrying inner meaning. What I and my research group have tried to do, initially in *Curriculum as a Political Problem* (Englund, 1986) and in later work, is to try to develop a theory not of the structure of an inner meaning but of an inner, *contingent*, not *a priori*-given, meaning-bearing content of education, implying a shift from a structuralist to a post-structuralist perspective.

What I tried to develop in my earlier studies on this theme was an understanding of the possible, and shifting, interpretation of the determinants of the meaning-bearing character of the curriculum in historical perspective and from within the perspective of struggling social forces. I sought to analyze the different world-views (not the structure) of the curriculum, proceeding from the curriculum as a document and the textbook curriculum in school subjects like history and social studies which deal with the relationship between the individual and society.

As regards the theme of *curriculum making*, I developed a view of curriculum making as a discursive production, but at the same time one which reflects political compromises, opening the way for different interpretations, both in the process of curriculum making and in its end-result—curriculum texts which could be interpreted in different ways. This line of development has led us to different kinds of text analysis (cf. Säfström 1994, 1996; Östman 1995, 1996).

I was, and still am, especially interested in the process of *creating a sense of community* and the tensions inherent in the creation of a political consensus and what can be interpreted as common meanings—while there is no consensus about how to understand and live such meanings (cf. Taylor, 1985). This is the specific paradox of curriculum making and its end result—there is always room for different interpretations of one and the same text.

One outcome of the research which I am still working on, and in which I am trying to develop an understanding of giving education different discursive meanings, are the three conceptions or metadiscourses which I originally outlined in my *Curriculum as a Political Problem* (Englund, 1986): patriarchal, scientific-rational and democratic. These conceptions refer to coherent, although not necessarily comparable, approaches to the fundamental dimensions shaping the design of education, with special reference to citizenship education, to the selection of its content, and to its status and character.

I was also inspired by the different strands of what came to be called the *reconceptualization* movement within curriculum theory, which emphasized the moral and political character of the curriculum and looked at education from a political philosophical standpoint. It is this political philosophical perspective which I have tried to develop: looking at education as a citizenship right (cf. Englund, 1994), the communitarian challenge to individualist notions of education, and so on.

The work of the research group can also—consistent with the reconceptualization movement understood in broad terms—be seen as *an attempt to rethink teaching as a moral act* (cf. Östman, 1994) while at the same time conceptualizing schooling as part of the process of *creating a public* (cf. Englund 1991a, 1996a; Ljunggren, 1996), *a public identity, and of creating citizens*.

Research Implications

Let me now offer a few words on the research implications of our perspective:

I do not like talking about anything's essence but perhaps one can say—to relate to the title of this section of this book— *that the essence of teaching is just that it is an offer of meaning or more adequate meanings: all teaching is meaning-bearing*.

My starting point—in line with what has already been said—is that *teaching is a kind of moral and social action implying different forms of choices*. The choices can be more or less conscious as expressions of historically institutionalized practices, a selective tradition, or very deliberate actions; whatever—there is a room for contingency in the teaching processes and the choices made (through textbooks, teachers and students) imply that students are offered specific, discursive meanings and others are excluded.

It is from this perspective on teaching that we have explored and developed theories and methods to make comparisons between different choices and to clarify the resulting meanings. To quote from our research program:

> The primary sources of inspiration for the development of curriculum theory and didactics we have found in the sociology of knowledge (especially Mannheim, 1952) and in pragmatism (Dewey, 1966, 1985), neo-pragmatism (Bernstein and Rorty) and post-structural theories of meaning (e.g., Cherryholmes, 1988). The tradition within the sociology of knowledge that we refer to focuses competing views of man, nature and knowledge; neo-pragmatism seeks to clarify meaning and post-structural theory of meaning tells us how meaning is created and can be investigated.

What the methods used have in common is that they build on comparisons and clarifications of meaning. They search for differences in order to make comparisons possible. In addition to historical and philosophically-based studies, including curriculum history, we are using and developing techniques of text analysis inspired by the traditions mentioned (cf. Englund, 1996a).

The meaning-bearing dimension is always present through the selection and constitution of meaning, implying that in socialization and communication processes "knowledge" is always discursively produced, perspective-giving, and argumentative. These processes are thus expressions of social actions of a very specific kind. To analyze discursively-produced knowledge, we need to show how different contextualizations carry different social meanings (Englund, 1991a; Säljö 1990). Moreover, different meanings can be constituted in the socialization process, and these are often mutually contradictory. Frequently, however, one of the meanings involved carries particular authority.

This means that educational research has to develop a language to describe the ever-present normative component, the meaning-bearing dimension of socialization and communication processes. For a long time the knowledge conveyed through these processes has been taken for granted or reduced to a psychological or sociological level, without any attempt to problematize the meaning of the knowledge and values concerned. That meaning has been characterized either as "good" or socially rational, by educational researchers drawing on the traditional sociology of education, or as an expression of the exercise of power, by those oriented towards the new sociology of education (Englund 1995; cf. Wexler, 1987).

However, analyses of the power and meaning associated with these processes can be seen as less black-and-white and their ethical and political significance defined more precisely if they are contextualized and related to the spectrum of perspectives represented by different social groups and political opinions and traditions (cf. Mannheim, 1952). This spectrum produces different ways of looking at the world, in turn imparting different discursive meanings to the knowledge offered and created in socialization and communication processes.

This leads us to the following concrete research implications: *It is essential, first, to try to uncover different socially based perspectives of knowledge and to give names to these different perspectives and, second, to treat and develop the possible confrontation between these different perspectives in both educational research and in actual teaching as communicative practice.*

As regards the first point, a possible way forward is to analyze and systematize different notions of knowledge by drawing attention to the different contexts in which it can be located and the social and political anchorage it can thus be given. These notions can in turn be linked to educational philosophies. These have been present, and have given different meanings to institutionalized socialization processes, even if they have not been explicit (cf. Englund, 1986: ch. 7–8) as a result of being hidden for a long time beneath a scientific-rational surface (Lundgren, 1979). More specifically, I wish to see different educational philosophies, didactic typologies and curriculum emphases for school subjects, etc., given names, substance, and a social context. If this is done analytically, the choices constantly being made within these processes, and their consequences, can be located and made open to comparison. As I see it, one of the central tasks of educational research should be the development of a language for these choices and that is what we are doing in some of our work (cf. Englund, 1986; Östman, 1995).

The second issue, to treat and explore the confrontation between different perspectives as a ground for teaching as com-

municative practice, implies a sophisticated relationship between research on teaching and the development of teaching
itself. Its common ground, however, is what I—from a Swedish
horizon—will call the *didactic* aspect: the possible
problematization of the content of education, of teaching and
learning. This leads to a specific demand on teacher education as a site for the development of *teachers' didactic competence*
(cf. Englund, 1991b, 1996b).

Consequences for Educational Research, Teacher Education and Teaching

In summary, the consequences of our starting points for (1)
educational research, (2) teacher education and (3) actual teaching are as follows.

In relation to educational research one is forced, as Rorty
(1983: 203–204) suggests, to

> emphasize, as Dewey did, the moral importance of the social sciences—
> their role in widening and deepening our sense of community and of
> the possibilities open to this community. Or one can emphasize, as
> Michel Foucault does, the way in which the social sciences have served
> as instrument of "the disciplinary society," the connection between
> knowledge and power rather than that between knowledge and hu-
> man solidarity.

However, there is, according to Cherryholmes (1988: 179–80),
a possibility to

> think of these paths not as heading off in different directions but as
> criss-crossing in irregular and unexpected ways. They are not mutu-
> ally exclusive. Furthermore, attending to Foucault's warning may be
> required for the success of Dewey's project.

Rorty's conclusion that Dewey is to be preferred because his
language creates the space and the potential to develop human solidarity by means of communication should be noted.
By seeing educational research as having the role of facilitating the prerequisites for communication we are pursuing an
educational philosophical standpoint where education is seen
"as the process of forming fundamental dispositions, intellectual and emotional, toward nature and fellow men, [where]

philosophy may even be defined *as the general theory of education*" (Dewey, 1916/1966 :328).

This path, this kind of analysis of the confrontation between different perspectives, leads us beyond objectivism and relativism (Bernstein, 1983) to a research emphasis which says that social science (and educational research) has to ask questions concerning what Aristotle called *phronesis* and *praxis*, i.e., to be able to say something about, or rather to analyze critically, how we should live and not be confined to mere technique (*techne*).

Secondly, the development of didactically competent teachers within teacher education implies the need to constantly problematize and scrutinize what is to be taught. The didactically competent teacher has to be open to different solutions, and be aware of and knowledgeable about the consequences of different choices of content and methods (cf. Englund, 1996b).

This problematizing perspective relates the content of education to a variety of contexts, giving it different social meanings. A more detailed presentation of this perspective can only be made in relation to specific (school) subject areas. The didactics of foreign languages, of Swedish as a first language, of mathematics, social studies, science and so on all have their specific starting-points and problems. Within every subject area, different didactic typologies, different ways of approaching the content, can be developed and distinguished, creating different preconditions for choosing the content and the meanings that it creates. The didactically competent teacher will be interested in and aware of these different possibilities, because school knowledge/classroom communication is necessarily something other than a recitation of decontextualized subject theory/scientific knowledge.

Within this perspective there is of course an awareness of the professional aspects that educationalists have emphasized for a long time—the need to consider and reflect upon one's practice in relation to the aims underlying the curriculum, a curriculum which, in Sweden at least, is the democratically agreed document on which the activities of schools are to be based.

Thus, what I want to particularly emphasize is the need to reflect upon and problematize not only the content of education, but also *the intentions behind the curriculum*. School knowledge as such can be seen as a question of democracy which invites an ongoing discussion about what to study and from what angle. This also raises the question of the balance between established and alternative subject areas, e.g. environmental and media studies, and of how the latter can be given legitimate space and how they are to be studied.

Of course the role of the teacher educator is central to developing the didactic competence of teachers. Teacher educators are their natural vanguard. They therefore have to move—if they have not done so already—from a focus on methods of instruction, on teaching the "right" way to teach, to a didactic perspective. With a didactic outlook, you distance yourself from the methods perspective and realize that the method you are choosing is one of many *and* comparable possibilities, possibilities which can be made the subject of didactic analysis. In the same way, a textbook (or parts of it) can be seen as a choice among different, comparable possibilities and, again, be subjected to didactic research.

Thirdly, the development of actual teaching in line with such a view implies a readiness to act reflectively, in relation to a vision. Our fundamental educational problem today is not, as Burbules (1993: 151) underlines:

> one of turning schools into better engines of increased economic productivity and growth, or of finding more and more directive ways to inculcate students with a body of "basic facts" that we presume they need to know. It is in finding ways to involve schools in creating and maintaining conditions in which inclusive, democratic, and open-ended dialogue can thrive. Such an endeavor is *basic* to our individual flourishing and to fostering the sociopolitical development of equality and freedom.

A critical pragmatism, in the spirit of the mature Dewey (1927):

> involves a conception of a critical public, free inquiry and communication, the growth of imagination, and the embodiment of purposeful habits of conduct as essential not only to the realization of inquiry but to the ultimate goals of life as well. With its claim that all knowledge is inescapably fallible, it radically opposes the fundamentalist tendencies of this age of abstraction toward final solutions (Rochberg-Halton, 1986: 18).

Translated into a communicative practice of teaching:

becoming a part of the public does not involve learning what the proper response is to an item stimulus. . . . [Rather] it is finding a way to enter the conversation about the significance of a flow of historical events and about the meaning that are to be attached to them (Feinberg, 1989: 136).

References

Bernstein, R. (1983). *Beyond Objectivism and Relativism: Science, Hermeneutics and Praxis.* Oxford: Blackwell.

Burbules, N. (1993). *Dialogue in Teaching: Theory and Practice.* New York: Teachers College Press.

Cherryholmes, C. (1988). *Power and Criticism: Poststructural Investigations in Education.* New York: Teachers College Press.

Dewey, J. (1916/1966). *Democracy and Education.* New York: MacMillan/Free Press.

Dewey, J. (1927/1985). *The Public and its Problems.* Athens, Ohio: Ohio University Press.

Englund, T. (1986). *Curriculum as a Political Problem. Changing Educational Conceptions, with Special Reference to Citizenship Education.* Uppsala Studies in Education 25. Lund: Studentlitteratur.

Englund, T. (1990). På väg mot en pedagogiskt dynamisk analys av innehållet (Towards a dynamic analysis of the content of schooling). *Forskning om Utbildning,* 17 (1), 19–35.

Englund, T. (1991a). Educational discourses and creating a public: A critical pragmatic view. Paper to the International Conference on "social reproduction, social inequality and resistance: new directions in the theory of education" at the Center for Interdisciplinary Research (ZiF), University of Bielefeld, October 2–4 1991.

Englund, T. (1991b). Didaktisk kompetens [Didactic competence]. *Didactica Minima,* (18/19), 8–18.

Englund, T. (1994). Education as a citizenship right: a concept in transition: Sweden related to other Western democracies and political philosophy. *Journal of Curriculum Studies,* 26 (4), 383–399.

Englund, T (1995). Narrow and broad didactics in Sweden: Towards a dynamic analysis of the content of schooling. In S. Hopmann & K. Riquarts (Eds.), *Didaktik and/Cur-*

riculum. Kiel: Institut für die Pädagogik der Naturwissenschaften, Universität Kiel, 125–150.

Englund, T. (1996a). The public and the text. *Journal of Curriculum Studies*, 28 (1), 1–35.

Englund, T. (1996b). Are professional teachers a good thing? In I. Goodson & A. Hargreaves (Eds.), *Teachers Professional Lives*. London: Falmer, 75–87.

Feinberg, W. (1989). Foundationalism and Recent Critiques of Education. *Educational Theory*, 39 (2), 133–39.

Ljunggren, C. (1996). Education, media and democracy. On communication and the nature of the public in the light of John Dewey, Walter Lippman and the discussion of modernity. *Journal of Curriculum Studies*, 28 (1), 73–90.

Lundgren, U. (1979). *Att organisera omvärlden. En introduktion till läroplansteori.* [Organizing the World Around us: An Introduction to Curriculum Theory]. Stockholm: Liber.

Mannheim, K. (1952). *Essays on the Sociology of Knowledge*. London: Routledge & Kegan Paul. (Originally published in German 1923–1929).

Rochberg-Halton, E. (1986). *Meaning and Modernity: Social Theory in the Pragmatic Attitude.* Chicago: University of Chicago Press.

Rorty, R. (1979). *Philosophy and the Mirror of Nature.* Princeton: Princeton University Press.

Rorty, R. (1983). *Consequences of Pragmatism.* Minneapolis: University of Minnesota Press.

Schilling, M. (1986). Knowledge and liberal education. *Journal of Curriculum Studies*, 18 (1), 1–16.

Säfström, CA. (1994). *Makt och mening. Förutsättningar för en innehållsfokuserad pedagogisk forskning.* [Power and meaning. The prior conditions for content-focused educational research]. Uppsala Studies in Education 53.

Säfström, CA. (1996). Education as a science within a scientific-rational discourse. *Journal of Curriculum Studies*, 28 (1), 57–71.

Säljö, R. (1990). Språk och institution: Den institutionaliserade inlärningens metaforer. (Language and social institutions: The institutional metaphors of learning). *Forskning om Utbildning*, 17 (4), 5–17.

Taylor, C. (1985). Interpretation and the sciences of man. In C. Taylor, *Philosophy and the Human Sciences: Philosophical Papers 2*. Cambridge: Cambridge University Press, 15–57.

Wexler, P. (1987). *Social Analysis of Education: After the New Sociology*. (London: Routledge).

Östman, L. (1994). Rethinking science education as a moral act. *Nordisk Pedagogik*, 3, 141–150.

Östman, L. (1995). *Socialisation och mening. No-utbildning som politiskt och miljömoraliskt problem*. [Socialization and meaning. Science education as a political and environmental-ethical problem]. Uppsala Studies in Education 61.

Östman, L. (1996). Discourses, discursive meanings and socialization in chemistry education. *Journal of Curriculum Studies*, 28 (1), 37–55.

Chapter 13

The Formation of Conscience: A Lost Topic of Didaktik

Peter Menck

> It's your job to change the pictures of the world.
> It's my job to change your world.
> Gudmund Hernes,
> Norwegian Minister of Education, Research and Church Affairs

A First Approach to the Problem

The problem I will deal with in this essay is well known within German Didaktik:

- Johann Friedrich Herbart introduced the frequently quoted term *erziehender Unterricht* ("educative teaching").
- A variant of Herbart's term, which I will take up in this essay, is the concept of *Bildung des Gewissens* ("formation of conscience"), used in the beginning of the 1960s by Josef Derbolav, who explicitly referred to Herbart.
- In his Kiel lecture Klaus Schaller (Schaller 1995) reminded us of a very old tradition, namely the unity of *scientia* and *conscientia* (knowledge and conscience), introduced by Jan Amos Comenius.

Taking up these traditions I will—again following Derbolav—address the *difference*, for Didaktik, between knowledge and conscience. What does this mean? Let me put the problem in a way every teacher is familiar with:

He teaches his small pupils how toads live in forests and ponds; in an ecological balance with other animals and plants;

occasionally protected by human beings when this balance is threatened. Can he—and how can he—make sure that his pupils will not go catching the toads (for now they know where to find them), pulling their legs off and slashing their bellies open instead of protecting them from car drivers and little rascals?

I will show that

- the problem as such was still known in the discourse of Didaktik in the Federal Republic of Germany around 1960. Franz Fischer (Fischer 1955) and Josef Derbolav (Derbolav 1962) discussed it extensively;
- it disappeared as a problem behind "affective teaching objectives;" and that
- it most recently is one of the motives morally legitimating the postulate of "hands-on learning."

In his *Guide to Lesson Preparation* Hilbert L. Meyer reports on the following situation:

In a teaching unit on agriculture several lessons were devoted to the topic of poultry farming. The aim was to compare the natural living conditions of hens with battery farming. In a first step the pupils and the five students who had planned and given this teaching unit together made life-size hens from old newspapers and much wall paper paste. On the next day the class was split in two groups; the first group was to built a hen house similar to natural living conditions, the second group was to make a battery farm, oriented to economical aspects.

The first group then started to build their hen-houses with the help of the most simple things (a sponge was used as a bowl; a cardboard box as a coop; grass was fetched from outside); they were completed within twenty minutes. In the meantime the second group was busy putting together cardboard boxes as batteries and then conjuring up two conveyor-belts with toilet paper rolls; one for the food and one for clearing away the excrement. In a third step the pupils had a look at each others' work and discussed reasons for building their coops this or that and not another way.

In Meyer's book the result of the pupils' work is given in these pictures (see Figure 1).

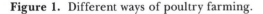

Figure 1. Different ways of poultry farming.

In their evaluation the five students reported on this part of their practice teaching:

> While we had more or less concentrated on teacher-orientation in the first two weeks we now realized that the pupils had far more fun during the lessons, that their reactions were more spontaneous, and that they used their imagination. Some pupils, who had not actively participated in the lessons before, really seemed to unbend. We experienced the same. The lessons were not planned so much in advance any more and there was room for spontaneity. Furthermore our teaching became more relaxed. By using different and—both for us and the pupils—new ways of teaching we succeeded in filling the pupils with enthusiasm for the topic of agriculture (Meyer 1980: 213–215).

I will return to this later in this essay. Before I deal with our problem let me offer a view on the situation of German Didaktik at the end of the 1950s.

The Situation in German Didaktik

The end of the 1950s and the beginning of the 1960s saw a diversified and fruitful discussion of the fundamental principles of West German Didaktik. I would view that discussion as follows:

No system of Didaktik like the one that Herbart's followers had developed in the 19th century, emerged. There was, however, a vast abundance of "practical inventions" above all in Reform Pedagogy, and of topics for discussion—some of them hundreds of years old—and only few of them incorporating related empirical disciplines. There was, furthermore, a framework created for the academic training of teachers, who were initiated into this knowledge. It must have appeared to them almost like an old house, built by the generations before them, homelike, but confusing, maybe even frightening.

The teachers of these prospective teachers must have been aware of this situation. For them, at the end of the 1950s

- compendia of Didaktik, for example, Karl Stöcker's (1960) *Modern Methods of Teaching*, were published. (The author's orientation towards a specific readership finds its expression in the title.)
- the training of teachers was reorganized, or, to put it more modestly, there were effective attempts to determine the place of practical teacher training courses within the preparation of teachers for the Volksschule (i.e., schools providing primary and secondary education). In Berlin there were Paul Heimann and Wolfgang Kramp, and Wolfgang Klafki was in Hanover.
- Derbolav's (1960) *Essay on the Philosophical Foundation of Didaktik* tried to explicate Didaktik as a science based on a unified principle—an attempt without consequences.
- Herwig Blankertz' (1969) *Theories and Models of Didaktik*, which aims at the same thing: a synopsis of the situation of Didaktik based on the theory of science, all of a sudden—and for a quarter of a century—dominated the scene. Blankertz' approach has been constantly subject to new variations, one of the last of which, developed by Werner Jank and Hilbert Meyer (1991), quite interestingly takes up older compositional components and incorporates elements of the literature of compendia as introduced by Stöcker. Maybe one could even regard the further development of these instructions for practical teacher training so that they become the so-called "Marburg Didaktik" or "Hamburg Didaktik" as steps from mere instruction to didactic theory.

This is the situation in German Didaktik as I see it. The overwhelming impression I have is the following: The classroom implies everything that teachers have to cope with. What do they have to pay attention to and how do they manage it? This perspective is not surprising: Didaktik is a vital part of teacher training—no matter whether Meyer explicitly states this in front of his students, or whether Blankertz claims it as the purpose of his undertaking in the preface of his work.

The Problem—Knowledge and Conscience

Derbolav expressed the problem of knowledge and conscience in the following way. In schools knowledge about the world is imparted, "positive" knowledge, i.e., knowledge about actual facts and their relationship to the world we live in: let us say knowledge about the origin and the basic principles of the American Declaration of Independence *and* the Declaration's binding character for the American political system. We assume that our pupils can actually benefit from this knowledge, after the lesson and even after they leave school. But how can we guarantee that a "theoretical insight into the world as our field of knowledge" implies a development of conscience, an imparting of "motives for action" within this world (Derbolav 1960: 22)? "Conscience" in this context is a code word for motives in general understood not in a moralizing but rather in a moral way, not as an expression of a certain moral system but rather as an expression of a subject's responsibility—a subject that acts and accepts responsibility for its actions. Derbolav—like Johann Friedrich Herbart many years earlier -- had no doubt that this conscience could be *formed*. But while we know that *reason* can be formed by means of knowledge, the question is how *conscience* can be formed.

To explore this Derbolav constructed a "Model of the Levels of Reflection" with the following elements:

1. First there is everyday life, dealing with things *in the world*. *Knowledge about* the nature of things is closely connected to knowledge about the right and correct ways of *dealing with* them.
2. By reflecting, man leaves a state of naïveté and builds up a certain distance from his own self and his environment,

a distance which enables him to see through things and come to correct conclusions *about the world*.

3. At the third stage responsible and independent acting *in the world* can be based upon a certain *knowledge about* man's situation in life—acquired at the second level. At the same time such action requires a set of motives which can be acquired—in ways analogous to the acquisition of knowledge—by reverting to the norms and customs guiding the ways of dealing with the world which are at hand, as it were, from the first stage (Derbolav 1960: 22).

The model seems to suggest a chronological succession with, first, the deepening of knowledge and, then, of the conscience. Such an understanding of knowledge and conscience as a chronological process would imply that there is no compulsion to actually do the one and the other. However, what Derbolav—quite logically—keeps apart should in practice happen as one—which does not necessarily make things easier. In other words, the connection between the model's elements should be understood dialectically. The unity of the didactic task as a whole should not conceal the difference between its aspects, and one aspect must not be left out at the expense of the other.

In other words, both acquisition of knowledge, which is an inevitable part of our dealing with the world, and acquisition of motives, which occurs in any event, should be the task of a school instruction which aims at contributing to the adolescents' maturity, i.e., responsible and independent living in the world. Herbart had the same aims in mind. Indeed virtually all educationalists agree on this purpose: the next generation should learn to master life in a human way—a purpose which justifies education in general and the school in particular.

An All Too Simple Solution: The Didactic Indicative

What does that mean? First of all it means that there should be a coherent situation lasting for 45 minutes. It also means that during this situation there should be an articulated process of joint and pedagogically legitimated work at the end of which problems and tasks are solved, topics thoroughly discussed, and the persons involved not hurt in their selfhood but, rather, enriched. In other words, pupils are expected to have learned something and the teachers have helped them with it. Furthermore, it is true that at the end of instruction and of schooling pupils have to face situations, examinations, where they will have to show whether they are able to solve certain tasks and problems on their own. In the Didaktik of our day it seems that exams and texts are regarded as not being necessary at all. In certain textbooks and in teaching curricula, we are told, and we learn, that success comes naturally, provided that we follow the suggested or advised way.

This assumption is expressed in a sentence we often come across in curricula: "The pupil learns . . ." And the Didaktik discourse, be it within the framework of hands-on learning, open classrooms, or new ways of education in environmental problems, is often dominated by this—as I call it—"didactic indicative." It would be much different if the language went— more honestly—like this: "In suggesting this we hope that the pupils will learn this or that," maybe followed by "It will have to be assessed, whether the desired success has been achieved."

In the training of teachers the didactic indicative has, to put it briefly, proved to be disastrous. Good intentions are passed off as reality; it is enough to "think school anew" (as Hartmut von Hentig [1994] puts it) and the school will then change automatically and, above all, its pupils will change with it. The ignorance of the problems on which the didactic indicative is based is equally disastrous in Didaktik. Reflection on teaching stops halfway through. Don't we have to think about whether we have achieved certain educational objectives or whether our instruction has made its contribution to the development of growing young people—a contribution to the establishment of stable orientations as a guidance for their lives within society? We have no reason to count on an automatism which will induce moral judgment in children after instruction based on the principles of reform pedagogy, developmental psychology, or any other principles.

About the Further Development of Motives

The issue I am exploring might be clearer if we remind ourselves of the problem we are exploring. It is a problem that is, first, posed to didactic theory in order to gain understanding and, second, posed to practice in order to be dealt with in teaching. But unfortunately, it is not an obvious problem. Derbolav himself did not make it easy for his colleagues and students to understand what he aimed at, and he did not explain how he intended to deal with the problem in detail. And soon after his essay was published the motivation to pursue the issue just disappeared in Didaktik. It is not even mentioned in Herwig Blankertz' *Theories and Models of Didaktik*. Where did it disappear to? Assuming the problem is really as important as I suggest it is, shouldn't there be something like a functional equivalent? There is one—and it comes in two variants, both of which can be identified as early as around 1960.

The So-called Educational Objectives

In 1962, Paul Heimann (1962) presented a structural analysis of teaching. It was his intention to disclose an "operational didactic field of reference" in the course of teacher training.

> Given that pupils in schools should alternately become aware of situations, be affected by them or realize something in them, we can divide teaching-intentions into the following categories:
>
> - the cognitive-active domain (knowledge, thoughts, basic convictions);
> - the affective-sympathetic domain (feelings, experiences, beliefs);
> - the pragmatic-dynamic domain (abilities, skills, habits, actions, completion of tasks).
>
> In other words these are "possibilities of development to be found in human nature, which the activity of teaching has to orient on" (p. 126).

This means that the development of beliefs and convictions as maxims of action are constitutive elements of instruction. Despite the lack of clarity with regard to Heimann's terminology, I see certain parallels between "convictions" and "beliefs" on his side and the "conscience" introduced in a more traditional terminology by Derbolav.

As we all know, a short while later a *Taxonomy of Educational Objectives* (Krathwohl 1964) was used as a means of classifying what Heimann called "intentions." However, instead of using the *Taxonomy* to define terms more precisely, a characteristic and momentous limitation of the awareness of the actual problem occurred in Didaktik: the "Affective Domain" became an "affektive Dimension" in the process of translation. The everyday use of terms then led to the connotations of the word "Affekte," meaning emotions or even passions. As a consequence, there was no more talk about the "preference for a value" or the willingness to "characterization by a value" and the like. The whole terminology was even further oversimplified—and this is still the case today—when the "Affective Domain" was merely defined in a negative way by contrasting it with the "Cognitive Domain." Therefore today we hear many complaints about a "purely cognitively-oriented teaching," and even about nonsense like "cognitive instruction contents." The "Affective Domain" is then regarded as a necessary corrective, often making use of Pestalozzi's formula "head, heart and hand." As a means of forming the heart—whatever that means —teaching procedures are suggested, especially those which grant freedom and a satisfying school life. The rest functions on its own.

Hands-on Learning

In the same year that Heimann developed his structural analysis, Klafki presented an essay entitled "The problem of an education towards responsibility" (Klafki 1962). In view of the public "complaints about the lack of willingness to accept responsibility among young people," he declared "a sense of responsibility," the willingness to "act in a responsible way or to accept responsibility for one's own actions" have to be regarded as constitutive elements of education. He proposed that both practical commitment and theoretical reflection could be means of "inducing the disposition to responsibility" (Klafki 1962: 49). Here again I see a functional equivalent to "conscience." The difference is that in Klafki's study the whole thing is completely devoid of any content.

But how can those basic convictions be induced methodically? Klafki suggests one solution—a partial abolition of school!

Maturing towards the acceptance of responsibility is achieved within a complex situation: The adolescent temporarily leaves the protected area of school and takes up the challenge of real-life experience, com-

mitment, responsibility and trial. He then returns to the protected
area. In this respect . . . the school's task lies . . . in critical reflection on experience. (Klafki 1962: 62)

One of the experiences he refers to are practical training
courses incorporated into the curriculum of secondary schools.
But these courses have had a somewhat sobering result: The
commitment, the seriousness, and the stimulus of those practical tasks, intended to induce a feeling of responsibility in young
people, were certainly there. What Klafki observed, on the
other hand, was a lack of critical reflection which was supposed to make the intended convictions available. The situative
context of action is so complex that the tasks themselves are
not clear anymore. As a consequence his considerations end
with a characteristic argument. Let me call it "schooling
utopia:"

> If the school is really serious about an education towards responsibil-
> ity it has to alter or extend its traditional way of seeing itself. It can
> not think of itself . . . as a relatively "protected area" any more, as an
> enclave for young people within the social-economical-political real-
> ity. . . . It has to . . . lead the adolescent temporarily to the experi-
> ences of fundamental interaction, commitment, and accepting respon-
> sibility in a reality *outside* school. (Klafki 1962: 71; my emphasis).

And this results in something like the cutting of the Gordian
knot:

> There should be no doubt that in the field of schools providing a
> general education, in the field of job training, evening classes, adult
> education, and teacher training important consequences regarding
> the theory of curricula and to methodology arise. (Klafki 1962: 71)

With this sword stroke of a new way of understanding ("thinking school anew") the picture of a new educational system seems
to develop logically and automatically, contrary to Alexander
the Great's experiences. However, educationalists are not politicians. And therefore, since then there has not been much
change in those areas pointed out by Klafki.

Let me be brief: In the Federal Republic of Germany of the
1980s schooling utopias like this gained many supporters. Their
motto was "Hands-on learning." It now does not seem to be
necessary any more to leave school because it is possible to

create certain situative contexts of action right in school. There is no more talk about a sense of responsibility. And Derbolav's "motives of action" are reduced to "motivation" as understood from a psychological point of view: "this is fun!"—that seems to be the only important thing in Meyer's hen battery report. I believe, however, that the moral pathos characteristic of the didacticians propagating the different varieties of hands-on learning has its roots in an unexpressed hope, in the hope that this kind of instruction promotes the formation of what we call "conscience." I assume that they do not dare to use this term because of its connection with a certain moral tradition. The fine examples—like the one I quoted at the beginning of this essay—which are intended to convince us of the usefulness of this Didaktik concept, make this assumption quite obvious. I will come back to this later.

The formation of conscience is not a topic in Didaktik today. Nevertheless I believe that it was part of the "educational objectives" of the 1970s as well part of the orientation of teaching to the principle of action of the 1980s—and it is a significant topic. In view of today's *practice* and, reverting to reflections within Didaktik of past times, I would now like to suggest how the problem could be rediscovered for today's didactic *reflection*.

Let me stress an important point immediately: I do not aim at producing a specific conscience for children and adolescents. I also do not seek means to securely implant historically-based moral values. This would be indoctrination—and nobody wants that. My problem is the *formation* of conscience, the cultivation of a moral authority, which enables the growing young people to see clearly the difference between good and evil, between use and abuse, and to choose one and condemn the other.

Let me make another observation. It was also in the 1980s that teachers, and even politicians, became passionately interested in Lawrence Kohlberg's (Kohlberg 1995) version of the problem of moral education—a version based on developmental psychology. I will not deal with this issue here. A sound knowledge of the moral development of children and adolescents is absolutely necessary for its formation. But this is not my central point of interest. First of all, it is essential to be fully aware of the *didactic* nature of the problem.

Once Again: The Problem

Usus atque abusus: The *Orbis sensualium pictus* and the primer

Jan Amos Comenius' fame has its roots in his illustrated readers for the little ones, in his *Orbis Sensualium Pictus* (Comenius 1658). Obviously they are far more than that, something that was well-known even in the 17th century. Let us take *The Fire* (see Figure 2).

The figure shows words in Latin and German, and also things presented as illustrations. And what else? A story, and a story with a moral—an obvious moral and a moral which is, however, not put into words. The story locates the place, the thing that is described, has in everyday life or, to put it more accurately, should have in everyday life. It tells us what to do and what to avoid. *Usus atque abusus*, use and abuse are shown in these pictures and in the corresponding stories—without moral reasoning, but simply by the choice of stylistic means and by their arrangement in these compositions. We are obliged to take care of the fire *without* any argument compelling, or even persuading, us to do so.

Now let's take *our* primers—the letters are embedded in stories; or take arithmetic books—the figures are incorporated in everyday situations (see Figures 3 and 4). Susanne and Alexander have to learn that $5 - 1 = 4$ and that $4/2 = 2$. At one and the same time they learn that they are able to—*and have to*—peacefully divide the candy Annette brought them.

Or let us recall that fine example of Meyer's hen battery. I am convinced that Meyer's students had intended to evoke certain feelings of "good " (Figure 1a) and of "bad" (Figure 1b) in their pupils. I am also convinced that Meyer himself selected these examples not only to demonstrate hands-on learning. *At the same time* he aims at inducing an awareness for environmental issues or creating a value judgment—without an artifi-

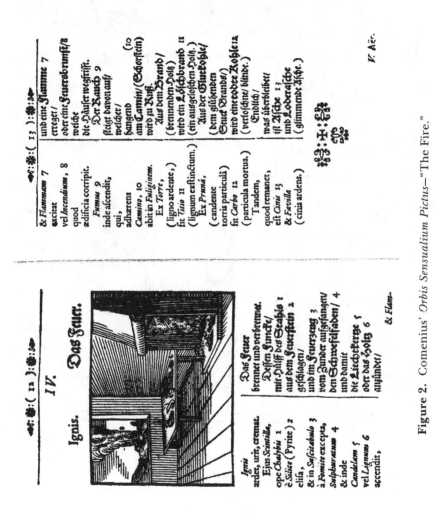

Figure 2. Comenius' *Orbis Sensualium Pictus*—"The Fire."

Figure 3. From a German primer: The letters "au," "s," "sz," "st." (1927).

cial moral but by merely looking at the pictures or, as the case maybe, the products of work.

We can find many other illustrations of this kind in the field of environmental education. There are fine examples of effective compositions, but there are also examples of compositions which do not seem to have the desired effect, and to which an artificial moral is then added, as it were. But one thing is missing. The inventors of those nice examples do not seem to fully understand what they are doing.

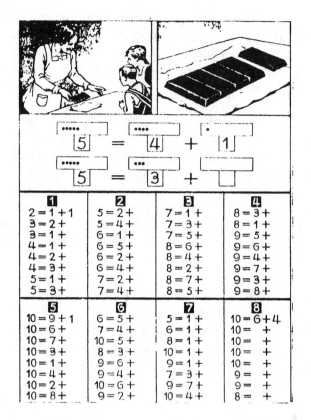

Figure 4. From a German arithmetic book (1937).

A Consensus on the Good

I will now explore what exactly happens in the cases described above. To do so I will go back to Derbolav's "Levels of Reflection" because, to my mind, it does allow us to clarify the issues:

- Susanne and Alexander start school. They learn about numbers, about natural numbers and fractions. These numbers are there only for calculations, and calculation is only done with numbers. Numbers as such do not really have anything to do with sharing candy.

- However, the story in the arithmetic book, the veiled arithmetic problem, directs our attention back to everyday life, where numbers and calculations *are* an aspect of sharing, e.g., "sharing" means dividing amounts and quantities among individuals.

Numbers—or whatever the topic of a lesson may be—*contain* a part of or an aspect of ways of dealing with everyday life, of human interaction. They *contain* an aspect of social practice. On the one hand this means that the practice is not visible, that it cannot be experienced directly; on the other hand it means that the practice of dividing is included in the notion of "fractions." It is our aim in developing a primer to re-establish the connection between school subjects and social practice.

However we have not yet dealt with the formation of conscience. It takes more to do that. Derbolav uses the long-winded phrases, "specific normative structures, implied in the contents" and the "norms worked out by the self in the educational situation, whereas at the same time a certain individually structured horizon of responsibility is gained" (Derbolav 1960: 27s.). How are we to understand this?

It is, after all, not only everyday life where it all comes. Everyday life is, furthermore and before all, guided by a consensus of what is good and bad. This consensus is not so much like the Ten Commandments' "thou shalt" but rather a "we do things, or things are done, in this or that way." This consensus can be reconstructed from the compositions and stories in the *orbis pictus* as well as from Johann Bernhard Basedow's *Elementarwerk* (Basedow 1770), and from my Nazi primer of 1941 (see Figure 5)

A Compulsion to the Good?

So what is good is given and not deliberately set by mere will. But how can we methodically form the conscience in any way, and, more particularly, in a way which guides human actions

- without the presence of physical force,
- without treating it as the consequence of a formal syllogism,

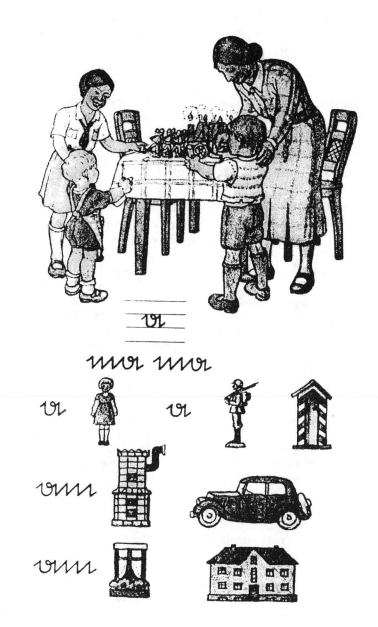

Figure 5. From a German primer: The letters "a," "am," "ma," "ma ma." (1941).

- without simply imposing moral principles, and, above all,
- without leaving the whole matter to the individual's responsibility—which is to be provoked, first of all, by teaching?

This is a didactician's, i.e., *our* question. Teachers in their classrooms know quite well how to do their job. What do they do? They tell stories and compose pictures, and they methodically arrange classrooms in such a way that the product of classroom work is convincing to the pupils' minds, so that they are prepared to willingly act in a humane way in the outside world.

Herbart conceptualized the logic of such practice in his famous Essay on *The Aesthetic Presentation of the World Being the Main Duty of Education*. He argues as follows:

> Education has to aim at morality. That means—in the terms of his psychology—that human inclinations have to be governed by will. What kind of judgment can convince the will to strive for the Good? The judgment in question cannot be a logical one as we do not look for logical consequences. Our aim is the constitution of a personality acting on moral principles and not the logical derivation of moral consequences. (cf. Herbart 1804: 105, 110, 111)

The only judgment remaining is the aesthetic judgment:

> Among all sorts of necessities for convincing [the will] there remains only the aesthetic necessity. It can be characterized as being able to create categorical judgments without any proof and without any kind of force. It is indifferent with regard to inclinations. And it develops from the perfect imagination of its object. (Herbart 1804: 110)

Now Herbart applies this to the relation of Man and Himself:

> When he finds a fundamental and practical, i.e., aesthetic necessity, a person acting on the basis of moral principles will direct his inclination to obey it." This self-reflection is possible "in so far as the self finds the very inclination contained within the object of the aesthetic judgment within himself, too. (Herbart 1804: 111)

For me this means, for example, that "in so far as the child just starting school finds his or her love of animals within the illustrations of his primer."

But with this, Herbart leads us into the depths of the philosophy of aesthetics and *Bildung*. I do not want to go into this any further. Let us go back to our didactic task instead—just as Herbart himself does in this very essay. First of all he supports "reading the Odyssey with boys." After that he thinks of all those "characters who enter the course of history, each of them illuminated if possible by his classic chronicler. Periods not described by a master and not inspiring a poet are worth very little in education" (Herbart 1804: 118). This is the neo-humanistic educational concept of the modern German Gymnasium.

To return to the beginning: Derbolav worked out this very idea in 1958 in his book on *The Example as a Principle of Education in the Gymnasium*. This is what I have been dealing with: stories, compositions, aesthetic creations in the broadest sense. In my book on the *Didactic Construction of Reality* (Menck 1986; see also Menck 1995) I speak more generally of the symbolic representation of reality: texts, pictures, and all kinds of things refer to reality; they symbolize everyday life, the social practice of man. In other words, in the classroom the presentation of reality is exclusively coded in the language of various symbolic systems. Now I can speak somewhat closer to the language of the classroom: stories are told, pictures are drawn, compositions are produced and settings are arranged.

Bringing Things Together

Let me now try to bring the threads of this account together: knowledge and conscience. But instead of an explicit argument let me present a picture (see Figure 6) and tell a story[1]

A "whining school-boy" in 1941 might have felt a strong desire to become a "soldier, jealous in honor" (Shakespeare, *As You Like It*, II. iv.) and fight battles against our enemies with mighty things like planes and cruisers. Susanne and Alexander sailed to Oslo in 1982. They read about the fate of the cruiser Blücher; they looked out for the battery of Oscarsborg; they helped their father to dip the ensign at the sight of the grave of more than 1,000 soldiers; they visited Fort Akershus; and they discussed the matter in great detail. I am sure that since then they *feel* things like war, occupation and resistance, death, and the ecological time bomb (because of the ammunition in that grave) when regarding pictures like this one and that they

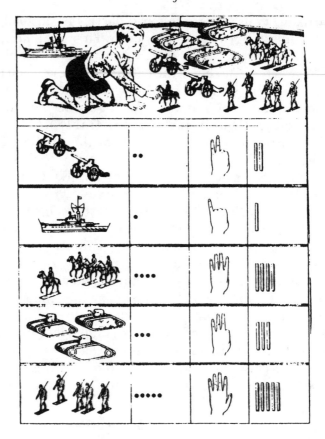

Figure 6. From a German arithmetic book (1937).

value the objects the pictures refer to accordingly. In short, their aesthetic judgment and their motives might differ somewhat from that of their father in 1941.

Knowledge is indispensable for an adequate interpretation of the pictures. And the aesthetic presentation is indispensable to provoke strong motivations towards the knowledge of what to do and how to do it.

Open Questions

German didacticians will inevitably make the following objection to my argument as a whole: Telling stories and composing pictures—that implies the risk of manipulation. Maybe that they are right. My answer to this is: Classroom is neither a stage nor TV. Stories and pictures are presented together with a task, and the presentations are followed by the pupils' work.

The lessons of Meyer's students began with an introduction about how hens live. This story provoked pictures the pupils already had in their minds. This was the beginning of the lesson and the *beginning* of a working process which *resulted* in a more appropriate and more complex conception of the world or at least of poultry farming.

So the didactician's next job is to reconstruct the structures of the double-sided process in the classroom: the process of the production of a product and, at the same time, of the formation of mind and conscience. This is one open question. There are more.

Let me refer to the Norwegian *Core Curriculum* (1994). Although this is not a textbook but, rather, a framework within which textbooks have to be produced, it is a wonderful example of what I wanted to explain here: Things and beliefs, the whole world Norwegians live in, and all that composed from the point of view of Norwegian culture—which is, by the way, in many ways the world we all live in.

This comment is more than an example of good will towards the hosts of our seminar. I mention it to allude again to the consensus on the Good. De facto this consensus is dependent on culture although, on the other hand, its *claim is universal*—otherwise we would not discuss it here. Above all this consensus is fragile and at risk. We are aware of that as well, even though in the didactic discourse we often seem to see the Good as consented—without really having agreed on it. The threat by the Bad in the world is even mentioned less.

But it is not only that. There is another problem which is not part of society outside the classroom, but is included in the methodology of the formation of conscience itself. Thus it is we, the didacticians, who are at risk. The means and the methods we use are ambiguous. There is, for example, something like an aesthetics of violence. We all are familiar with it from TV, but not only from there.

In the Norwegian *Core Curriculum* you find the picture presented in Figure 7. For me, this picture creates the feeling of strength; for Norwegians the aesthetic judgment of the "Sword

Figure 7. "Sword in Rock" (from the Norwegian *Core Curriculum*, p. 29).

in Rock," which reminds them of "the Battle of Hafrsfjord" (*Core Curriculum*: 29), may come to the conclusion of national identity. What I want to point out here may be illustrated by juxtaposing the monument against the adventures of the Viking "Roede Orm" (Bengtson 1978) so that we come to the conclusion of harm, death, and murder, too.

In other words, it is not enough to develop ways of methodologically forming the conscience to the Good. We should at the same time let Socrates guide us in changing our viewpoint. That means that the problem I have been discussing is, in a sense, already the second step. We should take the first step and, like Socrates, ask ourselves what the Good really is (see, e.g., Plato's dialogue *Laches*). And this is not something like a general philosophical or social-political problem, it is a basic problem in Didaktik. But since I am not Socrates I will leave it for a future discussion. For now, I conclude with one last picture (see Figure 8) and a simple definition of what school is.

"Schola est officina, in qua novelli animi ad Virtutem formantur"
(School is the workshop where young souls are formed to virtue).

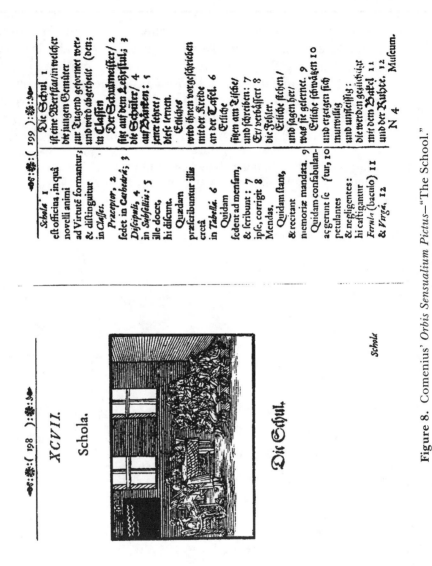

Figure 8. Comenius' *Orbis Sensualium Pictus*—"The School."

Notes

1   In Oslo, I began with the following remark: When you approach Oslo
     from the seaside you become aware of the old batteries of fort
     Oscarsborg near Drøbak. It was these batteries which destroyed the
     German cruiser Blücher on April 9, 1941. You know that the operation
     "Weseruebung" was the beginning of the occupation of Norway by the
     German army. I was not even 6 years old then, and Björg Gundem was
     around that age, too. Nevertheless, and be it even half a century later, it
     is not at all a matter of course that she and her Institute invited the
     aged German educationist to Oslo. And the warm reception we had in
     Oslo was not at all a matter of course either. Thank you all for that!

References

Basedow, J. B. (1770; 1972) *Des Elementarbuchs für die Jugend und für ihre Lehrer und Freunde in gesitteten Ständen erstes, zweites und drittes Stück. Mit dem Zubehör des Methodenbuchs und der Kupfersammlung etc.* Altona, Bremen; reprint Hildesheim: Olms.

Bengtsson, F. G. (1978) *Die Abenteuer des Roede Orm.* München.

Blankertz, H. (1969) *Theorien und Modelle der Didaktik.* München: Juventa.

Comenius, J. A. (1978) *Orbis Sensualium Pictus.* Dortmund: Harenberg.

Core Curriculum for Primary, Secondary and Adult Education in Norway (1994) Oslo: The Royal Ministry of Church, Education and Research.

Derbolav, J. (1960) Versuch einer wissenschaftstheoretischen Grundlegung der Didaktik. In *Beih. der Zeitschrift für Pädagogik, 2,* 17–45.

Fischer, F. (1955) Die Erziehung des Gewissens. In J. Derbolav & F. Nicolin (Eds.), *Geist und Erziehung. Kleine Bonner Festgabe für Theodor Litt* (147–188) Bonn: Bouvier.

Heimann, P. (1970) Didaktik als Theorie und Lehre. In D. C. Kochan (Ed.), *Allgemeine Didaktik. Fachdidaktik. Fachwissenschaft. Ausgewählte Beiträge aus den Jahren 1953–1969* (407–461). Darmstadt: Wissenschaftliche Buchgesellschaft.

von Hentig, H. (1994) *Die Schule neu denken.* München: Hanser

Herbart, J. F. (1964) Über die ästhetische Darstellung der Welt als das Hauptgeschäft der Erziehung. In W. Asmus (Ed.), *Johan Friedrich Herbart. Pädagogische Schriften,* Vol 1 (105–121). München: Küpper vorm. Bondi.

Jank, W. & Meyer, H. L. (1991) *Didaktische Modelle.* Frankfurt/Main: Scriptor.

Klafki, W. (1963) Engangement und Reflexion im Bildungsprozeß. Zum Problem der Erziehung zur Verantwortung. In W. Klafki, *Studien zur Bildungstheorie und Didaktik.* Weinheim: Beltz Verlag.

Kohlberg, L. (1995) *Die Psychologie der Moralentwicklung.* Frankfurt/Main: Suhrkamp.

Krathwohl, D., Bloom, B. S., & Masia, B. (1964) *A Taxonomy of Educational Objectives. Handbook II The Affective Domain.* New York: David McKay.

Menck, P. (1986) *Unterrichtsinhalt oder: Ein Versuch ueber die Konstruktion der Wirklichkeit im Unterricht.* Frankfurt/Main, Bern, Nancy, New York: Lang.

Menck, P. (1995) Didactics as construction of content. *Journal of Curriculum Studies,* 27 (4), 353–371.

Meyer, H. L. (1980) *Leitfaden zur Unterrichtsvorbereitung.* Königstein i. Ts.: Scriptor.

Schaller, K. (1995) Die Didaktik des Johann Amos Comenius zwischen Unterrichtstechnologie und Bildungstheorie. In S. Hopmann; W. Klafki; A. Krapp. & K. Riquarts (Eds.). (1995). Didaktik und/oder Curriculum. Beiheft 34 der *Zeitschrift für Pädagogik* (47–60). Weinheim: Beltz.

Stöcker, K. (1960) *Neuzeitliche Unterrichtsgestaltung.* München: Ehrenwirth.

Chapter 14

The Essence of Teaching

Erling Lars Dale

I would like to share with you some thoughts from my work on the notion of rationality in the educational system. I started out twenty-years ago (see Dale, 1972) as a critic of the means/ end model, of instrumentalism, in the educational system. My sources at that time were, especially, Max Horkheimer and Jürgen Habermas. Teaching is tied, I believed then and also believe today, to practical-moral principles, to the ethics of communicative acts. However the issue I would like to consider in this essay centers on rationality in the communicative act of teaching. What are the social conditions of communicative rationality in the performance of teaching?

The argument will run as follows: conscious deliberation, that is, the teacher's awareness when he or she chooses what to do (i.e., Aristotle's practical wisdom) in the classroom, is superficial. The decisions the teachers make when performing, in the act of teaching, have their background in the rationale of teaching, the underlying cultural teaching code. With reference to Ludwig Wittgenstein we call it agreement in judgment; or, with reference to the French philosopher Merleau-Ponty, in form of life and way of perception. I am going to reformulate the argument: the underlying cultural teaching code, the rationale of teaching, can socially produce irrationality in the performance of teaching.

I will divide this essay into four sections. Firstly, I will establish the context of rationality: the relation between curriculum, teaching and learning experiences. Secondly, I will discuss the concept of rationality. In the third section I will focus on the teaching performance. I will conclude by pointing to the life-experiences that we find most fruitful outside the "essence of teaching".

The Context of Educational Rationality

I distinguish between three levels of competence: the carrying out of teaching (C1), the construction of teaching programs (C2), and communicating in and constructing of a theory of teaching plans, the act of teaching itself, and the pupils' process of learning (C3). Carrying out teaching (C1) demands a sensitive presence in a situation which is more or less marked by forced action. The capability and the quality of learning activities in the immediate relation between teacher and pupil indicates the first level of competence. The second level of competence (C2), involving a weaker incentive to act, is about developing local teaching plans or, as they are defined here, as the construction of teaching programs.

This communication, within a community and giving priority to goal-setting, planning, and evaluation, should be as central a part of the practice of the teaching profession as the carrying out of teaching in itself. The third level of practice (C3) concerns presenting arguments, supporting points of view, and discussing, for example, what the ensuring of quality in the educational system means. Pedagogical research with its freedom from forced action belongs to this level of competence (C3). The basic themes are the goal of the teaching, its content, method, and evaluation; the construction of the theory of what should be learned, of ways of organizing and learning of content, and answers as to why, i.e. to legitimate the goal, the content, the method, and the evaluation.

Carrying out teaching (C1) according to a constructed teaching program (C2), legitimated by a theory of education (C3), represents professional teaching. The main feature of teaching is the realization of a curriculum with educational consequences in the student's learning experiences. By curriculum in this essay I mean what Hilda Taba (1962) called a "Teaching-Learning Unit," a teaching program developed by an individual schools with a national curriculum as general framework. A teaching program (C 2) is prior to the practice in the classroom (C 1). The national curriculum provides the guidelines which the teachers, together with their colleagues, have to interpret and analyze, and then construct the aims for their own specific teaching based on these interpretations and analyses. They have also to choose the concrete content for the actual teaching and organize the content in adequate learning sequences/episodes.

With Elliot Eisner (1994), I would emphasize the distinction between curriculum (C 2) and teaching (C 1). It is possible to appraise the intellectual significance of the curriculum independent of the teaching. The performance of teaching, the art of teaching (C 1), is a different context from the planning of series of educational events (C 2). I define teaching as a social system for goal-oriented learning based on communication between actors who participate in the interaction as pupil/student and as teacher (C 1). The organization of learning experiences is therefore "the essence of teaching," and one of the key-questions is how well a worthwhile curriculum is thought through?

We find the answer in the students' learning experiences, in the interaction between the learner and the conditions in the environment to which he responds. As Ralph Tyler (1949): put its "Learning takes place through the active behavior of the student; it is what *he* does that he learns, not what the teacher does". Learning experiences are, therefore, a context separate from the act of teaching, although the success of teaching is dependent on the active participation of the students. Their attention has to be attracted and stimulated towards the desired type of actions. Hilda Taba (1962) talks about the rhythm of learning activities, of the balance between input, reflection, synthesis, and expression; about the appropriate rhythm of absorbing and consolidating, internalizing, and reorganizing; about incorporating the dynamics of creative learning. This is a matter of vital importance. In John Dewey's (1966: 249) words: ". . . every subject at some phase of its development should possess, what is for the individual concerned with it, an aesthetic quality.." Students achieve educational learning experiences through aesthetic quality.

When the effect of teaching, through the aesthetic quality in the learning experiences, enters into the personality of the learner, influences his point of view and his attitudes, the results of teaching are meaningful for the students. This meaningful teaching take part in shaping their mental development. The essence of teaching is accomplished.

Educational Rationality

Rational behavior appears most typically in the willingness to expose oneself to criticism and to give reasons for what one does and says. The main point is that rationality shows itself in a form of behavior for which there are good reasons.

I want to underline four aspects of the notion of rationality: realization, consistency, critical analysis, and rational dialogue. Let us consider how rationality works in the following fundamental questions: Does the teaching realize the intentions of the curriculum? Are the students' activities consistent with the worthwhile development of the students?

In a specific situation inconsistency between the activities of the student and of the teacher, and the educational goal, does not illustrate irrationality. But if this inconsistency persists and this process, through repetition, becomes a structural phenomenon, educational irrationality is established. It is not the conflict between the educational goal and the actual learning experience that is irrational, but the permission given by the situation not to deal with the inconsistency through rational dialogue that deconstructs the essence of teaching

The Act, the Performance of Teaching

As mentioned earlier, by the word "teaching" I understand an organized social system for goal-related learning. Educational rationality is linked to three aspects of the system: the teacher's understanding of the goal, his or her interpretation of the situation, and sensitivity in the context. The ability to make rapid interpretations of situations and moods in the present moment of teaching is required along with some practical wisdom.

This way of teaching educational rationality has to be based on a rationale. Wittgenstein makes a distinction between agreement in opinion and agreement in form of life, between agreement not only in definition but also in judgment. Agreement in judgments is related, by what I understand by the rationale, to some kind of cultural constancy in the way of teaching, to the existence of a custom, to behavioral rules in the classroom.

A rationale signifies that the teachers are trained to follow a rule analogous to obeying an order or analogous to reacting to an order in a particular way. The rules of educational rationality are: to realize worthwhile curriculum intentions in teaching; to create a real consistency between worthwhile curriculum intentions and learning experiences. These rules are embedded in customs, institutions, etc. . Educational rationality is, therefore, a cultural practice. Decision-making within teaching as a game is conscious i.e., it has rationality, but when teachers make these decisions they are not the ones choosing the rules (the rationale). In the moment of deliberation (rationality) one obeys the rule blindly (the rationale).

Rationality and the rationale are, I think, comparable to the blind man's use of his stick when it has ceased to be an object for him. The stick (the rules of educational rationality) is no longer perceived as isolated; its point has become an area of interpretation and sensitivity. Learning to find one's way among things with a stick is an example of a perceptual habit. The rationale is the underlying code, the perceptual habit for some phenomena.

My thesis is: The rationale, the cultivation of educational rationality as a habit, is not established in public schools; a rationale for educational rationality is not at work in public schools. The term "the essence of teaching" is, therefore, a criterion of criticism.

In this respect I would like to refer some research (C 3)—to Linda M. McNeil's *Contradictions of Control* (1986) and John Goodlad's *A Place Called School* (1983). McNeil: "Adults who visit high school classrooms are often struck by the dullness of the lessons. Those who visit systematically note the overwhelming prevalence of boring content, dull presentations and bored but patient students.". And as an empirical fact of places called schools, Goodlad claims: "Boredom is a disease of epidemic proportions" and he refers to Andy Warhol's "The Haircut" to describe "all this sameness" in 38 schools, with 17,163 students and 1,350 teachers in more than 1.000 classrooms.

A rationale for educational irrationality, a defensive style of teaching of low instructional quality, is typical in public schools. The teacher learns to control the classroom by presenting the content in a way that requires limited, brief and correct answers, a content that is easily transmitted and graded. The potential richness of the content is transformed to subject content with simplistic "facts" (Linda McNeil).

A rationale that produces irrationality, is pathological. This concern about critical analysis of the relations between the curriculum, the teaching and the students' learning experiences is nothing more than a social, cultural and historical product of a rationale for educational research (C 3). The concept of teaching, rational dialogue about the essence of teaching, does not belong to the tradition of teaching, but to the research community.

But why is it not possible for teacher training to change the rationale in the schools so that they function more rationally from an educational perspective function ?

Changing the rationale of the level of practice (C 1) is not only a question within the school system. The forms of life within the schools, the internal logic of their functioning has to be analyzed within the framework of cultural reproduction and the educational system as an agency of exclusion and selection, a reproduction of class relations which (perhaps) functions more effectively when the pathological rationale in the public schools is concealed (Bourdieu, 1977). If this thesis is adequate to the case, we see that the society seems to have no need for a science of education with its rational dialogues on the essence of teaching (C 3)—nor for a link between the training of teachers and a critical science of education.

Life-experiences Outside the Essence of Teaching

I shall not discuss the irrationality of teaching further. The notion, the essence of teaching, becomes meaningful when we point to the life-experiences outside the organized learning process at school, to the world of leisure time. But surely we can in poetical teaching, as I seek to do in the following, draw attention to the world of tranquillity, where silence is the gate to feel harmony in the twilight.

Acknowledging the world outside the arranged processes of learning, we follow rock poet Van Morrison[1]

Got To Go Back!

Follow his story:

I used to look out
My classroom window
and dream
And then go home and
listen to Ray sing

It is outside the rational rooms of organized learning that time is good for

Meditation
contemplation too
(. . .)
For the healing goes on
with the dreaming.

Not until we turn away from a series of acts of goal oriented work and enter a state of calm meditation, do we let others in and experience

Oh The Warm Feeling

Van Morrison continues:

Like a child within the
kingdom
As we sat beside the sea
Oh the warm feeling as I
sat by you.
And it filled with devotion
(. . .)
And it healed all my
emotions
As I sat by you

In such a meditative, quiet mood, with closeness to the other sex, a possibility is given for blissful desires to join aesthetics— and we set out on a journey to

A Town Called Paradise

and experience the borderline of rationality

In The Garden.

Van Morrison continues:

> *And you went into a*
> *trance*
> *Your childlike vision*
> *became so fine*
> *And we heard the bells*
> *inside the church*
> *We loved so much*
> *And felt the presence of*
> *the youth of*
> *Eternal summers in the*
> *garden.*
> *And as I touched your*
> *cheeks so lightly*
> *Born again you were and*
> *blushed and we touched*
> *each other lightly.*

We are—

Just You and I and Nature–

and we understand the human value of metaphysical life-experiences beyond the educational rationality; we appreciate Van Morrison's words:

No Guru, no method, no teacher

Note

1   Reprinted from E. L. Dale: *Pedagogisk profesjonalitet*. Oslo: Gyldendal
    Norsk Forlag, 1989, (231–233) by permission of the publisher. All rights
    reserved.

References

Bourdieu, P. & Passeron, J.C. (1977). *Reproduction. In Education, Society and Culture.* Beverley Hills, CA: Sage.

Dale, E. L. (1972). *Pedagogikk og samfunnsforandring.* [Education and Change in Society] Oslo: Gyldendal Norsk Forlag.

Dewey, J. (1966). *Democracy and Education.* New York: Free Press.

Eisner, E. W. (1994). *The Educational Imagination,* 3rd Edition. New York: Macmillan.

Goodlad, J. (1984). *A Place Called School.* New York: McGraw-Hill.

McNeil, Linda M. (1986). *Contradictions of Control: School Structure and School Knowledge.* New York and London: Routledge.

Morrison, V. (1986*). No Guru, No Method, No Teacher. A CD.*

Taba, H. (1962). *Curriculum Development. Theory and Practice.* New York: Harcourt, Brace & World.

Tyler, R. W. (1949). *Basic Principles of Curriculum and Instruction* Chicago: University of Chicago Press.

Wittgenstein, L. (1984). *Philosophical Investigations.* Oxford: Basil Blackwell.

Chapter 15

Understanding Curriculum[1]: A Postscript for the Next Generation

William F. Pinar
William M. Reynolds
Patrick Slattery
Peter M. Taubman

The field is no longer moribund;
the field is no longer arrested.
There is turbulence now
(William F. Pinar & Janet L. Miller, 1982, p. 222).

The mood is invitation, and humbleness,
and deep search, first, for the germ of life
in oneself and, then, in [humankind]
(Ross L. Mooney, 1967b, 211).

An awareness of and sensitivity toward many
environments—physical, psychological, social, and
spiritual—are integral parts of postmodern
proposals which inform . . . curriculum
(Patrick Slattery, 1989, p. 156).

The time is certainly right for curriculum change.
So in an era of crisis and complaint,
we are cautiously optimistic and hopeful
(William E. Doll, Jr., 1983, p. 109).

The next century is ours
(Jacques Daignault, 1992, p.196).

Prefatory note: The curriculum field has achieved a new identity, one based on understanding rather than curriculum development. We come to this conclusion after a seven-year study of the field, published in 1995 by Peter Lang, entitled *Understanding Curriculum*. We present the final chapter which speaks, in a letter to the next generation, to the new identity of the American curriculum field.

I
Introduction

You're back. It has been a long journey, we realize, these past fourteen chapters. You were introduced to many, and sometimes complex, ideas. You heard a very large number of individuals speaking in their own voices. These ideas and voices required you to shift your ground many, many times, so that you could appreciate what these ideas were about, what these voices were saying, and why. And you thought curriculum was what the district office required you to teach, or what the state education department published in scope and sequence guides, or, if you are yet to teach, a list of books you were to read. As you know now, curriculum incorporates those literal and institutional meanings, but it is by no means limited to them. What you know now is that curriculum is a highly symbolic concept. It is what the older generation chooses to tell the younger generation. So understood, curriculum is intensely historical, political, racial, gendered, phenomenological, autobiographical, aesthetic, theological, and international. Curriculum becomes the site on which the generations struggle to define themselves and the world.

Curriculum is a extraordinarily complicated conversation. Curriculum as institutional text is a formalized and abstract version of conversation, a term we usually use to refer to those open-ended, highly personal, and interest-driven events in which persons encounter each other. That curriculum has become so formalized and distant from the everyday sense of conversation is a profound indication of its institutionalization and its bureaucratization. Instead of employing others' conversations to enrich our own, we "instruct" students to participate in others'—i.e. textbook authors'—conversations, employing others' terms to others' ends. Such social alienation is an inevitable consequence of curriculum identified with the academic disciplines as they themselves have been institutionalized and bureaucratized over the past one hundred years. Over the past twenty years the American curriculum field has attempted "to take back" curriculum from the bureaucrats, to make the curriculum field itself a conversation, and in so doing, work to understand curriculum. We invite you to participate in that conversation.

Without wishing to pre-empt the aims of your instructor who may have assigned this textbook, we appealed to you directly in chapter one not to regard this textbook as a catechism to be memorized and recited. We appealed to you to regard this textbook as the field appears to be suggesting that we—teachers and students—regard the school curriculum: as a provocation to reflect on and to think critically about ourselves, our families, our society. The point of the school curriculum is not to succeed in making us specialists in the academic disciplines. The point of school curriculum is not to produce accomplished test-takers, so that American scores on standardized tests compare favorably to Japanese or German scores. The point of the school curriculum is not to produce efficient and docile employees for business. The point of the school curriculum is to goad us into caring for ourselves and our fellow human beings, to help us think and act with intelligence, sensitivity, and courage in both the public sphere—as citizens aspiring to establish a democratic society—and in the private sphere, as individuals committed to other individuals. As feminist theory has shown, the two spheres are distinguishable in concept only. Once we shift the point of the curriculum away from the institutional, economic, and political goals of others, once we "take it back" for ourselves, we realize we must explore curriculum as a historical event itself. That is, as soon as we take hold of the curriculum as an opportunity for ourselves, as citizens, as persons, we realize that curriculum changes as we reflect on it, engage in its study, and act in response to it, toward the realization of our ideals and dreams. Curriculum ceases to be a thing, and it is more than a process. It becomes a verb, an action, a social practice, a private meaning, and a public hope. Curriculum is not just the site of our labor, it becomes the product of our labor, changing as we are changed by it.

This has been a backward-looking book in one sense. We wanted that. We wanted to link the field that exists now with the field that existed then. The curriculum field has been suffering a kind of identity crisis, and we wanted to help resolve that, by pointing to the continuities, as well as discontinuities, between the traditional and reconceptualized field. We hope we have, however modestly, succeeded. We hope that you, the student, can see how the complex, sometimes highly theoretical field that exists now, evolved out of a rather "practical" and bureaucratic field that existed until just twenty years ago. We also hope that by emphasizing the history of the field, and the history of the contemporary discourses, that you have come to appreciate that all fields of study have histories, all evolve, all suffer "paradigm" breaks, and all proceed in directions they might not have, had those who devoted their careers to these fields not existed. We hope you realize, then, that the American curriculum field is not a thing; it is not finished. Rather, the curriculum field, like other academic disciplines, is a conversation. And we hope you will consider joining it. In summary terms, what can we say about that conversation today?

II
The Curriculum Field Today: Problems and Possibilities

Few of us have the courage
to follow our thoughts wherever they might lead.
We all fear the dark at some level of our being
(Philip W. Jackson, 1994, p. 24).

Eurocentric analysis is viewed as linear.
 Rooted in empiricism, rationalism, scientific method and positivism,
its aim is prediction and control . . .
African epistemology, on the other hand, is circular . . .
and seeks interpretation, expression, and understanding
without preoccupation with verification
(William H. Watkins, 1993, p. 331).

Such a language would be . . .
 one that grows in the middle
(Ted Aoki, 1993, p. 14).

From Paradigmatic Unity to Particularism

We have seen how the field has moved from a paradigmatic unity—the Tylerian rationale—to particularism—the various contemporary discourses. The situation today is particularistic and even balkanized, but not the bland eclecticism that emerged after the struggle between social efficiency and progressivism in the second and third decades of the twentieth century. This proliferation of discourses can be traced to the vacuum created by the collapse of the Tyler rationale. In this vacuum scholars went to other fields as sources of new theory. This move away from curriculum as institutional text must be termed an astonishing success. The dying patient on which Schwab, Huebner, and Pinar commented from 1969 to 1978 has been profoundly revived due to the transfusions of important ideas from other fields. Yet, now that the patient is revived, there is another problem. How can we take the patient off the IV? That is, how do we encourage autonomy and self-sufficiency, which is not to say a new isolationism or self-importance. To change images, like a strong economy, the field must import—as well as export—important ideas to maintain dynamism. In the 1970s, in order to "jump-start" the economy of curriculum studies, ideas were imported from European fields. Now that the economy is thriving, it is time to begin to generate domestic ideas, without becoming protectionist. Indeed, it is clear that ideas from curriculum are being exported to other fields, including (and the following list is suggestive not comprehensive) early childhood education (Jardine, 1988; Swadener & Kessler, 1992; Kessler, 1991; Charlesworth, et al., in press), educational administration (Giroux, 1922b; Maxcy, 1991), science education (Jacknicke & Rowell, 1984; Good, 1992; Roscoe & Jacknicke, 1993), mathematics education (Frankenstein, 1983; Gordon, 1983) at-risk students (Donmoyer & Kos, 1993), special education (Warner, 1991, 1992; Szepkouski, 1993), teacher education (Giroux & McLaren, 1986; Gordon, 1986; Beyer, 1989, Grumet, 1989; Pinar, 1989; Shaker & Kridel, 1989; Schubert, 1989b; Beyer, Feinberg, Pagano, & Whitson, 1989; Block, 1993), curriculum evaluation (Eisner, 1985a, 1985b, 1991), English education (Giroux, 1992c; Hurlbert & Totten, 1992), social studies education (Stanley, 1992), language education (Edelsky, 1991; Walsh, 1991), reading (Block, forthcoming; Grumet, 1988a, 1988b; Hunsberger, 1988, 1992), higher education (Tierny, 1993), and teacher development (Hargreaves & Fullan, 1992), as well as to humanities disciplines such as cultural studies (Grossberg, 1993; Edgerton, 1992; Giroux &

McLaren, 1993) and literary theory (Leitch, 1992; see especially chapter 8 which reviews the history of the Centre for Contemporary Cultural Studies at the University of Birmingham).

Distance from the School

The current interest in becoming closer to practitioners may be an indication just how far apart from practice (i.e. the procedural) we have moved. Indeed, in the 1970s, when Pinar first called for the field to distance itself from the school and from teachers, he was in one sense merely acknowledging what he observed to be the case—that education professors were distant from teachers. In general, it was clear in the 1970s that teachers were skeptical of education professors. The expert-client relationship characteristic of the traditional field had failed. For many, undergraduate preservice teacher courses seemed intellectually lightweight at best—silly and arrogant at worse. True, Pinar observed that a minority of graduate courses were tolerable to students, and a fewer number still were considered exciting. But what was clear, even in the 1970s, was that most teachers did not regard us as friends, and certainly not as experts. Suggesting that the field move away from the school as the institution was merely acknowledging what was the case.

If there was ever a "paradise lost" of teacher-professor relations (during the first decades of this century?), no doubt it expressed a client-expert relationship. Not until we reconceive our role as strictly consultants and collaborators, as many working in the area of teacher development today are laboring to do, can this inequality and concomitant alienating consequences of distrust and misunderstanding be lessened. John Dewey wanted "experts" consigned to an "advisory role," as democratic education would require. Further, Dewey insisted that expertise must be subordinated to "fully participatory, deliberative, democratic politics" (Westbrook, 1991, p. 188), recalling the emphasis upon "deliberation" the Schwabian wing of the contemporary field has emphasized.

If teachers have been skeptical of the contributions education professors might make to school improvement, colleagues in arts and sciences, many politicians, and even the general public have been, at times, downright contemptuous. No matter that we education professors were even less responsible for the crisis in the schools than teachers themselves. Just as the students' achievement (or lack thereof) cannot be completely attributable to public school teachers, the failure of teachers cannot be laid entirely at the feet of university and college teacher educators. None of us teachers—at any level—is primarily responsible for how our students turn out; the process of education, interwoven as it is with family, history, and culture, is much too complicated to follow in a linear-causal fashion from the efforts of any one group. Furthermore, as Philip Wexler has suggested, identity formation in a "semiotic society" may occur largely outside school where the popular culture is imagistic, not print-based, as in schools. If Wexler is right, and education in an authentic sense now occurs outside school, and only incidentally inside, then the responsibility of educators is commensurately reduced further.

In the University

Where does this leave curriculum theorists? We are left in the university, a place of scholarship and teaching, where, instead of wringing our hands over lost influence in the schools and rejection by teachers and policymakers, we might commit ourselves to understanding what curriculum is, has been, and might be. It bears repeating that this does not mean fleeing from "practice", turning our backs on teachers, pretending to be like arts and sciences professors, as many educational foundations professors have pretended in the past. We curriculum theorists must still offer friendship and colleagueship to teachers; we must offer teachers our expertise as they request (and as circumstances permit it to be offered and to be accepted). We can offer politicians and policymakers that expertise but we ought not be surprised and certainly not deflated when they decline to employ it. After all, their interests in the schools are not necessarily educational, rather political and economic. We curriculum theorists must be firm that we are not responsible for the ills of public schools, especially given that our advice regarding how they can be improved, indeed transformed, has been and is so consistently ignored. Just as the field of economics is not to blame for the ills of the American economic system, or just as the field of political science is not responsible for the sorry state of the American political system, the field of curriculum is not primarily responsible for the condition of the schools. Or, as Bruce Kimball (1986), asks in regard to the liability of teacher education programs: "[what if] departments of art or music . . . were held responsible for the aesthetic sensibilities of American popular culture?" (p. 21). That is not to say we university teachers have not had a hand in the present dilemma, via teacher education (both pre- and inservice), but hardly our whole bodies.

In Order to Advance

Further, in our insistence that we must fix the schools (which cannot be fixed in any case, given present political and economic conditions and given that politicians will not let us try), an insistence that will only function to devalue our stock further, we undermine the only way we might develop the sophisticated understanding which—should the school establishment and politicians ever attend to our advice—might indeed help in significant ways. Such understanding must be grounded in educational experience (not necessarily schooling), but it must not remain there. Like physics or art, curriculum as a field cannot progress unless some segment of the field explores phenomena and ideas that perhaps few will comprehend and appreciate, certainly not at first and perhaps never. Our field will not progress beyond a certain primitive point unless we support a sector of theory—such as the work of Jacques Daignault—that perhaps most in the field cannot understand initially. Imagine physics progressing if scholars in that discipline were limited to work which beginning students readily understood. Imagine art progressing unless forms of painting and dance were supported which, initially, very few could appreciate. In any field there must be a sector of advanced work; otherwise, a field cannot advance.

Of course, the theoretical wing of a field must not pretend that its work is inherently superior to that which is institutional (or "applied," if we take the theory-practice relationship on a conventional continuum), but neither should the theory wing of a field be subjected to anti-intellectual tirades about "making a difference" in the schools or "improving practice" [see, for instance, Sears, 1992]. The theoretical wing of the field must not be ignored, as several synoptic textbooks continue to do. For books claiming to be surveys of the field to ignore the theory wing—or significant segments of it—is simple irresponsibility. If there were a professional society of curricularists, authors of such books would be expelled. Obviously, this is not to say books must not be written which reject particular theoretical positions, only those which ignore them.

The Near-term Future

How should the field progress in the near term? We would answer, "pretty much as it is." That faction of the field dealing with curriculum as institutional text is probably still too large, but conditions will continue which will reduce its size. One hopes it may never disappear altogether. Curriculum theory must not be collapsed into discourse. To understand educational experience requires being in the political, racial, aesthetic, spiritual, gendered, global, and lived world. There must continue some extension toward schools as institutions as they are, as thankless and Sisyphus-like this work often seems. However, the next generation of curriculum scholarship might move away from its sources in "parent" disciplines, such as phenomenology and poststructuralism, and away from the school, toward exploration of concepts indigenous to curriculum, independent of institutional agendas.

Toward Autonomy

However, the next generation's movement away from present sources to develop conceptual and methodological autonomy must not be in order to mimic the other disciplines, which, after all, regularly borrow from each other. Nor must a move toward autonomy be made simply in order to be considered a "mature" discipline, as such a title would be merely honorific. Rather, the field will move toward conceptual and methodological autonomy because staying near our sources pulls us toward a posture of "application" or "implications for curriculum." To understand curriculum further we must capture its internal dynamics and moments, i.e. its movements (flashes, raptures, intensities) of educational experience, so that curriculum does not appear to reside apart from the ideas which elucidate it. Such work does not imply a rejection of ideas conceived in other disciplines; it means that such work will not proceed in a linear causal manner from source to application. Rather, our work with sources will mirror the mediations and transformations that characterize educational experience.

Contemporary Discourses Transitional

Much of the work reported in this textbook, we can say, exhibits, in the context of this discussion of the field's next step, a transitional character. Having rejected the narrow instrumentalism of the Tyler period, the field has moved toward theory, and intelligently enough, employed some of the most current and sophisticated theory available at the time, ideas from social theory, phenomenology, feminist theory, and so on. This phase is not played out yet, but perhaps nearly so, as we see a proliferation of studies that are in their conceptual structure, similar, and close to their sources, like pressure building on a fault line. A "leap" or shift in conceptual "plates" may be forthcoming, when not only themes but conceptual structures will change, and we think it is possible that this "hybrid" theory will come, to change images, through cross-fertilization.

Several sectors of curriculum scholarship reported here exhibit porous borders already. For instance, feminist theorists would insist their work is profoundly political, and prominent political scholars have been moving rapidly away from class into race and gender. Their current boundaries result from being close to the parent disciplines which themselves are boundaried. As well, a certain loyalty to the parent discipline is a likely concomitant to immature appropriations of them. The transitional character of these sectors as well as the coming hybridization is implied by the current breakdown of borders associated with the sectors we have reported here, although this is still generally in an early stage. For instance, Giroux's notion of bordercrossings (1992a) might apply here, in one sense, that is, of moving easily across borders that before seemed to employ customs agents. For true hybridization to occur, however, the identity of the traveler must fuse with those with whom he or she travels and visits.

Giroux's work may further illustrate this point. He can be said to have moved from a nearly exclusive political emphasis to concerns for curriculum as racial and gendered text, but these later aspects seem to be, in the context of his opus, "add-ons." That is, the basic theses do not seem to have changed much from the "language of possibility," struggling for a more democratic public sphere, resistance to the status quo, and so on. Giroux seems to have "added on" concerns for race, gender, and postmodernism in his most recent writing, leaving intact his core theme of "critical pedagogy." We make this observation not as a criticism of Giroux—both his importance to the field and his achievement are indisputable—but to offer a specific example of how the work of Giroux's generation, which is to say, the work which functioned to reconceptualize the field in the 1970s, may not take us to the next generation of scholarship. While Giroux's generation may have taken the field through the violence of a paradigm shift, a contribution of which those of us in that generation might feel justifiably proud, we will not, most likely, be the ones to take the field to the next step. That next step probably will not constitute another paradigm shift, but a maturing conceptually and methodologically toward independence and autonomy, and away from the parent disciplines.

One example of this next stage might be hinted at by thinking about theory and ethnography. For many mainstream scholars theory now seems to some to be separated from schools. Ethnography, fashionable even among mainstream scholars in the early 1990s, claims to describe what occurs in schools. For these mainstream scholars, then, theory is considered to be stripped of practice, but ethnography seems stripped of theory. Many of us realize that this is not true, but there is on the surface a commonsense appeal to this binary distinction. Our point here is that in the next stage of the field's development we might see theory which is very much explicit in depictions of school life, and we might see explicit depictions of school life in theory. Wexler's Becoming Somebody [see chapter 13] and the work of Margo Figgins [see chapter 11; also Ebeling, 1992] are current examples of possible moves in this direction.

Philip Jackson, as we saw in chapter 1, presents the field as currently moving in two directions, one pointing toward practitioners and the other pointing away. It is not an either/or choice, of course. The fact is that the contemporary field is moving in both directions simultaneously, as this textbook makes clear. As we suggested earlier, the move closer to practitioners may be compensatory, but it is important and it is to be supported. In the next generation of work it may be merged with some strands of work in the theory wing. In a certain sense, this movement within the contemporary field represents a "second wave" (Pinar, 1988, p. 13) of Reconceptualization, however modest its program of action and intervention.

History Important

The current and growing emphasis upon the history of the field is important; we hope it will continue and intensify. Recent publications by curriculum historians such as Craig Kridel (1989), Herbert Kliebard (1987, 1992), Larry Cuban (1984/ 1993), Daniel and Laurel Tanner (1990), Daniel Tanner (1991), Ivor Goodson (1983), and O. L. Davis (1976, 1986) highlight this important emphasis in the contemporary field. Organization such as the Society for the Study of Curriculum History (Kridel & Tanner, 1987) perform a significant service in institutionalizing this interest. Departments of Curriculum and Instruction ought to hire at least one historian, in addition to several theoreticians, to join with those whose work is close to schools. An American Curriculum Studies Association might be formed to monitor the professional interests of the field so that the field receives appropriate institutional support for curriculum history and theory.

The Institutional Sector Recedes

To understand curriculum comprehensively requires understanding curriculum as institutional text. Because the topics and functions of this sector of the field tended to be opponents in the 1970s decade of struggle for Reconceptualization, it has been somewhat difficult to write completely impartially about these areas. It is quite important here to distinguish between our own research programs and theoretical commitments, and what the field is saying, and where we think the field ought to move. First, we suspect there will always be an institutional sector of the field, partly, as Goodlad and Su (1992) suggest, because the categories of curriculum development, design, and evaluation are time-honored. Unlike Goodlad and Su, however, clearly we do not see a simple reassertion of the traditional wing in the aftermath of the Reconceptualization. Curriculum as institutional text is a smaller "nation" than before; it has ceded considerable territory to the contemporary discourses, as the simple distribution of pages in this textbook makes clear.

There has been a second change as well in the effort to understand curriculum institutionally. To a striking extent, the very nature of this sector has changed, and changed in ways sometimes closely consonant and sometimes identical with the themes and programs of the reconceptualized field. For instance, Elliot Eisner has advanced a rationale for curriculum evaluation remarkably free of previous schemes' bureaucratic and pseudo-scientific elements. The notions of "educational criticism" and "connoisseurship," as he himself acknowledges, rest comfortably in the Deweyan and Schwabian traditions, intersecting but diverging discourses. Also indicative of this change is the groundbreaking work of Lee Shulman, as well as the work of F. Michael Connelly and D. Jean Clandinin, which takes seriously the complex uses of knowledge by both teachers and students, and suggests strategies for acknowledging and supporting these in curricular and school practice generally.

Overlapping Efforts

The next stage of the field, as we have suggested, will require that scholars not only read their own discourses, including new source material for that discourse, but material outside their sector as well. The careful reader of this textbook will have noticed overlapping ideas in several discourses. For instance, within the autobiographical/biographical sector, efforts to develop "personal practical knowledge," "teacher lore," and "collective autobiography" overlap. Hermeneutics is significant to several sectors of curriculum research, especially the phenomenological and theological (Pinar & McKnight, in press). Illustrative of overlapping across discourses might be Shulman's notion of "pedagogical content knowledge", Daignault's "passage," and Grumet's "middle way." Poststructuralism may function like a virus for political scholarship, undermining its present structure and function. Racial scholarship may well become an integrative sector in which political, feminist, phenomenological, poststructuralist, aesthetic, theological, and international elements are recombined and synthesized into a sophisticated, autonomous theory of curriculum. The point here is to build on what has been done already. At this point in the field's development we risk balkanization, building nearly identical fiefdoms which do not contribute to a "common faith" or to movement in the field as a whole. Perhaps we need a "United Nations" of scholarship sectors to formalize dialogue across discourse borders.

III
What is the Field Saying?

> The outbreak of crime and violence is a
> symptom of lives not lived deeply enough. . . .
> At the end of the twentieth century we are in a
> boundary situation. We can transform ourselves, or not
> (Mary Aswell Doll, 1994, p. 15).

> Emancipatory pedagogy is
> the freeing of one's mind
> to explore the essence and influence
> of the African-American race
> through the world, and the ability to pass
> on that information as a foundation
> upon which to build
> (Beverly M. Gordon, 1993, p. 278)

> Liberatory education can help us create
> a dialogue across differences
> (Elizabeth Ellsworth, 1990, p. 12).

It is not possible to answer this question in summary fashion. To attempt it is to risk composing a "masternarrative," creating the illusion that we, or any observer, stands apart from the field, and can distill the complex discourses we have reported into a single narrative. Theory is not such a narrative. In the reconceived field, theory is intended to undermine such pretensions to definitiveness and universality. Bowers is right when he observes: "In the hands of liberal-technicist educators, theory has become the talisman for centralizing authority over the decision-making process and increasing the efficiency of control and predictability. We all are quite clear that an 'objective' position is in principle impossible" (Bowers, 1984, pp. 14–15). With this acknowledgment of our "positionedness," we think it is possible to make a very general statement regarding what the reconceptualized field of curriculum might be saying.

No Longer Arrested

The place to begin a summary statement is that the field is no longer arrested. When that allegation was made—first by Schwab in 1969, then by Huebner in 1975, and by Pinar in 1978 that the field was moribund and arrested, respectively—the traditional field was in place. However, the Tylerian paradigm was collapsing, from both internal difficulties which Kliebard, Huebner, Eisner, Macdonald, and others made clear in the 1960s and 1970s, and by external developments, such as the National Curriculum Reform Movement of the 1960s, as well as the changing political terrain of schools and departments of education, as we described in chapters 3 and 4. The fact that a generation of curriculum professors remained in place whose careers were invested in a paradigm that had collapsed made for a crisis in the field. Naturally, this generation was not about to say, "Oh, it's over, is it? Okay. Here, take the microphone." Nor did we rebels—would-be revolutionaries—ask for the microphone politely. As perhaps in any paradigm shift, emotions intensified and overstatements were made.

A Relatively Rapid Shift

Despite these excesses, the field made a relatively rapid reconceptualization [10 years approximately is our estimate for the shift to have occurred], and as this textbook indicates, the reputations of the major scholars associated with the too-broad [see Hlebowitsh, 1992] concept of "traditionalists" remain in tact. Even Tyler himself, who has not always been treated completely fairly, remains an enormous figure, whose shadow is very much cast still today. Of course, the field is today hardly "one happy family." Even during periods of so-called "normal science," when a paradigm is securely in place and faces no insurmountable challenges from within or destabilizing circumstances externally, differences in viewpoint bring tensions and even acrimonious disputes, as the controversies in the political sector [chapter 5] or the theological sector [see chapter 12], for example, indicate. Other disputes occur across discourse borders, as feminist critiques of political and poststructuralist scholarship illustrate. Other sectors seem relatively free of significant criticism, either internally or externally, as the phenomenological movement indicates. There are signs that the phenomenological movement is extending beyond its own borders to influence scholarship in other sectors, for instance, Aoki's work with teacher voice [see chapter 13], Carson's phenomenological revision of curriculum implementation [see chapter 8], his political efforts to promote peace education [see chapter 5], and his interest in international and global education [see chapter 14]. The theological and international sectors too often tend to be ignored. So, what does this somewhat smooth although dynamic situation tell us, very generally speaking?

We do not wish to homogenize the distinctiveness of the various individual discourses. For example, political scholars should press toward activism. Yet, while respecting tendencies toward "extremism" in individual discourses, we must realize that no one discourse offers final answers to curriculum questions. We may wish a comprehensive theory of curriculum, but it cannot pretend to be a "totalizing" one. We can avoid totalization by realizing that such a comprehensive theory is, to borrow McCarthy's (1990) term, nonsynchronous, not merely additive, i.e., two parts political, two parts race, one part theology. Rather, we might appreciate that according to time, place, and voice—which include our individual institutional situations—we enact various elements of a comprehensive point of view, we become infused by them as it were, and in Deweyan fashion, move our practical situations forward. Unlike Lasch (1991), we believe progress is possible, despite the often illusory nature of progress, its contentiousness, persisting ethical, moral, and political dilemmas associated with the concept, and its technological dangers. We believe in—and accept theological grounding for—a moral view of humankind that asserts the primacy of human study, teaching, and understanding.

We now understand the curriculum to be even more complex than our predecessors understood it to be, certainly much more complicated than most politicians and many colleagues in arts and sciences realize. In this respect, we are in the odd position of knowing much more than other groups who act as stakeholders in the curriculum, but, in real political terms, we are the least politically powerful group to be able to act on that knowledge. Perhaps that is one price of understanding, although one would hope not, for it is those working in educational institutions who suffer most as a result.

Textbooks are the Beginning

It is an understatement to observe that curriculum does not imply those materials made by experts or by textbook writers; textbooks are the beginning. That second clause might sound flippant, perhaps arrogant. Of course, what is recorded as human knowledge in books and on computer discs is of unspeakable importance. That is not in question here. What is in question is what the reconceived field has studied: what has been made, what is made, what can be made, what might be made of human knowledge in our time, for our ends, given the great political, racial, aesthetic, and gender issues of our day? There is no devaluation of the "tradition" when we use the simple and bureaucratic word "textbooks." Tradition and textbooks are the ground against which, in honor of which, all curriculum study can be said to occur and proceed. It is we who live now, and those coming to live after us, who become the figure in this gestalt. The curriculum question becomes: what do we make of this knowledge, which is to say, what do we make of the world, what do we make of ourselves?

Movement

From different traditions toward different ends each of the contemporary discourses points to an understanding of curriculum in terms of movement, even, we might say, velocity, knowledge prompting questioning that moves the student (a broad category to include the teacher and scholar as well as the student) from one "location" to another, a location we hope as educators is more intellectually complicated, more developmentally mature, more passionate and compassionate. This movement may be like skating on the frozen surface of facts, generalizations, theories, but it may also create the sense of intellectual space being extended, enlarged, and multiplied so that intelligence itself may be multiplied as well as "sharpened." In this view, curriculum is not only particles moving through space, but it is the space in which the particles move, and the velocity and intensity of movements. The passages are intellectual and bodily, and they are relational, gendered, racial, political, and phenomenological. Some would term such movement cosmological (Oliver & Gershman, 1989). Velocity and intensity decrease and cosmology becomes obscure when curriculum becomes encrusted with ideology, with politics, with the bureaucratism of institutions so that the "free play of the signifier," that is, the free movement of ideas, is reduced. To the extent the curriculum reproduces or resists a status quo, it is "lifted out" of its passages, and bores crevices in the mind, creating ruts and rituals that decrease movement, and produce inauthentic knowing and static, bureaucratic knowledge. Similarly, teaching for tests subverts the movement of curriculum, recapitulating the recitation of the nineteenth century faculty psychology and classical curriculum.

This is not to say that velocity and intensity imply an anarchy of teaching and learning, although "chaos" as a concept in curriculum has achieved legitimacy (Doll, W., 1993a). It does suggest, however, that the organizing designs of the curriculum are only superficially in the books we read and the lectures we give and the small group discussions in which we participate. The organization of curriculum occurs in the lives of educators and students, involving political, racial, gendered, phenomenological, autobiographical, aesthetic, theological, international configurations as well as institutional ones. School curricula are discursive formations and configurations of facts, feelings, etc., which reflect the temporality, historicity, and provisionality of knowledge. Curriculum designs and organizations are a little like kaleidoscopic configurations of what we know, traces of what we have forgotten and suppressed, distributed through the echoes and shadows of life history, popular culture, and laced with desire. Put another way, Bowers (1984) has observed:

> Existential choice is thus expanded in proportion to the complexity of the symbolic code the individual acquires. A complex symbolic world provides the means for choosing among different interpretational schemes, as well as imagining future possibilities that would result from different scenarios. . . . What cannot be imagined cannot be chosen. (p. 47)

Then and Now

Like Dewey, Bode (1927) spoke about the psychological (as opposed to logical) organization of subject matter. Bode made a compelling if "folksy" (Bullough, 1981, p. 4) defense of Deweyan progressivism. These were the heydays—the late 1920s and the 1930s—of curriculum construction. In his introduction to the 1927 edition of Bode's *Modern Educational Theories,* Bagley spoke of the receptiveness of schools to professional, presumably, university-originated ideas of curriculum making. The questions he asked are still, to a degree, questions regarding what knowledge is of the most worth, but he located the answers in the organization of subject matter, the construction of curriculum. That was taken-for-granted. There was opportunity on a grand, public scale.

Today the location of opportunity is different. There is little curriculum construction to do on the scale and in the senses that Dewey, Bobbitt, and Bode argued over. Today curriculum construction is located in the multinational textbook conglomerates, in state textbook adoption committees, in district or ministry curriculum guidelines. The era of local construction of curriculum materials, certainly at the secondary level, is over. Where curriculum can be constructed now is in the "lived space" of the classroom, in the lived experience of students and teachers. In such space and in such experience, the knowing teacher and student can find passages from what is given (indeed, mandated) to the what might be, "a middle way" between strict adherence to the facts and to participation in flights of fancy, a "midpoint" between the idiosyncrasy and spontaneity of chaos and intimacy, and the predictable formalism of bureaucratic officialdom. Passages, middle ways, and midpoints can be discussed via the "pedagogical content knowledge" of a self-knowing teacher, a teacher who knows that her or his pedagogical obligation is not to deliver someone else's mail (not a little of it "junk" mail at that), but, with his or her students, to compose our own correspondence (cf. Figgins & Pinar, 1993) regarding the knowledge the textbook publishers and district curriculum guidelines have decreed.

The Return of Dwayne E. Huebner

Another perspective on the historical shifts in the field became available in a recent and important paper by Dwayne E. Huebner (1993) [see chapters 3 and 4.] More than fifteen years after leaving Teachers College, Columbia University and the curriculum field for the Divinity School at Yale University and the field of religious education, a 70-year old Dwayne Huebner returned to curriculum theory by composing a paper focused on the spiritual in curriculum. Huebner's paper was in response to an invitation to speak in New Orleans to a seminar on spirituality and curriculum, sponsored by three near-by universities, organized by William E. Doll, Jr. In a powerful reading, Huebner returned to many of the themes that had preoccupied him—and the field—over a life-span. Huebner appreciates that the problem of the field remains one of language (Huebner, 1966; see chapters 3, 4, 8, and 11):

> How can one talk about education, specifically, curriculum, and also talk about the spiritual? The problem is one of language. . . . Thanks to Macdonald, Pinar, Apple, and a variety of other curriculum writers who stand on their shoulders, we no longer have the horrendous hegemony of technical language (drawing primarily on learning theory and ends/means structures) usurping discussion of education. (p. 1)

Huebner acknowledges that, while not dominant in the scholarly field, technical language remains embedded in the schools, i.e. in the talk of schoolpeople. To some extent he blames the field he left for the present predicament of educators, lost in the technical, pseudo-scientific language of bureaucratic legitimization which erases not only the spiritual but the imagination as well. In a "we" that includes educators and especially educational psychologists, he reminded us that: "We have forgotten or suppressed that imagination is a foundation of our givens" (1993, p. 1). Evoking a notion of educational journey that he had employed over two decades ago (1975), he dismissed once again the language of educational psychology, and especially that of learning theory: "Learning' is a trivial way of speaking of the journey of the self" (p. 4). It is this pseudo-scientific and profoundly distorting language that had led Huebner to become skeptical of mainstream research: "Several years later I began to question the educator's dependency on the research enterprise" (p. 1). In part, it is the pretense of certainty of the social and behavioral sciences fields that is so reprehensible. It is awareness that there is a "beyond" to our knowledge that is the beginning of the theological: "It is a 'moreness' that takes us by surprise when we are at the edge and end of our knowing" (p. 2). What other damage has technical language done as he looks back at thirty years? In language which reminds us of Robert McClintock's strong essay on study published in that memorable 1971 issue of Teachers College Record [see chapter 4; also McClintock, 1971; Jennings, 1971] Huebner (1993) observed:

> Similarly, the significance of the word "study" has been destroyed. Students study to do what someone else requires, not for their own transformation, a way of 'working' on their own journey, or their struggle with spirit, the otherness beyond them. Just as therapy is work—hard work—but important for the loosening of old binds and discovering the new self; so too should education as study be seen as a form of that kind of work. (p. 8)

From students and study, Huebner moves to teachers and teaching. Sounding not only theological but phenomenological (cf. Aoki 1992; Aoki & Shamsher, 1993), Huebner (1993) reminded the audience that: "teaching is a vocation. . . . A vocation is a call" (p. 8). Indeed, the vocation of teaching, he continued, involves three aspects: "Three voices call, or three demands are made on the teacher. Hence the life that is teaching is inherently a conflicted way of living. The teacher is called by the students, by the content, and by the institution within which the teacher lives. . . . Spiritual warfare is inherent in all vocations" (1993, p. 9). Given such complexity of this calling,

Huebner (1993) understands that: "The pain of teachers, unable to respond to the call of some students, is often too much, and they seek relief by hardening their hearts" (p. 10). How can teachers respond to the demands of their profession? Huebner (1993) tells us:

> It is also quite clear to me that it is futile to hope that teachers can be aware of the spiritual in education unless they maintain some form of spiritual discipline. This needs to be of two kinds. Given the inherent conflicts involved in teaching, and the inherent vulnerability of their vocation, teachers need to seek out communities of faith, love, and hope. . . . The second discipline is a disciplining of the mind, not in the sense of staying on top of all the educational research and literature, but in the sense of developing an imagination that has room for the spiritual, such that when you look out over the educational landscape you see not only what is there and recognize your call to respond with love, truth and justice; but so you can also see the principalities and powers, the ideals and the spiritual possibilities hidden behind all of the forms and events that are taken for granted. (p. 11)

Here Huebner has pointed to the center of understanding curriculum, especially as theological text. He enables us to appreciate that finally our struggle to teach and to study with others and with God is precisely that: a call for labor, for discipline, sustained by faith, love, and hope. The effort to understand curriculum as theological text is not a separate specialized sector of scholarship; it is call to live with others morally and transcedentally: "The need is not to see moral and spiritual values as something outside the normal curriculum and school activity, but to probe deeper into the educational landscape to reveal how the spiritual and moral is being denied in everything" (Huebner, 1993, p. 11). In seeing how the moral is denied we glimpse how we might work toward its realization.

Dwayne E. Huebner returned to the curriculum field November 20, 1993, on the campus of Loyola University in New Orleans, but it was clear he had not left us. As our abbreviated and simplified reports of his work in this textbook make clear, he and a very few others—such as his friend and colleague James B. Macdonald—helped create the world we inhabit now and labor to recreate as educators and theoreticians. His generative influence has been evident in many discourses, including the political, the phenomenological, and the aesthetic as well as the theological. Huebner may have left the field partly in grief over what has happened in the schools, and partly because he was unable to find solace in the emerging scholarly field which his own work had made possible. His own journey has been remarkable, highly significant for an entire field of study. As he retires in spring 1994, Huebner remains one of the most important minds the field of curriculum has known.

Changed and Still the Same

In these ideas we see how the field has changed and how it has stayed the same. No longer are we asking and acting upon our answers to the fundamental curriculum question—what knowledge is of most worth?—by constructing curriculum materials. We answer the question via our own discursive "moves" with our students and with ourselves. These moves, the field is suggesting, are complicated, but they can be passages away from the curriculum as literal, as institutional, as officially decreed. These moves are political, racial, gendered, autobiographical, phenomenological, aesthetic, theological moves, deconstructed moves, and moves away from the provincialism of the United States of America toward global and international understanding. The reconceived field of curriculum understands that its raison d'être is seeking answers to fundamental questions—including what knowledge is of most worth?—and, in this one specific sense, in the struggles of the 1970s the reconceptualists were reasserting a past that had been allowed to be forgotten. In seeking to answer these questions, curriculum development as a paradigmatic organizing concept and activity has been largely abandoned. The field still seeks to befriend its constituency in the schools and, to a lesser extent, in the government, but having been largely abandoned by the latter, segments of the field have redoubled their efforts toward the former, in programs called "teacher lore," "personal practical knowledge," and "collective autobiography." As well, the field has created a theoretical wing to ensure that it does not again collapse on the social surface of existing bureaucratic institutions, as it did in the triumph of Bobbitt and Tyler that became the traditional field.

IV
Conclusion

The prism hangs in my study window,
swaying slighting with the spring breeze.
It turns, and I watch new patterns emerge in the crystal planes
as blooming forsythia meld into green branches.
I see that I cannot turn the prism for others
in a complete or constant manner,
just as I cannot possible view all the patterned colors
detailed by its movement. I struggle with the story of my own teaching,
knowing that this is only half the telling
and that even this half is refracting only scenes,
slight segments of the process of teaching and thinking about
    curriculum.
Still, some students, as they leave our class,
speak of never being able to think about curriculum
in quite the same ways again
(Janet L. Miller, 1990, p. 95).

Theory is the result of our desire
to create a world we can understand
(Elliot W. Eisner, 1985c, p. 29).

We have portrayed the field as it is today, a field just recently reconceptualized, animated, filled with two thousand voices. It is a vital and energetic field, not one smooth and neatly subdivided as, for instance, academic psychology. As William A. Reid (1992) writes, reflecting on the shift in the 1970s: "Yet, fifteen years on, there still seems to be little agreement about what the 'reconceived' field should be like" (p. 193). That is true. There remains little agreement. Cherryholmes (1988) thinks there will not be, that the character of curriculum is controversy. However, we do not regard that as a terrible problem.

A more serious problem, we believe, is the apparent inability of the various sectors to speak to each other, to move into an independent "middle" from their various "corner" positions, and to develop a literature on curriculum at some distance from sources in other disciplines. These issues of disciplinary sources and the field's autonomy are not new. Fifteen years ago Pinar wrote:

What is crucial for reconceptualists . . . is to remember that these [European] traditions are sources for the Reconceptualization. We must use their insights to create our own. We are Americans not Europeans; we are curricularists not philosophers or psychoanalysts. We must avoid the temptation to uproot insights from these traditions and "apply" them to the educational issues of our time. Such work is by definition derivative and distorting, involving as it does reduction of complex issues to conceptual systems created in other times, on other soil, for other purposes. To become scholars of phenomenology or of Marxist theory first and curricularists second is to betray our historical calling. These origins are important; I do not demean them. But they are origins only, and we must create our own intellectual and practical discipline, independent of its sources, sensitive and responsible to our present. (1979, pp. 97–98)

Being sensitive and responsible to our present is one typification of the educator's challenge, inviting us to do the order of educational labor laid out by each of the contemporary discourses. In the accomplishments that understanding such work may bring, we move toward independence. Pinar wrote:

We must take seriously our responsibility to face the educational issues of our time, both in their surface forms as well as in their deeper theoretical significance, a significance we must identify. This means being willing to speak in our own voices, with words which while clearly related to established theoretical traditions, strictly speaking belong to no one discipline. Almost as a kind of by-product we must be willing to attempt what our predecessors and contemporaries may have wished but never achieved. We must make curriculum studies . . . into an autonomous discipline, with its own distinctive research methods and theoretical emphases. Of course, these methods and emphases will bear significant relation to the traditions from which they originated. However, they will not be identical or reducible to them. (1979, p.99)

In remaining loyal to our sources, the contemporary reconceptualized field may be placed in danger of being torn apart by tendencies toward "particularism" or "localisms" in the contemporary discourses, not unlike the nationalisms which we have seen in world politics in the early 1990s. The field is threatened by being taken too far to the left by the Marxists; by focusing too narrowly on gender by certain feminist theorists; by focusing too narrowly on phenomenological pedagogy by phenomenologists; by focusing too righteously on the Western Judeo-Christian contribution by theological scholars; by focusing too preciously on art by those who understand curriculum as aesthetic text, and too exclusively on life history by the autobiographers. What the next generation might explore is a political phenomenological understanding of curriculum, influenced by gender analysis, autobiographical theory, situated internationally in a multiracial global village. This is not to suggest a bland eclecticism, i.e. understanding curriculum as political, racial, etc. etc. etc. The various dimensions of curriculum must be interrelated non-synchronously rather than as parallel aspects (McCarthy, 1990) [see chapter 6].

Believing that "curriculum is essentially public and institutional in character" (p. 172), William Reid (1992) asks: "Could curriculum inquiry reintegrate the new-found humanism of the reconceptualists with the insistence on the public nature of curriculum as subject matter which we find in the tradition which they sought to replace?" (p. 174). We believe that the answer the field makes to Reid's question is yes, a qualified yes. We cannot share without modification Reid's insistence that "curriculum is intrinsically and historically an institutional conception" (p. 174). Historically yes; intrinsically no. We see work—autobiography, for instance—that is not identified with institutional interests. We do agree with Reid (1992) that "those interested in curriculum inquiry should, in the 1990s, be taking stock both of what the work of the last 20 years has achieved, and what it has failed to achieve. The limitations of "traditional" approaches has been exposed" (p. 177). We disagree that "on the other hand, we have not, as yet, equipped ourselves with criteria for understanding how far the various kinds of experiments in which we are engaging might, in combination with elements of the more established schools of thought, contribute to a 'reconceived' tradition of curriculum inquiry with a distinct and coherent character" (p. 177).

We believe this textbook demonstrates that the field has evolved to exhibit a "distinct and coherent character." Like no other specialization in education, influenced as it is by the humanities, arts, and social theory, curriculum is a hybrid interdisciplinary area of theory, research, and institutional practice. True, it is balkanized and particularized; there are problems of cross-discourse communication. Clearly, however, the contemporary curriculum field is distinctive and coherent. The problem is consolidation, and this Reid (1992) understands. As we opened this textbook with his question for the 1990s, so we close it:

Whether the 1990s will be indeed prove to be a period of consolidation and integration, based on broadly humanistic approaches . . . remains to be seen. It would be a worthy agenda (p.177). We agree.

One effort at consolidation and integration is the scholarship of Peter S. Hlebowitsh whose reconsideration of the Tyler Rationale in light of the Reconceptualization we reported in chapter 4. In another essay, Hlebowitsh (1992) suggests that Dewey's work can provide one line of thematic continuity between the traditional and reconceptualized fields. A renewed appreciation (Schubert, 1989) for this line could help mend the fractured identity of the contemporary field, thus supporting a moment of consolidation and integration. Hlebowitsh (1992) suggests that the distinction between procedure (linked with Bobbitt) and method (as conceived by Dewey) is the thematic line that links the reconceptualized field with aspects of the traditional one. He writes:

> The difference between procedure and method in the curriculum is the difference between Bobbitt and Dewey; it is also the difference between Bobbitt and a number of "traditionalists", including Tyler, Taba, and the Tanners (to mention three generations of curriculum scholars). Method is in the spirit of Dewey's pragmatism; it is the thread with which the divided nature of **curriculum scholarship may begin to receive mending.**
> (Hlebowitsh, 1992, p. 82, emphasis added)

[Hlebowitsh's most recent work (1993) seems to have forsaken the project of mending.]

Understanding Curriculum

What we teachers and students make of what is given to us is in large measure determined by our willingness to explore the questions implicit in the various discourses reported in this volume. Just as it is not enough for teachers to work with a model of teaching in which they simply transmit a body of knowledge or a set of skills to students, just as it is not enough for students to regard learning as reproducing such content and such skills, so it is not enough for curricularists to view the object of their study as "out there," waiting to be described and represented to teachers as formulae and recipes. What is required is more profound understanding of curriculum. By understanding curriculum we do not mean the ultimate and definitive representation of what is there already, waiting for the right words. Nor do we mean that educational experience can be collapsed into discourse and become simply the object our practice forms. Rather, understanding curriculum implies remaking both experience and its discursive representations so that we see the past and present more clearly, and where our seeing might lead us. Thanks to political scholarship we are clear that we must see the curriculum as an ideological document which both expresses and requires particular forms of labor embedded in the reproduction of power. We understand that to resist politically means linking forms of the curriculum with the larger society, with analysis of the "selective tradition," with cultural capital made available to different populations differentially. To understand curriculum politically leads us to racial and gender investigations (and they lead back to politics), as both sets of representations function to distribute knowledge and power differentially. Phenomenological, aesthetic, autobiographical, and theological experience both expresses political privilege and undermines it. International understandings of curriculum help us to bracket the taken-for-granted, and the intertextual understanding of curriculum that the reconceptualized field offers can lead us to ask, with greater complexity and sophistication, the traditional curriculum questions: what knowledge is of most worth? What do we make of the world we have been given, and how shall we remake ourselves to give birth to a new social order? What John Dewey said in reference to philosophy might be said in reference to the contemporary curriculum field:

> A [curriculum theory] which was conscious of its own business and province would then perceive that it is an intellectualized wish, an aspiration subject to rational discriminations and tests, a social hope reduced to a working program of action, a prophecy of the future, but one disciplined by serious thought and knowledge. (Dewey, quoted in Westbrook, 1991, p. 147)

Here Dewey unites self-realization and society (Westbrook, 1991), two of the major currents in contemporary curriculum scholarship. An intellectualized wish expressed as a social practice, thoroughly theorized and subject to rigorous critique which functions to reformulate the wish, re-expressed as practice: a moving form, that is understanding curriculum today.

V
Prologue

Curriculum is our memorial to an old intentionality.
Remembered, resymbolized, a former relation to the world
is reviewed and then arranged for someone else. . . .What
curriculum theory strives to return to the reception of curriculum
is the reflexive moment that was there in its creation
(Madeleine R. Grumet, 1990, p. 193).

Any discussion of curriculum reform
must address issues of representation
as well as issues of unequal distribution
of material resources and power
outside the school door
(Cameron McCarthy, 1993b, p. 291).

That's how a textbook might end, is it not? A summary statement in which 3200 references are incorporated, requiring, it
is true, notching up the level of abstraction, but summing it up
in the process. Doesn't work, does it. Even summoning the
grand ghost of Dewey isn't enough. [We are not trying exhume
Dewey for the 1990s; see, for instance, Paringer, 1990; Doll,
W., 1993b). Why? Charles Ives doesn't sound like Aaron
Copeland. Unlike the Grand Canyon, curriculum is not a thing
of nature, but of culture [Kieran Egan (1992) reminds us that:
"our culture is our nature" (p. 118, emphasis added).] And culture is contentious. Furthermore, we are arguing over what to
tell the children (and what not to tell them). We are reinvent-
ing the world, although we manage often to present it in schools
as a museum piece, something dead to be revered or at least
memorized. In this book we have worked to present the sound
of silence breaking (in Janet Miller's memorable phrase; Miller,
1982), of the cacophony that occurs when everybody is moved
into the same room. No one note—no matter how abstract, how
melodious—can capture what is multiple, contradictory, contentious. A modest aspiration, perhaps, but we find ourselves
in a field where most pretend theirs is the only discourse worthy of study. Now that everyone is in the same room, what is
next?

While the field may always be cacophonous, we think the
scholars in the field might choose to be kinder to each other,
might acknowledge each other's presence more frequently and

more respectfully. As you can see, a number of people are working on similar problems, inspired by similar traditions, aspiring to like ends. There is no reason why these people might not work together a bit more. The curriculum field, it has been pointed out, is a disciplinary community (Pagano, 1981), and there is much to be gained if we started acting a bit more like one. Feminist theory might represent a model that is more genuinely collaborative.

We are not suggesting, of course, that the field requires more order, that its diversification is a problem. On the contrary, we call for collaboration, conversation, and disciplinary autonomy to increase the complexity of the field. We agree with Henry Louis Gates, Jr., who, writing in regard to his own field of African-American Studies, endorses critical inquiry: "We are scholars. For our field to grow, we need to encourage a true proliferation of ideologies and methodologies, rather than to seek uniformity or conformity" (1992, p. 126). Like Gates, we seek growth and proliferation. Our hope is that this book supports that movement.

You can see that this field is very much a conversation, despite the efforts of some to pretend others do not exist. It is a conversation that invites your participation. Unlike more mature fields, curriculum theory remains, relatively speaking, open. You needn't search for a niche, for some small area that has not yet been explored. The new, reconceptualized field—the contemporary field—of curriculum theory is hardly more than a generation old, and the frontier is all around us. You might find that inviting. It is a field where your interests can be pursued. From our point of view, the most important motive for entering a field is that it is interesting, that it appeals, that one's interests can be supported and developed.

Perhaps the most exciting areas may be ones we have not identified in this book. They may be areas—hybrid ones—that will evolve out of existing sectors, across discourses, identifying areas of focus and specialization of which we cannot conceive at this time. Because the field is relatively young, somewhat unstable, still quite open, such work may find warmer welcomes than it would in a more conservative and mapped field. As you have seen, the conversation in the field shifted rather dramatically just twenty years ago, and it might shift again, in a direction we cannot foresee at this time. This is the excitement of working in the curriculum field. And it is the promise of excitement not of prudence that we think should inform your choices regarding graduate study in education. We invite you to join us. The next moment is yours.

Note

1   The contribution of William F. Pinar at the Oslo Conference was the concluding chapter of W. F. Pinar, W. M. Reynolds, P. Slattery and P. M. Taubman, *Understanding Curriculum*. New York: Peter Lang, 1995.

References

Aoki, T. (1992). Layered understandings of teaching: The uncannily correct and the elusively true. In W. Pinar & W. Reynolds (Eds.), *Understanding curriculum as phenomenological and deconstructed text* (17–27). New York: Teachers College Press.

Aoki, T. (1993). In the midst of slippery theme-words: Toward designing multicultural curriculum. In T. Aoki & M. Shamsher (Eds.), *The call of teaching* (87-100). Vancouver, British Columbia, Canada: British Columbia Teachers' Federation.

Aoki, T. & Shamsher, M. (Eds.). (1993). *The call of teaching.* Vancouver, British Columbia, Canada: British Columbia Teachers' Federation.

Beyer, L. (1989). Reconceptualizing teacher preparation: Institutions and ideologies. *Journal of Teacher Education,* 22–26.

Beyer, L., Feinberg, W., Pagano, J. & Whitson, J. (1989). *Preparing teachers as professionals: The role of educational studies and other liberal disciplines.* New York: Teachers College Press.

Block, A. (1993, June 27-July 1). My Lord I have not the skill: On the relation between theory and practice. Paper presented to the International Conference on Teacher Education, Tel-Aviv, Israel.

Block, A. (forthcoming). *Occupied reading.* New York: Garland.

Bode, B. (1927). *Modern educational theories.* New York: Macmillan.

Bowers, C. (1984). *The promise of theory: Education and the politics of cultural change.* New York: Longman.

Bullough, Jr., R. (1981). *Democracy in education—Boyd H. Bode.* Bayside, NY: General Hall, Inc., Publishers.

Charlesworth, R., Hart, C., Burts, D., & DeWolf, M. (in press). Advances in early education and day care.

Cherryholmes, C. (1988). *Power and criticism: Poststructural investigations in education.* New York: Teachers College Press.

Cuban, L. (1984/1993). *How teachers taught: Constancy and change in American classrooms 1890–1980.* New York: Longman.

Daignault, J. (1992). Traces at work from different places. In W. Pinar & W. Reynolds (Eds.), *Understanding curriculum as phenomenological and deconstructed Text* (195–215). New York: Teachers College Press.

Davis, Jr., O. (Ed.). (1976). *Perspectives on curriculum development 1776–1976.* Washington, DC: ASCD.

Davis, Jr., O. (1986). ASCD and curriculum development: The later years. In W. van Til (Ed.), *ASCD in retrospect: Contributions to the history of the Association*

Doll, M. (1994, April). My body, my self: The alma materia of knowing. Paper presented to the annual meeting of the American Educational Research Association, New Orleans, LA.

Doll, Jr., W. (1983). Practicalizing Piaget. *JCT,* 5 (4), 92–110.

Doll, Jr., W. (1993a). *A post-modern perspective on curriculum.* New York: Teachers College Press.

Doll, Jr., W. (1993b). Curriculum possibilities in a post-future. *Journal of Curriculum and Supervision,* 8 (4), 277–292.

Donmoyer, R. & Kos, R. (1993). *At-Risk students: Portraits, policies, programs, and practices.* Albany, NY: State University of New York Press.

Ebeling, M. (1992). *Knowing-in-action: A naturalistic inquiry into first world critical pedagogy.* Charlottesville, VA: University of Virginia, Curry School of Education, unpublished doctoral dissertation.

Edelsky, C. (1991). *With literacy and justice for all: Rethinking the social in language and education.* London, England: Falmer.

Edgerton, S. (1992). *Cultural studies and the multicultural curriculum.* Baton Rouge, LA: Louisiana State University, Department of Curriculum and Instruction, unpublished Ph.D. dissertation.

Egan, K. (1992). *Imagination in teaching and learning*. Chicago, IL: University of Chicago Press. [Published in Canada by the Althouse Press, London, Ontario. References are to this edition.]

Eisner, E. (1979, 1985a). *The educational imagination: On the design and evaluation of school programs*. New York: Macmillan.

Eisner, E. (1985b). *The art of educational evaluation: A personal view*. London, England: Falmer.

Eisner, E. (1985c). Aesthetic modes of knowing. In E. Eisner (Ed.), *Learning and teaching the ways of knowing*. Eighty-fourth yearbook of the National Society for the Study of Education (23-36). Chicago, IL: University of Chicago Press.

Eisner, E. (1991). *The enlightened eye: Qualitative inquiry and the enhancement of educational practice*. New York: Macmillan.

Ellsworth, E. (1990). Educational films against critical pedagogy. In E. Ellsworth & M. Whatley (Eds.), *The ideology of images in educational media* (10–26). New York: Teachers College Press.

Figgins, M. & Pinar, W. (1993, October). Dancing behind the mirror: A Performance of letters. Presentation to the Bergamo Conference on Curriculum Theory and Classroom Practice, Dayton, OH.

Frankenstein, M. (1983). Critical mathematics education: An application of Paulo Freire's epistemology. *Journal of Education*, 163 (4), 315–339.

Gates, Jr., H. (1992). *Loose canons: Notes on the culture wars*. New York: Oxford University Press.

Giroux, H. (1992a). *Bordercrossings*. New York: Routledge.

Giroux, H. (1992b). *Educational leadership and the crisis of democratic culture*. University Park, PA: Pennsylvania State University, University Council of Educational Administration (UCEA).

Giroux, H. (1992c). Textual authority and the role of teachers as public intellectuals. In M. Hurlbert & S. Totten (Eds.), *Social issues in the English classroom* (304–321). Urbana, IL: NCTE.

Giroux, H. & McLaren, P. (1986). Teacher education and the politics of engagement: The case for democratic schooling. *Harvard Educational Review*, 56 (3), 213–238.

Giroux, H. & McLaren, P. (Eds.). (1993). *Between borders: Pedagogy and the politics of cultural studies.* New York: Routledge.

Good, R. (1992, September). Notes from Bergamo. *Journal of Research in Science Teaching*, 29 (7), 635–636.

Goodlad, J. & Su, Z. (1992). Organization of the curriculum. In P. Jackson (Ed.), *Handbook of research on curriculum* (327–344). New York: Macmillan.

Goodson, I. (1983). *School subjects and curriculum change.* London, England: Falmer. [2nd edition: 1987; 3rd edition: 1993, with foreword by Peter McLaren.]

Gordon, B. (1993, 1985). Toward emancipation in citizenship education: The case of African-American cultural knowledge. In L. Castenell, Jr. & W. Pinar (Eds.), *Understanding curriculum as racial text: Representations of identity and difference in education* (263–284). Albany, NY: State University of New York Press. [Also (1985) in Theory and Research in Social Education, 12 (4), 1–23.]

Gordon, M. (1983). Conflict and liberation: Personal aspects of the mathematics experience. In H. Giroux & D. Purpel (Eds.), *The hidden curriculum and moral education* (361–383). Berkelely, CA: McCutchan.

Grossberg, L. (1993). The formations of cultural studies: An American in Birmingham. In V. Blundell, J. Shepherd & I. Taylor (Eds.), *Relocating cultural studies: Developments in theory and research* (21–66). London & New York: Routledge

Grumet, M. (1988a). Bodyreading. In W. Pinar (Ed.), *Contemporary curriculum discourses* (453–473). Scottsdale, AZ: Gorsuch Scarisbrick.

Grumet, M. (1988b). *Bitter milk: Women and teaching.* Amherst, MA: University of Massachusetts Press.

Grumet, M. (1989, January-February). Generations: Reconceptualist curriculum theory and teacher education. *Journal of Teacher Education*, 13–18.

Grumet, M. (1990). The theory of the subject in contemporary curriculum thought. In J. Willinsky (Ed.), *The educational legacy of romanticism* (189–209). Waterloo, Ontario, Canada: Wilfrid Laurier University Press.

Hargreaves, A. & Fullan, M. (Eds.). (1992). *Understanding teacher development*. New York: Teachers College Press & Cassell (UK).

Hlebowitsh, P. (1992, Winter). Critical theory versus curriculum theory: Reconsidering the dialogue on Dewey. *Educational Theory*, 42 (1), 69–82.

Hlebowitsh, P. (1993). *Radical curriculum theory reconsidered: A historical approach*. New York: Teachers College Press.

Huebner, D. (1966). Curricular language and classroom meanings. In J. Macdonald & R. Leeper (Eds.), *Language and meaning* (8–26). Washington, DC: ASCD.

Huebner, D. (1975). Autobiographical statement. In W. Pinar (Ed.), *Curriculum theorizing: The reconceptualists* (213–215). Berkeley, CA: McCutchan.

Huebner, D. (1993, November 20). *Education and spirituality*. New Haven, CT: Yale University, The Divinity School, unpublished manuscript. [Presented to the Seminar on Spirituality and Curriculum, November 20, 1993, on the campus of Loyola University in New Orleans, sponsored by Louisiana State, Loyola, and Xavier Universities.]

Hunsberger, M. (1988). Teaching reading methods. *The Journal of Educational Thought*, 22 (2A), 209–218.

Hunsberger, M. (1992). The time of texts. In W. Pinar & W. Reynolds (Eds.), *Understanding curriculum as phenomenological and deconstructed text* (64–91). New York: Teachers College Press.

Hurlbert, M. & Totten, S. (Eds.). (1992). *Social issues in the English classroom*. Urbana, IL: NCTE.

Jacknicke, K. & Rowell, P. (1984). Reaching for possibilities in science education. *Curriculum Praxis Series, Occasional Pa-*

per No. 33. Edmonton, Alberta, Canada: University of Alberta, Faculty of Education, Department of Secondary Education.

Jackson, P. (1994). Stopping, yet again, to consider Frost's evening traveler. Chicago, IL: University of Chicago, Department of Education, unpublished manuscript.

Jardine, D. (1988). "There are children all around us." *The Journal of Educational Thought*, 22 (2A), 178–186.

Jennings, F. (Ed.). (1971). Curriculum: Interdisciplinary insights. *Special issue of Teachers College Record*, 73 (2).

Kessler, S. (1991). Early childhood education as development: Critique of the metaphor. *Early Education and Development*, (2) 2, 137–152.

Kessler, S. & Swadner, B. (Eds.). (1992). *Reconceptualizing the early childhood curriculum: Beginning the dialogue*. New York: Teachers College Press.

Kimball, B. (1986). The training of teachers, the study of education, and the liberal traditions. *Educational Theory*, 36 (1), 15–22.

Kliebard, H. (1987). A century of growing antagonism in high school–college relations. *Journal of Curriculum and Supervision*, 3 (1), 61–70.

Kliebard, H. (1992). *Forging the American curriculum*. New York: Routledge.

Kridel, C. (Ed.). (1989). *Curriculum history: Conference presentations from the society for the study of curriculum history*. Landham, MD: University Press of America.

Kridel, C. & Tanner, L. (1987). The uncompleted past: The Society for the Study of Curriculum History celebrates its tenth anniversary. *Journal of Curriculum and Supervision*, 3 (1), 71–74.

Lasch, C. (1991). *The true and only heaven: Progress and its critics*. New York: Norton.

Leitch, V. (1992). *Cultural criticism, literary theory, poststructuralism*. New York: Columbia University Press.

Maxcy, S. (1991). *Educational leadership: A critical, pragmatic perspective.* New York: Bergin & Garvey.

McCarthy, C. (1990). *Race and curriculum.* London, England: Falmer.

McCarthy, C. (1993b). After the canon: Knowledge and ideological representation in the multicultural discourse on curriculum reform. In C. McCarthy & W. Crichlow (Eds.), *Race, identity, and representation in education* (289–305). New York & London, England: Routledge.

McClintock, R. (1971). Toward a place for study in a world of instruction. *Teachers College Record*, 73 (20), 161–205.

Miller, J. L. (1982). The sound of silence breaking: Feminist pedagogy and curriculum theory. *JCT*, 4 (1), 5–11.

Miller, J. L. (1990). Teachers as curriculum creators. In J. Sears & D. Marshall (Eds.), *Teaching and thinking about curriculum* (85–96). New York: Teachers College Press.

Mooney, R. (1967b). Perspectives on ourselves. *Theory into Practice*, 6 (1), 200–211.

Oliver, D. & Gersham, K. (1989). *Education, modernity, and fractured meaning: Toward a process theory of teaching and learning.* Albany, NY: State University of New York Press.

Pagano, J. (1981). The curriculum field: Emergence of a discipline. *JCT*, 3 (1), 171–184.

Paringer, W. (1990). *John Dewey and the paradox of liberal reform.* Albany, NY: State University of New York Press.

Pinar, W. (1979). What is the reconceptualization? *JCT*, 1 (1), 93–104.

Pinar, W. (1988). Introduction. *Contemporary curriculum discourses* (1-13). Scottsdale, AZ: Gorsuch Scarisbrick.

Pinar, W. (1989, January/February). A reconceptualization of teacher education. *Journal of Teacher Education*, 9–12.

Pinar, W. & McKnight, D. (in press). The uses of curriculum knowledge: Notes on hermeneutics. *International Journal of Educational Research.*

Pinar, W. & Miller, J. (1982). Feminist curriculum theory: Notes on the American field. *Journal of Educational Thought*, (16) 3, 217–224.

Reid, W. (1992). The state of curriculum inquiry. *Journal of Curriculum Studies*, 24 (2), 165–178.

Roscoe, K. & Jacknicke, K. (1993). *An experience of curriculum change: Science, technology, and society*. Paper presented to the Bergamo Conference on Curriculum Theory and Classroom Practice, Dayton, OH.

Schubert, W. (1989). Reconceptualizing and the matter of paradigms. *Journal of Teacher Education*, 27–32.

Sears, J. (1992, Summer). The second wave of curriculum theorizing: Labyrinths, orthodoxies, and other legacies of the glass bead game. *Theory into Practice*, 210–218.

Shaker, P. & Kridel, C. (1989). The return to experience: A reconceptualist call. *Journal of Teacher Education*, 2–8.

Slattery, P. (1989). *Toward an eschatological curriculum theory*. Baton Rouge, LA: Louisiana State University, Department of Curriculum and Instruction, unpublished Ph.D. dissertation.

Stanley, W. (1992). *Curriculum for utopia: Social reconstructionism and critical pedagogy in the postmodern era*. Albany, NY: State University of New York Press.

Szepkouski, G. (1993). "I'm me own boss!" In D. McLaughlin & W. Tierny (Eds.), *Naming silenced lives: Personal narratives and the process of educational change* (177–197). New York: Routledge.

Tanner, D. (1991). *Crusade for democracy: Progressive education at the crossroads*. Albany, NY: State University of New York Press.

Tanner, D. & Tanner, L. (1990). *History of the school curriculum*. New York: Macmillan.

Tierny, W. (1993). *Building communities of difference*. Westport, CT: Bergin & Garvey.

Walsh, C. (1991). *Pedagogy and the struggle for voice: Issues of language, power, and schooling for Puerto Ricans.* New York: Bergin & Garvey.

Warner, M. (1991). Objectivity and emancipation in learning disabilities: Holism from the perspective of critical realism. Paper presented to the Bergamo Conference on Curriculum Theory and Classroom Practice, Dayotn, OH.

Warner, M. (1992, April). Metatheory in special education: Critical pragmatism from the perspective of critical realism. Paper presented to the annual meeting of the American Educational Research Association, San Francisco, CA.

Watkins, W. (1993). Black curriculum orientations: A preliminary inquiry. *Harvard Educational Review, 63* (3), 321–338.

Westbrook, R. (1991) *John Dewey and American philosophy.* Ithaca, NY: Cornell University Press.

Wexler, P. (1992). *Becoming somebody: Toward a social psychology of school.* [With the assistance of W. Crichlow, J. Kern, & R. Martusewicz.] London, England: Falmer Press.

Chapter 16

Characteristics of Critical-Constructive Didaktik

Wolfgang Klafki

Preliminary Remarks

"Critical-constructive Didaktik" is the term I use for the conception of Didaktik I hold today. The elaboration of this conception has been one of the main centers of my work in education for more than twenty-five years. I cannot, of course, give a detailed account of the development of this concept within the space of one essay, nor can I present all the presuppositions and systematic differentiations the concept includes (cf. Klafki 1994). Most unfortunate of all is the fact that I can make only brief reference to examples of the research and practical development work this conception of Didaktik has inspired.

On the Development of Critical-Constructive Didaktik

This conception of Didaktik has a long prehistory, but just a few comments here must suffice. It is important for me to emphasize that from the beginning of my activity as an educationist I have regarded Didaktik as a subdiscipline of educational theory. When I began, in the late 1960s, to elaborate the concept of Didaktik I am about to present to you, the work ran parallel to my contributions to the development of a general science of education as critical-constructive theory. In this paper, however, I shall confine myself to Didaktik.

My first publications on Didaktik (and general theory of education) in the late 1950s and the beginning of the 1960s were still wholly influenced by the thoughts of "Geisteswissen-schaftliche Pädagogik". It is difficult to translate this term into English. Perhaps "human-science oriented pedagogy" may be suitable. But I use the German term in the following.

For those unfamiliar with German educational theory, I will present some background: "Geisteswissenschaftliche Pädagogik" was a movement which, after the First World War, became the most influential in German pedagogy until the end of the Weimar era. After the Second World War it was developed further and played a leading role in West Germany until around 1960. The main names associated with this movement since the 1920s, who were inspired by the theory of the "Geisteswissenschaften" (human sciences) of the philosopher Wilhelm Dilthey, are Eduard Spranger, Herman Nohl, Theodor Litt, Erich Weniger and Wilhelm Flitner. To characterize "Geisteswissenschaftliche Pädagogik" I shall now sketch four of its main attributes.

The **first** is a close relationship between pedagogical theory and pedagogical practice. "Geisteswissenschaftliche Pädagogik" was understood as theory *of* pedagogical practice *for* pedagogical practice, as enlightenment of the preconditions, opportunities and limits of pedagogical practice.

The **second** attribute is emphasis on the relative autonomy of education in theory and practice in relation to all other political, social and cultural influences. This claim to relative autonomy (or, synonymously, "relative independence" = relative Eigenständigkeit) was understood as an achievement of modern pedagogy since Rousseau and the Enlightenment, deriving from the responsibility of pedagogical theory and practice to provide opportunities for children and adolescents (and adults, as applicable) to develop towards a state of independence and responsibility for their own actions—"Mündigkeit"—linked up to Kant's notion.

A **third** fundamental characteristic of human-science pedagogy is its conception of pedagogical theory and practice in a historical context. This means that all concrete phenomena of pedagogical practice and all statements of pedagogical theory regarding content must be understood in their historical character.

For a few proponents of "Geisteswissenschaftliche Pädagogik", particularly for Herman Nohl, Erich Weniger and

Wilhelm Flitner, at least one more characteristic should be mentioned. These educationists and their students and followers saw themselves in close affinity with German reform pedagogy and international progressive education, or at least with the significant branches of the reform pedagogy and progressive education movement of the first half of this century. These proponents of "Geisteswissenschaftliche Pädagogik" saw themselves, so to speak, as the critical conscience of these movements of pedagogical reform.

As a student at Teachers Training College in Hanover 1946-1948 I made my first nodding acquaintance with the tenets of "Geisteswissenschaftliche Pädagogik". When I returned to university after a few years working as a school teacher committed to reform pedagogy, I became a student of Weniger and Litt. Later, as a lecturer and theorist in education myself, I tried, among other things, to develop on Weniger's theory of Didaktik and bring it to practical fruition.

The concept of "didactic analysis" (cf. Klafki, 1963, 1995 b), for example, dates from this period. It was intended to help teachers prepare their lessons and concentrated on the content element of instructional design.[1] I feel obliged to point out, however, that the approach I endorse today is an adaptation and extension of the earlier version (Klafki, 1994). It appeared first in 1980, originating in the wake of the development of critical-constructive Didaktik. But the questions of lesson preparation are only part of Didaktik.

Since the mid-1960s I have been in constant, fruitful correspondence with a large number of German proponents of Didaktik, including many who specialize in the Didaktik of particular subjects. This exchange has brought not only mutual stimulation and cooperation, but of course also critical debate. It was necessary to define my position and to distance myself from conceptions which were incompatible even with human-science Didaktik and as such all the more incompatible with approaches, including my own, to revise human-science Didaktik in the spirit of critical-constructive Didaktik.

Here I can only outline the most important influences at work on my conceptions of educational science in general and Didaktik in particular, at first wholly dominated by human-science pedagogy, and later by what I have come to term "critical-constructive Didaktik". One crucial factor was the emergence of empirical research as a virtually new feature of German pedagogy from the 1960s onwards. A second was the increasing weight in many areas of West German pedagogy of the issues, methods and reflective approaches of the social sciences, particularly the sociology of education. One of the most important fields here was the question of social class in connection with educational opportunity. A third influence were the new social and political movements to which the decade gave rise, such as extra-parliamentary opposition, the student movement, demands for more democracy throughout society and fundamental social criticism. At the academic level this included the reception and critical discussion of theories and conceptions influenced, or at least stimulated, by Marxism and other critical social theories, particularly the critical social philosophy of what is known as the "Frankfurt School", represented by Adorno, Horkheimer and, later, Jürgen Habermas, to name just a few.

As I said at the beginning, I have no space to enlarge here. But I would like to stress that from the outset I did not regard the productive reception of these new impulses, particularly those of the "critical theory" of the Frankfurt School, as a one-way process of absorption, as though educational science and its subdiscipline Didaktik could or had to be based on a completely new ground, or indeed derived completely from "critical theory". I was and am convinced that the confrontation between educational science (and Didaktik) and critical theory can only be successful if educational science does not forget or jettison those issues and insights which have been elaborated in the long course of pedagogical thinking, especially since the age of Enlightenment. Thus it may well be that critical-constructive educational science has to make criticism of some statements relevant to pedagogy stemming from the "Frankfurt School". But that is not my topic here. The points in common are crucial, and the most important of these, as I see it, is as follows: Critical social theory and critical-constructive educational science influenced by critical social theory, particularly critical-constructive Didaktik, agree that the development of opportunities for self-determination on the one hand and co-determination on the other are dialectically linked and mutually conditional. By self-determination and co-determination I mean the development of individual responsibility and independence and the development of corresponding economic, social, political and cultural conditions. The subject, the individual as a person is always influenced by history and society, is "mediated," yet is never completely absorbed by his social role, is never determined by society alone, but in principle always has opportunity to criticize society, to take action with a view to change, and to make independent decisions. It is the central objective of pedagogical practice and pedagogical theory in the conception described here to create such opportunities in the educational process (cf. Klafki 1976).

Main Characteristics of Critical-Constructive Didaktik

I shall now focus on a few characteristics or groups of characteristics of the conception I hold. First I shall address the question, What does the term "critical-constructive" mean?

Let us first take the component "critical" and link up with some of the comments I made in the last section. "Critical" implies an interest in knowledge insofar as this approach to Didaktik is oriented towards the goal of guiding all children and adolescents to greater capacity for self-determination, co-determination and solidarity. At the same time it takes seriously the fact that the reality of society and its educational institutions in many cases does not correspond to this objective. From here stems the insight that further developments and changes—in the sense of permanent reform—can only be driven forward in conjunction with attempts to democratize society as a whole, attempts which must assert their influence in the face of strong countercurrents and sociopolitical resistance. Didaktik must, therefore, examine and articulate—often with recourse to appropriate sociological, political and psychological research—the manifestations of such inhibitions which stand in the way of teaching and learning in the sense of developing the capacities for self-determination, co-determination and solidarity. At the same time it must test and research teaching and learning processes which will be appropriate to develop these capacities as far as possible, if necessary in direct confrontation to the inhibiting factors.

The second attribute is "constructive", indicating the constant reference to practice, the interest in action, design and change which is constitutive of this didactical conception. It

sets out not only to create awareness by practitioners of prerequisites, opportunities and restrictions of pedagogical action, but is aimed also at the possibility of anticipations by
didactical theory, suggesting models for possible practice,
producing well-founded concepts for reformed or reforming
practice, for humane, democratic school and instruction. At
the same time, it suggests new models of cooperation between
"practice" and "theory".

But the term "constructive" should not be misunderstood in
a technological sense. The abilities of self-determination, co-
determination and solidarity cannot be directly induced by
didactical action. They cannot be "made", and thus didactical
theory cannot provide the practitioner with rules, technologi-
cally speaking, and "means", technically speaking, which guarantee that instruction will produce these abilities.

Education and Society

A further characteristic of critical-constructive Didaktik concerns the relationship between society and education. This is
not understood as a one-way relationship with the dependence
all on one side, as though the theory and practice of education were directly dependent on social facts and trends, just as
they happen to be and to develop. The authors of critical theories and concepts of education grounded in general sociology,
social philosophy and the sociology of education, maintain that
education has the opportunity and the responsibility not only
to re-act to social conditions and processes, but to judge them
and influence them in the interests of each young person or
indeed of any adult wishing to continue his or her education.
Forward-looking education can and must be based on recognition of the necessary link between the aptitude to perceive basic
personal rights and the image of a fundamentally democratic
society, a consistently liberal and social democracy.

On the Roots of Critical-Constructive
Didaktik in Theory of *Bildung*

In describing the second characteristic of critical-constructive
Didaktik, I touched upon a point I would now like to deal with
as a third characteristic. Here, too, I can give only a brief out-

line and must refer you to my other work for more details (cf. Klafki, 1994).

As I understand it, critical-constructive Didaktik is founded in Bildungstheorie. As most of you will be aware, Bildung cannot be adequately translated by "education". In this section I shall refer to Bildung rather than education to emphasize my reference to this particularly German concept. There is here a connection with human-science pedagogy, but with a more differentiated and critical determination of the relationship between Bildung and society.

The concept of Bildung on which critical-constructive Didaktik draws is rooted in the multifaceted understanding of Bildung which developed mainly in the period around 1770–1830. It was elaborated particularly in the German-speaking areas of Europe, but had from the beginning a world-wide perspective. This conception absorbed stimuli from the European Enlightenment: Lessing, Kant, and Herder, Goethe and Schiller, Pestalozzi and Herbart, Schleiermacher, Fichte and Hegel, Froebel and Diesterweg, all contributed to its development. Despite all the differences, and in places contradictions, in the ideas put forward by these thinkers, a few fundamental points in common emerged, not least the idea of the self-responsible, cosmopolitan person, contributing to his own destiny and capable of knowing, feeling and acting. I cannot here go into the history of the Bildung concept in the latter half of the 19th and in the 20th century. Human-science pedagogy and its theory of Bildung would need to be taken into account, for instance. And if we were to look beyond the circle of German-speaking authors, we would encounter, say, John Dewey's philosophy of education. But above all we would have to name approaches from the last three decades, such as the work of Hans-Joachim Heydorn, Theodor W. Adorno, Max Horkheimer, Jürgen Habermas, Herwig Blankertz, Dietrich Benner and others.

I have tried to summarize these developments in reflection on Bildung with respect to our current pedagogical tasks and to the future, as far as predictions are at all possible. I have condensed the many facets of the concept into three elements (or three abilities) which Bildung is to promote: self-determination—co-determination—solidarity. These require a brief explanation:

— Self-determination: Each and every member of society is to be enabled to make independent, responsible decisions about her or his individual relationships and interpretations of an interpersonal, vocational, ethical or religious nature.

— Co-determination: Each and every member of society has the right but also the responsibility to contribute together with others to the cultural, economic, social and political development of the community.

— Solidarity: As I understand the term, it means that the individual right to self-determination and opportunities for co-determination can only be represented and justified if it is associated not only with the recognition of equal rights but also with active help for those whose opportunities for self-determination and co-determination are limited or non-existent due to social conditions, lack of privilege, political restrictions or oppression.

The task of critical-constructive Didaktik is first to examine existing theories and concepts for institutionalized teaching and learning, particularly in school, as well as the practice of teaching and learning, to ascertain the extent to which it harmonizes with the three principles I have named. Second the task is to develop, test and evaluate concepts of teaching and learning which are oriented to those principles, as far as possible in cooperation with practitioners.

The Semantic Range of the Concept "Didaktik"

For the sake of greater clarity Table 1 presents a schematic view of the aspects covered by Didaktik. My aim is to emphasize the complexity of Didaktik as a research field and an applied discipline.

I suggest that in order to encompass the complex structure of Didaktik on our present level of knowledge we must take at least the main sections and subsections of the table into consideration. In the literature on the field it has often been stressed, and quite correctly so, that the individual elements of this complex structure are mutually influential and can thus only be appropriately understood and applied with some kind

Table 1
RANGE OF MEANING OF THE TERM "DIDAKTIK" IN THE CONCEPTION OF "CRITICAL-CONSTRUCTIVE DIDAKTIK"

Didaktik = educational research, theory and conception-building, related to all forms of purposeful and (to some extent) reflective teaching (instruction) and learning connected to teaching. (Here with main emphasis on teaching and learning in schools.)

D i d a k t i k

Reference-disciplines:

- psychology of learning and social relations
- pedagogical socialization -research and -theory
- research and theory on school as an institution/organization
- didactics of other pedagogical fields, e.g., didactic of adult-education, leisure-ed., museum-ed., extra - school youth work etc.

Three problem-levels

- *General Didactics* (Allgemeine Didaktik)
- *Domain D.s* (Bereichsdidaktiken), which cover some subjects or aspects of subjects, e.g., "social sciences", "polytechnic", d. of modern foreign languages etc.
- *Subject D.s* (Fachdidaktiken), e.g. math. -d., history-d. etc.

Dimensions, regarding the three levels:

- Dimension of decisions concerning
  - *curricula* (Richtlinien bzw. Lehrpläne)
  - *reasons* for decisions regarding curricula
  - *processes* of decision making and developing reasons
  - *conditions*, relating to such processes
- Dimension of concrete teaching and learning
  - *planning* instruction
  - *realizing* teaching and learning
  - intended and not-intended *results* ("hidden curriculum") of teaching and learning

Aspects:

- *aims* and *objectives*
- *contents* of teaching/learning
- *organizational forms* and *methods* of t./l.
- *media* of t./l.
- *forms* of *examining/judging/ evaluation* t./l.

of reference to the whole. How these interrelationships can be determined more precisely is a difficult question!

Teaching and Learning in School as a Nexus of Interaction, Social Learning and Content-Related Acquisition of Knowledge and Abilities

For critical-constructive Didaktik, school instruction must be designed and explored as a nexus of interaction, social learning and content-related acquisition of knowledge and abilities. Let us look first at interaction.

The objective of the interactive process of instruction is for learners, with the support of teachers, to gain—in a process of increasingly independent learning—knowledge and methods of knowing, as well as ways of perceiving, shaping, judging, evaluating and acting, in order to be able to confront their socio-historical reality actively and reflexively. This process includes acquisition of the ability to continue learning, in other words, the students are to "learn how to learn".

These abilities can, however, only be gained through confrontation with contents, with themes, either within subjects or within interdisciplinary structures: methods of statistics, certain laws of nature, the rise of fascism, ecological processes, techniques of art, and so on. When designing learning processes such as these it is important to know, among other things, that at the beginning of teaching-learning processes, instructional themes are usually only relatively roughly sketched preliminary drafts. They contain more or less broad latitude for interpretation and concretization. Their shape, i.e., what the learners actually acquire as the content *for them*, how they understand and interpret the problem involved, is decided in the course of the instructional process itself. Depending on the type of topic, the result may vary considerably from student to student.

But teachers as well can and should constantly subject themselves to new learning processes through interaction with the learners. This allows them not only to get to know their students better, but also to learn something new about the topic or theme through renewed reflection when planning and preparing the instruction, as well as in the instructional process itself, for example through the original ideas which the students contribute or through reflection of the learners' problems of understanding.

This interpretation of instruction as a process which must be interactive is bound up with its nature as a *social process.* Various social perceptions, attitudes, prejudices and ways of acting enter into instruction via the social and individual biographies of teachers and students. Such social perceptions, attitudes, prejudices, ways of action are strengthened or suppressed or modified, lead to conflicts and disturbances, contacts and compromises, transpositions or defensive reactions. Once this fact is recognized, the unreflected social learning, which is constantly taking place during the instructional process, must be consciously included in the setting of objectives and the making of decisions about instructional themes, and not simply from the point of view of instructional method, but with respect to democratic social education. Social learning must be consciously designed in such a way that the content dimension of the social concept is articulated within it. What sort of image do I, student A or student B, create for myself and the other students with whom I am learning, cooperating or competing in learning processes? Do I perceive foreign classmates as outsiders, as alien? If the answer is yes, what is it about them that makes me feel this way? And vice versa: what could they find in me to class me as different, foreign or an outsider? Or what strategies are used, for example, in our learning group, to resolve conflicts, to build up or break down hierarchical differences? Are they the same strategies we practice in groups outside school? Analogous questions should also be asked with regard to teachers.

Student Participation in Instructional Planning and Design

If teaching is to facilitate a learning process in the sense of the first five theses, then the aims and contents or themes, as well as the methods and media must be planned and justified with the learners in mind and in discourse with them. To put it another way, the principles of self-determination and co-determination must be implemented in the teaching-learning process.

Participation of students in planning and designing of instruction should increase gradually over time, with the students confronting tasks of increasing difficulty and facing up to growing demands for co-planning and evaluating instruction or phases of instruction, in other words experiencing "instruction about instruction". These are elements of a conception which is currently being discussed quite intensively under such headings as "open" or "student-oriented" instruction.

Research Conceptions in Critical-Constructive Didaktik: the Linking of Historical-Hermeneutic and Empirical Methods with the Methods of Social Analysis and Ideology Critique

In this section I deal with approaches to research. My thesis here is that critical-constructive Didaktik can only fulfill its commitment to promote capacity for self-determination, co-determination, and solidarity and thus provide help for pedagogical practice by linking at least three method groups, namely

- historical-hermeneutical methods,
- empirical methods, and
- methods of social analysis and ideology critique.

The synthesis of these three is not a simple addition. Nor is it bound to previous self-interpretations of these groups on the level of theory of science. Indeed, the groups at times create the impression of being irreconcilable. I do not believe that this is correct, but there is no time to give the reasons for this assertion in any more detail at this point (cf. Klafki 1994: 98–114, 135–138; 1978: 146–167; 1995 a: 63–80). Instead I should like to present an alternative thesis, and I trust that it will at least seem plausible.

If any one of these groups of methods is applied to questions of Didaktik, then consistent scientific reflection will inevitably confront the researcher with preconditions or limits which can only be overcome with the help of the other approaches. In other words: when the knowledge which can be gained using any one of these method groups has reached its limits, it becomes apparent that the epistemic process can only be advanced with the help of one of the other approaches. When this happens, constructive method synthesis is necessary.

As a footnote here I should like to refer back to the beginning of this section, where I stressed the necessity of a synthesis of at least three method groups. It is possible that there are other method groups besides hermeneutics, empirical analysis and social analysis/ideology critique, or that other fundamentally new approaches will be developed in future. As far as the present state is concerned, I am uncertain whether, for example, phenomenological methods as they have developed over the past decades—and which, as far as I can see, now bear little resemblance to the phenomenology, the "Wesensschau", of early Husserl—must be addressed as a separate method group or whether they are in terms of theory of science a specific branch of hermeneutics or a particular combination of hermeneutic and empirical approaches.

Now to the next step of my argument. I hold that the combination of hermeneutics, empirical analysis and social analysis in combination with ideology critique must be tackled from the historical-hermeneutic perspective. This also applies to Didaktik because instruction, i.e., the institutionalized teaching and the learning it generates, always denotes meaningful and purposive actions and processes. But it also holds that all of the learners' actions and processes which refer to the didactical actions of the teachers are meaningful actions, irrespective of whether they fulfill the teachers' intentions. In a similar sense, Pertti Kansanen, in his " Outline for the Model of Teachers' Pedagogical Thinking", describes "purposiveness as the characteristic of education" and of the "teachers' pedagogical thinking" (Kansanen, 1993: 52).

Historical-hermeneutic methods aim to clarify, to decode meaningful phenomena in a scientific manner. They serve as tools in comprehension; in the interpretation of meaningful documents (e.g., curricula, textbooks, written or oral records, pictures or pedagogically relevant architectural products such as school buildings or the design of rooms within them); in the interpretation of didactical decisions, actions and processes which are to make possible instruction, prepare for it or influence its course. By this I mean decisions, actions and processes through which teachers on the one hand and students on the other affect running instruction. In the case of learners, for example, this applies even when they wish to evade the teachers' intentions or when they disturb instruction.[2]

All problems of Didaktik are set within the wider context of educational history and, beyond that, the context of social history, often with an international perspective. This applies regardless of whether those concerned—curriculum developers, teachers, students—are aware of the fact or not. But at the same time, the didactical meanings mediated socio-historically, which are contained in, for example, curricula, instructional concepts, school books, instructional planning, etc., refer to presumed or desired future history, by which I mean those situations, tasks and opportunities in life which today's children and adolescents will probably encounter in the future. The didactical meanings, the intentions, the purposes for teaching and learning also contain certain ideas concerning the meaning of human life, the relationship between the individual and society, the significance of childhood and adolescence in the process of life, in other words philosophical and, not least, ethical preconditions.

The historical-hermeneutical approach aims at the nexus of questions I have just outlined. Didaktik in an historical-hermeneutical perspective therefore aspires to clarify the sense of decisions, developments, discussions, mechanisms in or relevant to Didaktik by means of appropriate scientific methods. It is supposed to work out the hidden historical conditions, the concepts of future, the philosophical implications, to make them intersubjectively verifiable and discussible and thus help those who have to act and decide in the name of Didaktik—such as curriculum planners and teachers, but also the students—to become aware of what they are actually doing, what they are deciding and acting about and under what historical conditions, in other words: What really lies in and behind their decisions, deliberations, actions.

Time is too short here to present and explain the sources of historical-hermeneutical research, in other words the various types of texts, ranging from elaborated theories of Didaktik to record instruction documented in writing, on audiotape, on videotape, as well as the processes and rules of the interpretation of such texts.

Next I shall look at the significance of the empirical method group as it interlocks with the historical-hermeneutic method group. Where historical-hermeneutic studies refer directly to current problems of teaching and learning, the inclusion of empirical research processes is imperative. Meanings which can be gleaned from didactical documents—such as curricula, written theories, teacher manuals, teachers' lesson plans, the objectives of a pedagogical reform movement, school books or other materials—no doubt influence or can influence the reality of school design, of instruction, of communication and interaction of teachers and students, but they are not the whole reality of Didaktik. A historical-hermeneutical approach can be taken to decode the didactical meanings embedded in a mathematics or history curriculum, but it cannot be ascertained by historical-hermeneutical means whether the instruction taking place in schools corresponds to these meanings or is far removed from it, not even if the teachers identify with the curriculum and believe that they are teaching in keeping with it. Questions such as these require different, in this case empirical research methods: surveys, interview procedures, field experiments, systematic observations, the use of tests, etc..

It should not be assumed, however, that in using these methods we step into a whole new world of research completely free of hermeneutical problems. I firmly believe that empirical research misunderstands its role if it sees any necessity or possibiblity to distance itself from hermeneutics as a perceived antonym or mere pre-stage of science. It must be recognized that empirical research and its "objects" are themselves full of hermeneutical problems, interwoven with and surrounded by hermeneutics.

This applies in three respects:

Firstly, every empirical study presupposes an issue, has a pre-understanding of some kind. Let us assume, for example, that an empirical research team is doing groundwork for the development of new curricula for political education and wish to build up a catalogue of the political experiences, knowledge and abilities students should acquire within general education or in a specialized school by questioning experts. If the researchers now conduct a survey by questionnaire or interview, such an approach implies a number of interpretations or pre-sumptions. It will already have been assumed, for instance, that it is necessary i.e., that it makes sense to aim for political education in school, that school should offer the students opportunities to confront certain situations and the political phenomena they contain and so on. Yet these are not interpretations, definitions of meaning which should be taken for granted for instruction. They are pre-decisions, which of course can be discussed and supported by argument, but cannot be regarded as mere "facts" which could be "ascertained" by supposedly interpretation-free empirical observation.

In short, if an empiricist wishes to elucidate and justify his own questions by rational means, then he is engaging—whether he realizes it or not—in hermeneutics, i.e., the interpretative exposition of his pre-comprehension. If not, then he does not know what he is actually doing as an empiricist!

Secondly: Not only the questions of empirical research contain premises which can and ought to be illuminated by historical-hermeneutical means. Its "objects" too—such as the actions, relationships, institutions, processes and conditions which it sets out to examine through observations, surveys, experiments, etc.—are meaningful phenomena, at least partly determined by meaning-contexts, and not sense-less facts. And this applies whether the educational games of teachers at various schools or the effects of different games on learning achievement or learning motivation or social behavior of students are to be tested, or whether the effects of certain methods such as group instruction or programmed instruction or teacher-led instruction on the development of students' scientific understanding, scientific problem-solving capacity, arguing skills, artistic perception or musical skills are to be ascertained.

The consequence is: The research procedures and the forms in which they are carried out must match the character of the objects of research, which are meaningful expressions of human beings within systems of didactical significance. But this does not appear to be true of many of the empirical procedures which instructional research has brought forth so far. Take, for example, the categories developed by Bales (1950), Bellack (1974) or Flanders (1970) for classroom interaction analysis. In principle we can say that empirical didactical research, with respect to this embedding in systems of meaning, proves to be a task which is bounded by considerably more preconditions and is more difficult than has often been assumed until now.

In my opinion, procedures from what is termed "qualitative social research" would follow from here. They have been in use in pedagogical research, including Didaktik, for quite some time: some were even developed specifically for this field. They are sometimes expressly described as forms of "empirical-hermeneutic" or "hermeneutic-empirical" research. To list just a few examples:

— Participant observation of instructional processes.
— Transcription or video/audio recording of group discussions, e.g., among teachers.
— Narrative interviews, i.e., non strictly pre-standardized interviews, perhaps with students discussing their leisure activities outside school or their friendships within school.
— Intensive or in-depth interviews, e.g. to ascertain the causes and variations of fear and failure in students.
— The procedure of "retrospective thinking-out-loud," where teachers follow audio or video recordings of their lessons and reconstruct what they were thinking at "difficult" moments.
— Collection and analysis of biographical documents in order to reconstruct longer-term individual developments, e.g. with respect to the constancy of or changes in teachers' attitudes to their work in the course of their careers, or with respect to students' educational biographies.
— Analysis of teachers' diaries recording their perception of teaching and day to-day life in school.

Thirdly, let us briefly consider the concluding phase of empirical research. That this phase has a deeply hermeneutical character is at least indirectly expressed in the fact that even traditional empirical researchers designate it as "interpretation of the obtained data". If dealing with systems of meanings—in methodological terms, hermeneutics—is required at the beginning of an empirical didactical study to clarify the main query and methodically detach it from the complex structures in which it is embedded, and if the data collection phase also proves at least partly determined by systems of meanings, then after data collection interpretation is once again required to integrate the facts into the wider systems of meaning from which the specific question first had to be detached. Re-integration into more complex contexts is a productive hermeneutical achievement, during which existing systems of meaning can be elucidated or modified or new systems of meaning can be worked out. This achievement cannot be taken for granted—as the large number of over-hasty conclusions drawn from empirical studies show. These misplaced conclusions, some of which have affected the political debate on education, for example, have often arisen because neither the preconditions of a particular study nor the wider contexts into which the evaluation should place the findings have been recognized. In other words, no thorough hermeneutical clarification has taken place beforehand and no thorough hermeneutical evaluation has taken place afterwards.

I shall now move on to the third group of methods which must be integrated into didactical research if it is to warrant the adjective "critical-constructive".

I have already intimated several times that all didactical institutions and decisions—the organization of instruction in school, curriculum design, teaching style, content and form of school books and all other didactical materials, etc.—are inevitably influenced by the conditions and notions of society and have social consequences. There is no pedagogical or didactical province outside society. The relative independence of education in theory and practice, and thus the relative independence of school and instruction, must be legitimated and implemented within and with critical reference to the social context. This generates particular queries and research tasks for Didaktik, and makes it necessary to develop corresponding research methods. I see two interlocking tasks here.

The first task can be formulated as the question: How are social conditions and developments reflected in the following dimensions of the field of operation of Didaktik?

— In the objectives and contents of guidelines, syllabi, curricula.

— In the explicit and implicit processes of in-school assessment and in the selection procedures.
— In the contents of school books and other teaching and learning materials.
— In the organizational forms of teaching and learning, e.g. in the decision to create heterogeneous or homogeneous groups of students for teaching.
— In the teachers' attitudes and pedagogical actions, e.g., their ways of dealing with boys or girls, which often differ.
— In the students re-actions to the ways in which they are addressed by the teachers.
— In the social relationships between the students, and so on.

Now to the second task: We must do didactical research work in the sense of ideology critique, i.e., targeted at certain forms of social consciousness. "Ideology" is understood here in its narrower, stricter sense of a form of wrong social consciousness, produced by certain conditions of social power and dependence. Ideologies in this sense are covering and seemingly legitimating existing social power structures and dependencies, for example where persons believe that the domination of one group of people by another is justified, imputing the latter group to be "naturally" more intelligent and more talented, or where people are convinced that women are "naturally" less fitted to science or politics than men, when in fact it can be demonstrated or at least assumed with a high degree of probability that the conditions of inequality are phenomena resulting from certain historical and social processes and conditions.

These examples show that ideologies match with the interests of certain socially powerful or privileged groups. But it is particularly significant that ideologies can also be considered true by the very people whose rights they actually restrict. In this case, the disadvantaged parties have themselves internalized the ideologies.

Ideology, false social consciousness of the type sketched out here, can be represented and mediated through Didaktik with the very best of intentions as long as the hidden social motives and the unreflected social consequences of curricula, teaching and learning materials, forms of differentiation, and teaching and learning processes do not come to light. The picture of the family drawn in books for language arts, foreign language or social science teaching is often motivated by the unreflected conventions of certain social groups; men and boys, women and girls are often portrayed in unquestionably stereotyped roles; the "slices of life" which some school books or other teaching media present are often laundered of all social inequalities, unemployment, wage disputes, strikes, crass contrasts between the wealthy suburbs and the inner-city slum, and so on. And such aspects of reality are correspondingly rare in recommendations for role-playing and class discussions. Indeed, reference to any sort of conflict, be it in the family or any other part of the social environment, is all too often studiously avoided. The students are presented with an essentially harmonious, intact image of reality, of a society in which the principles of freedom, justice, democratic civil rights, etc. would appear largely implemented. Often this is supported by the pedagogical stance that children cannot yet process psychical and intellectual the contradictions, the hard facts, the shortcomings of reality. They would need a polished, idealized image of reality in order to gain confidence for life.

This stance may well be adopted with the best of pedagogical intentions. But a form of Didaktik which has recognized the problem of the social preconditions and consequences of school teaching and school learning must draw on ideology-critique and ask: Who benefits—by design or by accident—from this type of education? Who benefits and who does not benefit when young people do not learn to see their world realistically and critically? We must, for example, confront our western societies which claim to be free and social democracies, in which superfluous domination, inequality and oppression have either been eradicated or are being consistently eradicated not only in political debates, but also in education with countervailing tendencies and facts, and we must give our pupils the chance to put questions for possible reasons for discrepancies between agenda and reality.

It is obvious that these reflections have significant consequences for the understanding of hermeneutics and empirical analysis in Didaktik. Not only is it necessary to integrate these two method groups. It is also necessary to integrate questions

of social analysis and ideology critique into historical-hermeneutic interpretation of didactical institutions, programs, theories and practices.

The same consequences must be drawn for empirical research, particularly with regard to the development of queries
and to evaluation and interpretation of study findings: Empirical research is also indispensable from the point of view of
the social analysis/ideology critique approach. But within the
framework of critical-constructive Didaktik it has an unambigu-
ous task. It can no longer be understood formally as a "neutral", supposedly value-free study of effectiveness, but must
rather concentrate on two assignments:-

— The first is the exploration of the conditions responsible
for unequal opportunities in the development of young
people (and, where appropriate, of adults) within the institutions of education and outside.
— The second is innovation research. In conjunction with
reforms of school and instruction guided by humane and
democratic objectives, it should explore the possibilities
for achieving these objectives for all young people, which
means not least for those who have so far been disadvantaged, usually from the socially weaker groups in the population.

A Closing Remark

I only became aware of reconceptualization as an element of
North American curriculum theory when preparing for the
Oslo-Conference "Didaktik and/or Curriculum" (August 1995),
thanks to Stefan Hopmann. If I have read William Pinar's 1978
essay, "The Reconceptualization of Curriculum Studies", correctly, then the reconceptualists' position is similar to critical-
constructive Didaktik in significant areas.

Notes

1. I learned later that this concept also became known in parts of Scandinavia and that, for example here in Norway, some teachers encountered it during their training. More recently—before the 1993 symposium in Kiel—I was astonished to discover that some American educationists were interested in the approach, and in the early version in particular. An abridged version was published in English translation in the *Journal of Curriculum Studies*, 27 (1995), 13–30.

2. The Greek term "hermeneuein" meant to interpret, to make something understandable which was originally incomprehensible or difficult to understand, to grasp its meaning.

References

Bales, R. F. (1950). *Interaction Process Analysis: A Method for the Study of Small Groups.* Cambridge MA: Addison-Wesley.

Bellack, A. A., Davitz, J., Kliebard, H. & Hyman, R. (1974). *Die Sprache im Klassenzimmer.* Düsseldorf: Schwann Verlag

Flanders, N. (1979). *Analyzing Teacher Behavior.* Reading MA: Addison-Wesley.

Kansanen, P. (1993). Outline for the Model of Teachers' Pedagogical Thinking. In P. Kansanen, *Discussions on Some Educational Issues IV, Research Report 121* (51–65). University of Helsinki: Department of Education.

Klafki, W. (1963, 1975). Didaktische Analyse als Kern der Unterrichtsvorbereitung. In W. Klafki, *Studien zur Bildungstheorie und Didaktik* (126–153). Weinheim: Beltz Verlag.

Klafki, W. (1976). *Aspekte kritisch-konstruktiver Erziehungswissenschaft.* Weiheim and Basel: Beltz Verlag.

Klafki, W. (1978). Ideologiekritik. In L. Roth (Ed.), *Methoden erziehungswissenschaftlicher Forschung* (146–167) Stuttgart: Kohlhammer Verlag.

Klafki, W. (1991). Can Education Science make a Contribution to Substantiating Pedagogic Aims? *Education: A Biannual Collection of Recent German Contributions to the Field of Educational Research.* Tübingen, Institut für Wissenschaftliche Zusammenarbeit. Vol. 44, 35–45

Klafki, W. (1995a). Zum Problem der Inhalte des Lehrens und Lernens aus der Sicht kritisch-konstruktiver Didaktik. *Zeitschrift für Pädagogik,* 33 (Beiheft), 91–102.

Klafki, W. (1995b). Didactic analysis as the core of preparation of instruction. *Journal of Curriculum Studies,* 27 (1), 13–30.

Klafki, W. (1996). *Neue Studien zur Bildungstheorie und Didaktik: Zeitgemäße Allgemeinbildung und kritisch-konstruktive Didaktik.* Weinheim and Basel: Beltz Verlag.

Pinar, W. F. (1978). The Reconceptualization of Curriculum Studies. *Journal of Curriculum Studies,* 10 (4), 205–214.

Conclusion

Didaktik Meets Curriculum: Towards a New Agenda

Stefan Hopmann
Bjørg B. Gundem

. . . an American coming to Europe for education, loses in his knowledge, in his morals, in his health, in his habits, and in his happiness.
(Thomas Jefferson, 1785)

When Jefferson toured Continental Europe in late 18th century, he was especially interested in visiting educational institutions like schools, seminars, and universities. As far as we
know, and as the quotation indicates, he was not very much
impressed. In fact he believed that the young states of the newly
established United States could offer a better education than,
for instance, Prussian schools. It is not quite clear whether or
not most contemporary American educators shared Jefferson's
view, but we do know that his successors from around the 1840s
had a completely different view on the European scene. From
Horace Mann to John Tilden Prince at the turn of the century
dozens of American educators and politicians went to Europe,
first and foremost to Prussia, studying the structure and achievements of the school systems of the old world, admiring their
teacher education, and learning from their educational theories. Names like Herbart, Hegel, Froebel and Wundt became
familiar within the American educational community, key
sources and study books were translated, school models and
research tools copied. However the American scholars of education of the time remained almost unknown to their European contemporaries, even if they had toured the mainlands
of educational discourse, Germany and France.

Whereas the 19th century was so clearly one of educational export from the old world to the new, the 20th century saw quite the opposite pattern. From around the turn of the century Continental European names, especially German ones, vanished from the American discourse. But in the 1920s educators in the old world got more and more curious about what was going on on the other side of the Atlantic. Obviously, something about "democracy and education," "progressive education," or "scientific curriculum making" could be learned from the United States. Key sources, such as Dewey's early works, were translated in almost all European languages. After the second world war curiosity turned into a willingness to learn from the leading nation of the western world, and from around 1965 American educational research swept through the old continent, and was especially influential in areas like research on teaching and curriculum studies. Being at an international standard meant being on a level with what was going on in the United States. For some areas, like educational psychology, this is still the case. But in other areas the last decade has witnessed the beginning of a new era. After two centuries of one-way communication it seems the time is ripe for a period of interchange and mutual understanding. And this turning of the tide is what the dialogue project "Didaktik meets Curriculum" has been about.

Initiated in 1990 by Stefan Hopmann and Ian Westbury, the dialogue project aimed at contributing to this change of perspectives at least in two fields, curriculum studies and teacher education. But unlike most other international projects (like the international co-operation in research on teacher thinking, in the field of curriculum history, or assessment studies, etc.) the project "Didaktik meets Curriculum" explicitly focused on the dialogue itself, using different topics from the field only as examples through which differences and commonalities could be made visible. To achieve this, a series of transatlantic conferences was staged, key sources translated, and joint publications edited (cf. the introduction to this volume).[1]

The conference at Oslo and a symposium at the AERA Annual Meeting in 1996 in New York mark the end of the project group's joint efforts.[2] This chapter is not an attempt to sum up, outline or examine what was done or written within the project, or to discuss the outcomes. The variety of issues raised and contributions offered would require an additional volume—and the important outcome of the project is this very variety of papers, written with the purpose of not only of presenting a position but of achieving mutual understanding. Moreover the dialogue is not finished. It has gained a momentum of its own and lead to a considerable number of joint and transatlantic efforts in different fields. However, before talking about this ongoing work and future perspectives, a retrospective discussion of some experiences within the project might be helpful for those to who have participated in our activities and to those who might be interested in taking part in future dialogues.

Besides important contributions to research topics and practical issues, the dialogue has given valuable insights into some conditions and constraints on mutual understanding. First of all, there is the problem of language, not only as a problem of translation, but more fundamentally as a mirror of deep traditions in "talking about education." This issue leads directly to a second problem crucial for the dialogue, the acknowledgment and understanding of structural differences in the way educational discourse and research are organized. Finally there is the question if and where fields of mutual interest emerged, what should or could be taken on in the future. At the bottom of this question lies naturally the more basic one, whether or not there is a need for a new research agenda within the fields of curriculum studies and teacher education.[3]

1. Didaktikk, Didaktik, Didactique, Didactics— or What are we Talking About?

It was late in the evening at a dinner party following an international conference on curriculum research that an American colleague asked spontaneously: "What on earth is this Didaktik you are always speaking about?" For a Continental European scholar of education this would have been a curious question as it is virtually impossible to become a teacher or move into the field of education without having experienced Didaktik—in university courses, in teacher training, at school board meetings, and the like. So it should not have been difficult for us to answer the question from our American colleague. But it was!

In fact we needed a whole project to come to terms with this question, and we are still not convinced that we have given an adequate or even a satisfactory answer, leaving no doubt about what Didaktik is. This would not matter if Didaktik was not the core of our business, if most of us do not use the word to sum up the focal point of our professional life.

First of all, we had to explain that Didaktik is not what Anglo-Saxons call "didactics." In English "didactics" has a somewhat old-fashioned connotation, referring to practical or methodological issues with a pejorative overtone. "Didactic" is someone "inclined to teach or lecture others too much" or "teaching or intending to teach a moral lesson" (*Webster's Unabridged Dictionary*, 1989). In German or the Scandinavian languages "to be didactical" can have the same meaning, but in the field of education the word encompasses much more than a teaching style. The professional knowledge of teachers is called "Didaktik" and most of teacher education deals with "Didaktik." An administrator writing a new state curriculum would call his work "Didaktik," and the same goes for the researcher doing an empirical study on learning in schools.

We can identify at least three different levels which together define the core components of Didaktik:

- a theoretical or research level, where the word denotes a field of study;
- a practical level, where Didaktik is exercised, comprising among others the whole fields of teaching, curriculum making and schooling; and
- a discursive level, where Didaktik names "the frame of reference" (in the sense of Alfred Schütz' theory of knowledge) as in case of professional dialogues between teachers, teachers and other groups outside school discussing school matters or other issues of teaching and learning. In this sense we speak, for instance, about subject matter Didaktik, the Didaktik of school levels, the Didaktik of lesson preparation, etc.

Institutions naming the core of their business "Didaktik" can be found in the fields of educational research (e.g., Germany's Institute for the Didaktik of Mathematics), teacher education (e.g., departments of general Didaktik and subject matter Didaktik), school administration, curriculum making, and text book production, and last but not least, wherever teachers meet, in schools, in teacher associations or in in-service training courses.

Didaktik is also neither an equivalent of curriculum studies or other familiar branches of the Anglo-Saxon discourse on education, nor just a habit or a practical approach, but is embedded in almost all professional activities dealing with teaching and schooling. It can be characterized as a language, with a vocabulary and a group of "native" speakers, who have a certain kind of professional education and/or a certain field of professional work in common. Historically, this language is bound to a certain structure of schooling and teacher education in which anyone participating professionally in teaching and schooling is expected to be able to explain "the reason for any particular method or practice . . . in a way, which leaves no doubt as to his sincerity . . ." (Prince 1897, p. 273)—and this reason has to be an explicitly educational one, based on "Didaktik" reasoning. Within the American discourse this could be compared to the "language of curriculum," as it is used on functionally equivalent levels and within equivalent institutions. However, Didaktik subsumes "curriculum" as merely one issue beside and interwoven with other issues like teaching and learning, schooling, school administration, etc.. Moreover, both languages tend to put their central issues into different perspectives as some examples taken from the conference minutes of the Kiel symposium of the project group may illustrate (cf. table 1).

In that Didaktik has its own vocabulary, direct translations based on a dictionary can be misleading. *Bildung*—one of the central conceptions of Didaktik—is by no means identical with "education;" in fact the German or the Scandinavian equivalents of "education" (*Erziehung, oppdragelse*, etc.) are often used in combinations like "*Bildung & Erziehung*," "*dannelse & oppdragelse*," flagging the fact that these terms refer to different aspects of the educational process. *Lehren* (*læring*) connotes something different than "teaching" or "instruction," and *Lehrplan* (*læreplan, læseplan*) something different than "curriculum" or "syllabus." To transport the meaning of these concepts

Place	Type	Image'
1. School (as place of teacher education)	training on the job	teaching as "Autodidaktik"
2. Normal School	a) basic course	teaching as imitation
	b) advanced course	teaching as application
	c) training course	teaching as method
3. Seminar	advanced course plus ...	teaching as a way of living
4. University, college	a) preparation of administrators	teaching as service
	b) preparation of educators	teaching as educating
	c) preparation of second. teachers	teaching as introduction
	d) counseling, research & development	teaching as planned behaviour
5. Administration	a) school administration	teaching as "Gestaltung"
	b) planning & development	
	c) INSET	
6. Associations & Unions	a) unions & general associations	teaching as profession
	b) subject matter associations	
7. Publishers & Producers	a) publishers	teaching as working with material
	b) other producers	

Table 1: Types of Institutionalization of Didactic Cultures (Hopmann 1994b)

into an Anglo-Saxon frame requires at least a footnote, if not a chapter on what is meant by using these expressions. More specialized concepts like *didaktische Reduktion* (a certain kind of transforming content into school matter) or *Bildungsgehalt* (the educational substance embedded in a school content) cannot be translated appropriately without referring to the strands of Didaktik they are placed in and the specific meaning enclosed. The same has to be said about core concepts of the American discourse like "pedagogical content knowledge" or "reconceptualization," which carry concept-based connotations a direct translation would not necessarily mirror. David Hamilton, who participated in almost all of the conferences of the project group and supported its efforts with friendly critique, has repeatedly pointed to the fact that this is also true in those cases where the different languages use words of same origin, for instance words emerging from the joint heritage from Greek, Latin or baroque sources like "curriculum" and "Didaktik" or "didactics." He believes that the history of the words itself, of their use and transformation in history, could be a key to understand what has been different, even though— as he added—this might not necessarily reflect, let alone explain the differences of today. Thus a dictionary of education would have to be both, comparative and historical, if the user is to be aware of what certain translations may omit or add to the original.

The language problem could be ignored, if one could agree upon "what the matter is," without being mislead by the use of certain concepts. But unlike technical languages based on definitions, or conventions, the matter itself is constituted by the very language at stake. Thus even everyday expressions like "content" (*Inhalt, innhold*) can mean very different things, if, for example, an American or a German researcher were to explain the issue of "content coverage" within a comparative project on school achievement (cf. Hopmann & Riquarts, 1995b).

The fundamental language problem cannot be solved; it can only be taken into account. Thus one important lesson from our project is that all kinds of comparative research have to have a meta-level of communication, against which the interchange is screened and checked continuously for potential misunderstanding and mismatches. For each concept with meaning-bearing importance, the chosen or implied range of application has to be explained. In other words, comparative research as well as international exchanges need comparative topics of the kind Aristotle developed to deal with meanings within practical discourse. And just as Aristotle proposed (and Joseph Schwab sought to introduce into the field of curriculum studies), topical knowledge can only emerge from a practical discourse, i.e., from an explicit dialogue between those involved. It would not be sufficient to exchange statements or to translate papers, because only an ongoing "self-referential" interchange between both discourse levels can indicate where understanding is reached or where it is not reached. For this to succeed, international exchange needs a much longer time-line than is typical, and much more continuity, to secure and enhance the quality of understanding. The never-ending discussions on whether results of comparative projects like the international studies on literacy, mathematics and science are meaningful and trustworthy indicate that it is not just a question of research ethics, but also one of political and cultural importance.

So what were we talking about? The reader of the different publications which emerged from the project will find a wide range of issues from teacher education and from the field of curriculum studies. We decided that the best way to come to an understanding would be to ask contributors from the different backgrounds to speak about what seemed to be the same issue, e.g., about "how to prepare a lesson" or "what kind of ethic in educational research." So in most cases the same issue was addressed by one speaker from an Anglo-Saxon background, one from a German-speaking country and a Scandinavian one. The differences in how our participants presented their case, where they failed to reach a mutual understanding, and what remained unclear or insecure served as indicators of where "meta-discourse" was needed. Sometimes the results could hardly be recognized as answers to the same question (e.g., the contributions dealing with the ethics and the tact of teaching in this volume and in Hopmann & Riquarts, 1995a). Sometimes the contributors themselves tried to carry on the meta-discourse by reflecting on how the other side might or might not understand what they wanted to present (e.g., the contributions dealing with paradigm-shift in this volume). Sometimes there was no difference visible, at least not at the level of presentation (cf. the joint contribution concerning math teaching by Pereira & Keitel in Hopmann & Riquarts, 1995a). Even though the speakers from different "language backgrounds" were chosen from different, often conflicting strands of their home "language" (e.g., reconceptualists as well as followers of more "traditional" approaches to curriculum studies), the "natives" normally had more in common than those coming from different languages who used similar tools and theories (e.g., building their argument on critical theory/hermeneutics or on empirical data from field research). (Unfortunately the project did not have the money to tape and transcribe the discussions, which evolved on basis of those experiences and which in many respects were the core of the conferences.) Only by following the change in style and language from the first conference in Aarau (1991) to the last symposium in New York (1996), as it is reflected by the different conference volumes, one might sense that those participants who were continuously involved in the project's activities became more and more aware of the implications and fallacies of a transnational discourse on education.

Based on these experiences one could write an ethnography of international discourse within the field. Issues like rhetoric (how to start a presentation or underline arguments), structure (what kind of argument-related evidence, how important is systematic elaboration, etc.) and tradition (how to relate arguments to the history of the field) would have to be addressed. These differences were especially felt on the occasions where "foreign" contributions were to be published in "native" journals. The journal editors expected in almost all cases that the language and structure of the papers be adapted to their "native" standards, even though this meant that an important source of information was omitted. Internationally experienced colleagues were able to write their papers according to these requirements, adapting themselves to "American-style," "Scandinavian style" or "German style." But—by doing this—a loss of "native flavor" was unavoidable, a serious loss insofar as the "native" traditions at stake reflect the differences in language and understanding. It would go beyond the purpose of this afterword to go to explore this further. Bilingual readers will recognize those differences anyway by comparing the project's publications. However, the bottom line should be mentioned. Analyzing the Kiel conference one colleague told us: "Americans tell stories—Germans explain histories—Scandinavians have had their experiences"!

2. In Search of Difference

Differences are not always obvious, at least not in educational discourse. Take for example speaking about "pedagogy" (*Pädagogik, pedagogikk*). In the Anglo-Saxon tradition "pedagogy" means "the art and science of teaching," especially the "instruction in teaching methods" as provided by educational psychology (*Websters Unabridged Dictionary*, 1989). For a German or a Scandinavian "the art and science of teaching" is just one of dozens of subdivisions of *Pädagogik* (*pedagogikk*). For them the expression covers the whole field of educational theory and practice. Thus most professors of *Schulpädagogik* (*skolepedagogikk*) would normally not reduce their activities to "pedagogy," but most likely deal with a wide range of questions like the impact of school as an institution, curriculum studies or school development, issues which at an American university would most probably be the research field of educational sociology or curriculum. The reason for this difference might be found in the different histories of teacher education (cf. Hopmann & Riquarts, 1995b). It is an important issue in that more than half of all German professors of education hold professorships officially devoted to *Schulpädagogik*.

As in this case, transatlantic dialogue has to take into account that the educational discourse and research are organized quite differently in the respective traditions. Embedded in these institutionalized traditions are different patterns of argumentation and validity, different rhetorical cultures and different cultures of theory development. To give just a few examples:

- In Germany, almost all professorships of education are directly connected to teacher education (or to other educational professions like social work). For most of these professorships year-long practical experiences within schools or other educational institutions are required. Graduate schools of education without direct involvement in teacher education are unknown.

  It is different in Denmark, where most educational research is based at Denmark's Lærerhøjskole (the Royal Danish College of Teacher Education), an institution of further education for teachers already working in schools.

Only one Danish university has an educational department (as part of the department of philosophy, rhetoric and education), a small one with few resources. In Norway colleges of education and university departments exist side by side, the latter providing both professional education and graduate studies, but no teacher education (at university level this is provided by a special department of teacher training). Where they do not constitute faculties of their own, most university departments of education in Germany are part of the humanities (the faculty of philosophy), in Scandinavia they have often been combined with the social sciences (sociology, psychology, etc.).

There exists no comparative research on how these differences affect research and teaching at the university level, but the contributions to our dialogue project clearly reflect these different affiliations.

Even more striking are the differences in the field of curriculum control. In most European states there is no doubt that the state has the right to set curriculum guidelines for both schools and teacher education (cf. Hopmann, 1990). Most states have established state research institutes to get the necessary research and development work done. The guidelines themselves are, in most cases, written in close cooperation with experienced teachers and combine state control with a "license" for teachers or teacher educators to make their own plans within this framework. As the predominant mode of curriculum control since the mid-19th century, this pattern gave birth to Didaktik: it was and is the language by which state administrators, principals, teachers, and all others involved in the process of education could communicate about how to work within the framework. The requirement to teach within the frame of social expectations laid down in the guidelines supported the development of professional abilities to fulfill these expectations by a vast variety of instructional designs and contents, *and that is what subject matter Didaktik is about.* Locally- or teacher-based curriculum decision making leads naturally to another set of abilities, in that the questions decided upon by state-issued guidelines now have to be taken up at the school level. However, in many cases the choice of a school book (which has traditionally been a more important issue within the Anglo-Saxon pattern of schooling than in Continental Europe) or the achievement expectations laid down in assessment tests or the entrance requirements for subsequent education substitute for the decisions made in the Continental pattern by state-issued guidelines (cf. Ben-Peretz, 1990). How much "freedom" teachers are allowed within one or the other pattern may be very much the same or completely different, but in any case it leads to different kinds of teacher thinking (cf. Biehl, Hopmann & Ohlhaver, 1996).

One implication of these institutional traditions is that the relation between academic research and practice has developed quite differently. The American field of curriculum studies, for example, has a strong tradition of university-based developmental projects, providing complete curriculum guides including all the necessary teaching material. However, one has to be aware of that this kind of academic research has had almost no impact on what is going on in curriculum development in schools, in school districts or at state level (cf. the contributions of Frances Klein and O. L. Davis in this volume). In recent years many curriculum theorists have distanced themselves willingly from school, understanding the curriculum discourse as an intellectual "journey" and not a field of first and foremost practical activities (cf. William Pinar in this volume). This is completely different in Germany. A recent survey by Biehl, Hopmann & Ohlhaver (to be published in 1997) indicated that almost all university-based activities in the field are closely connected to practical work in curriculum development, school book writing, etc., mostly in direct cooperation with state administrations, state institutes, and the teachers themselves. The most influential curriculum theories unanimously agree that curriculum development is a social process within the society and its school system in which academic research should play a supportive role (cf. Gundem, 1992, 1995; Hopmann & Künzli, 1994). Thus one German professor of education who participated in our discussions and plays a significant role in German discourse on curriculum making called the reconceptualist approach as presented by Pinar irresponsible and totally unacceptable to morally serious scholars of education. In fact, neither American-styled curriculum development by university departments nor academic curriculum discourse without practical affiliation have ever played a significant role in Germany (except for a few years around 1970; cf. Hopmann, 1988). Whereas the Norwegian situation resembles mostly the German tradition (with less involvement of the academics), the curriculum field in Sweden has until recently been shaped by a strong tradition of cooperation between research and state-run curriculum development (cf. Erik Wallin and Ulf P. Lundgren in this volume).

"Americans tell stories—Germans explain histories—Scandinavians have had their experiences;" these differences are probably directly connected to the history of institutional affiliations and the embedded history of methodological preferences. Coming from a tradition shaped by subjects like theology, philosophy and history the average German professor of education has to build any basic argument on teaching, schooling or learning on the history of educational thinking. It is quite usual to start an argument by going back to Schleiermacher, Herbart or Comenius, even if the topic at stake is not a historical one, but an issue of today. Like their Scandinavian colleagues German scholars of education are again and again astounded by the almost history-free research and theory development presented by their American colleagues. And it is not very difficult for them to show that many of the leading curriculum theories and models of today are "re-inventions of the tool," remakes of ideas developed way back in the history of educational discourse. Take for example Max van Manen's surprise that the "tone" and "tact" of teaching has been an issue of continental educational theory since the days of Schleiermacher and Herbart (cf. van Manen in Hopmann & Riquarts, 1995a) or the fact that Lee Shulman's concept of different types of professional knowledge has very much in common with traditional models of Didaktik—like the Didaktik of Heinrich Roth from around 1950 (cf.

Hopmann, 1994). A historically grounded check of the
vast variety of curriculum proposals reported by Pinar *et
al.* in their seminal *Understanding Curriculum* would reveal that even the most recent inventions are remakes,
e.g., that a recently developed "romantic" approach to
curriculum making can lead towards a Herbartian structure of the school curriculum—without even noticing it
(cf. Pinar *et al.*, 1995, 692ff.). Given the one-way character of the transatlantic discourse, at least until recently, it
is no surprise that (especially) non-American precursors
are practically unknown today—even if they played a significant role in the early years of American education (like
Herbartianism until the turn of the century). Sometimes
this leads to the somewhat curious situation, that an
American educational model is exported to Continental
Europe without any indication of its Continental roots,
where it is treated as an American invention without connecting it to its local prehistory. Thus the project method
made its European career as an invention of American
progressive education, even though it originally stems
from Continental pedagogy of the 18th and 19th century
(cf. Knoll, 1991).

One of the curious things about this situation is that,
at the same time, non-educational European theories have
had a significant impact on educational discourse in the
United States. Habermas, Gadamer, Heidegger and Foucault are just a few examples of European philosophers
who have had a great impact on some strands of American curriculum theory in recent decades. The work of
Michael Apple, Henry Giroux and of many of the
reconceptualists could hardly be imagined without these
sources. The same flow of ideas can be observed in the
opposite direction. From Parsons to Rawls there is hardly
an American social theory of importance which has not
been used, and discussed, in the old world. But, on both
sides of the Atlantic divide, the scholars of education who
draw on these theories have never found similar interest
in their work. Thus the predominant German educational
theories of the 1970s and, 1980s, the works of Wolfgang
Klafki, Herwig Blankertz and many others inclined to
critical theory, are practically unknown in the United

States. The same could be said about the critical strands of American curriculum studies, which have found almost no resonance in Germany (with the exception of some works in the field of educational sociology like Dreeben's *On What is Learned in School* and Jackson's studies on the hidden curriculum). However, the different strands which draw on the same sociological, philosophical, etc. sources, for example critical theory, meet each other in the Scandinavian discourse, especially in Denmark and Norway where the German tradition has always been strong but where, at the same time, paradigm shifts within American educational research have been given much attention. German critical educational theories stand, curiously enough, much stronger in Denmark and Norway than in Germany itself where they have lost ground in recent years to other approaches like system theory and postmodernist approaches.

Even though some of these examples sound like clichés about the respective traditions, one could continue with similar observations concerning, for instance, the placement of research of teaching within the academic field and its relation to curriculum studies (cf. Westbury & Doyle, 1992). Or one could point to new developments, like the renewed interest in the relation of subject matter and teaching, which have lead both traditions to quite similar research questions and models of explanation (cf. Gudmundsdottir & Grankvist, 1992). These and other examples have been discussed in more detail in the different publications of the working group (cf. for instance Gundem, 1996, Hopmann, 1990, Haft & Hopmann, 1990, Hopmann & Künzli, 1992, Hopmann & Riquarts, 1995a, Hopmann *et al.*, 1995). What these examples illustrate is the fact that the participants involved in the dialogue do not only represent their personal brand of theory, but are also deeply rooted in far-reaching structures and traditions which shape their choices, their awareness of each other, and their abilities to understand what their colleagues from the other side are talking about. The search for such often unnoticed differences, for differences in the everyday life of educational theory and practice, is crucial if mutual understanding is to be possible.

However to achieve more than this rather simple insight would require a good deal of comparative knowledge (cf. for instance the contributions of William Reid and Ian Westbury in this volume). And even if this insight might sound rather simple-minded, it is not the conventional wisdom of the field. Why, for example, do so many publications in the field of comparative education not explicitly deal with these questions? Even the *International Encyclopedia of Education*, edited by Husén *et al.*, 1994) lacks any systematic treatment of these problems.

3. Towards a New Research Agenda

The project "Didaktik meets Curriculum" has highlighted some known and some lesser-known differences and commonalities which may or may not have an impact on the transatlantic dialogue about education. To enhance mutual understanding is a worthwhile task—but the question remains of assessing whether or not more can be gained from the dialogue. When our American colleague asked "What on earth is Didaktik," his question represented not only intellectual curiosity but also a quest for knowledge which might enhance the state-of-the-art of curriculum studies from a till-then neglected source. It was the newly developed research interest into subject matter's role in professional knowledge, teacher thinking and teaching that had lead him to the speculation that something supporting this kind of research might be gained from a better acquaintance with the Continental European tradition of subject-matter Didaktik. It was in fact a paper on math Didaktik, presented by a German colleague at an international math education conference which had stirred his curiosity. The paper had dealt with concepts like "didactical reduction" and "didactical transformation" which indicated that there was a developed analytical framework at hand to do both practical work in schools and research. Like him, almost all of our American colleagues involved into the dialogue were most interested in this feature of Continental Didaktik. The Europeans, on the other hand, saw in the newly developed strands of research on teaching and of curriculum studies a welcome support to their own efforts to give general and subject matter Didaktik a better empirical foundation. Thus on both sides there is an actual need, which might be dealt with on basis of a developed dialogue leading to joint efforts in the field.

Therefore it seemed to be appropriate to close the Oslo conference with the issue of whether there is a need for a new agenda in educational research and what the dialogue might contribute to this agenda. Many contributions to this closing debate addressed known but not yet adequately addressed issues like the tendencies to a world-wide unified curriculum and the important role non-educational agencies like supranational organizations or the World Bank seem to have in this respect (Birgit Brock-Utne, Kurt Riquarts). Implicitly the same problem was articulated by a contribution dealing with the implications of multi-culturalism and multi-ethnicity and with the challenge to develop a concept of education which deals with these implications in a multi-faceted way, and not in terms of an "integration" pedagogy reducing minority cultures to deviance (Kamil Özerk). A similar argument was made about the role of gender in educational research and practice, calling for a non-patronizing approach to difference and inequality (Kirsten Reisby, William Pinar). These issues are evidently of mutual interest on both sides of the Atlantic.

The most challenging issue seems, however, to arise from a few participants surprising observation that both curriculum studies and academic research on Didaktik find themselves in a comparable messy situation at the end of this century. Frances Klein's and O. L. Davis' (in this volume) sharp critique of the practical irrelevance of contemporary curriculum studies had striking similarities with the ways in which some Norwegian scholars of education, and some of their German colleagues, experience their own situation. Parts of the Norwegian educational research community, for instance, feels itself set aside by the politicians and the curriculum practitioners who are unleashing one of the biggest school reforms in Norwegian history. Obviously, modern educational thinking has lost its anticipatory and guiding force outside its own academic environments, at least in the field of curriculum making. The question "whose fault" found quite different answers. Some accused the researchers of being too far from what is going on outside the academic ghetto; others claimed that the research community is set aside because of its critical stance to what is going on. Whatever the diagnosis, there can be no doubt that the respective academic milieus have to think about their future role in shaping educational realities.

Historically seen, there is nothing new about this challenge. Joseph Schwab in the United States and Herwig Blankertz in Germany raised the same issues some twenty years ago and there is a history of similar deliberations since the days of enlightenment (Oelkers & Neumann, 1984). Scholars of education have pictured themselves throughout history as being in a state of fading impact. Probably this is a necessary part of dealing with the unavoidable distance between them and those on the "front-line." What is different today, however, is the reality that academic research on education is far from the only provider of educational research and scientific knowledge to the field. On both sides of the Atlantic, public and private research institutes and other enterprises have gained a considerable share in delivering the kind of evaluation research and knowledge actors in the field of schooling are asking for. State administrations and other sponsors of academic research are becoming more and more specific in their expectations about what they are prepared to pay for, setting academic research in a position somewhat similar to the research done by state-run institutes or private contractors. Thus the question How do we (re)gain influence? rises to a new level of significance, at least for those who measure the importance of educational research by its impact on practice.

Naturally, a conference series like ours cannot provide a compact and comprehensive answer to such a question. But many of the debates following the different contributions focused on what kind of research should be developed to change this situation. Not surprisingly, most proposals extended the new research topics presented at the conferences, for instance, combined research on curriculum and teaching, looking closer to the relation of content and classroom-management (Walter Doyle), the role of "pedagogical content knowledge" (Lee Shulman, Sigrun Gudmundsdottir), the social construction of subject matter inside and outside schools (Roland Lauterbach, Ian Westbury), or the rationality and meaning-bearing implications of teaching (Erling Lars Dale, Tomas Englund). Also the debates about the ethics of teaching showed clearly that the "critical" and the "practical" are intertwined aspects of any Didaktik or curriculum theory aiming at responsible teaching (Wolfgang Klafki, Klaus Schaller, Peter Menck, etc.). Following these directions some members of the working group have decided to start a new dialogue effort focusing on "subject matter as a frame of reference" dealing, for instance, with the emerging research on school subject matter knowledge and the role of subject matter in constructing and controlling the curriculum. Another project attempts a comparative view on curriculum making and lesson planning in five European states and the development of analytical tools to compare state-run and locally-based curriculum decision making. A third effort focuses on the exploration of comparative topics in educational discourse.

More issues and research options could be added. The bottom line of most of them was a change of attitude or the renewal of an old virtue—as Peter Menck would put it—asking for a scholarship of education which sees itself as an active, responsive and responsible partner in the field, which shares the needs and endeavors of those teaching and educating. Research strategies supporting self-determination and autonomy and respecting the perspectives present in the field are needed. Perhaps the combination of some models and approaches from both traditions, Didaktik and curriculum, may provide the necessary tools and theories to move on in this direction (cf. Gudmundsdottir & Grankvist, 1992, Doyle & Westbury, 1992, Gundem, 1996, Hopmann & Riquarts, 1995b etc.). Because of this, the working group behind the dialogue-project "Didaktik meets Curriculum" is delighted that the most important task of the project was fulfilled: the strategy of "making people meet" should encourage mutual understanding and cooperation by bringing leading scholars from the different strands together. Not only the publications of the working group, but more so the newly established working relations within the field seem to be promising: Scandinavian scholars touring Germany and hosting German and American colleagues at their own institutions, Scandinavian and German scholars of Didaktik taking part in American conferences on curriculum, publications on Didaktik in Anglo-Saxon journals (like the *Journal of Curriculum Studies*) and by American publishers as well as extensive discussions about new paradigms in curriculum research in European journals give hope that we are indeed on our way to a new era of interchange and dialogue. If the project has contributed to this development, it was truly successful.

Notes

1   The list of references at the end of the chapter contains all joint publications, which have emerged from the work of the project group. Besides this, numerous books, articles and papers closely connected to the project's ideas have been published both in Europe and the United States.

2   Also the New York symposium will be documented within the frame of a reader presenting important historical sources of Didaktik and examples of its contemporary use to the American audience (cf. Hopmann, Riquarts & Westbury 1996).

3   The conclusions drawn here are naturally inspired and influenced by our colleagues and friends, which have participated in the project's development. However, as outlined here, they are in the responsibilty of the authors alone. All quotations carrying a name, but not indicating a publication, are taken from discussions and statements, which have been made in the course of the project.

References

Achtenhagen, F. (1992). Zur Notwendigkeit einer Renaissance der Curriculum-Diskussion. *Unterrichtswissenschaft*, 3, 200–208.

Ben-Peretz, M. (1990). *The Teacher-Curriculum Encounter: Freeing the Teachers from the Tyranny of Texts.* Albany: SUNY Press.

Biehl, J., Hopmann, S. & Ohlhaver, F. (1995). Wie wirken Lehrpläne. *Pädagogik*, 1, 28–32.

Doyle, W. & Westbury, I. (1992). Die Rückbesinnung auf den Unterrichtsinhalt in der Curriculum- und Bildungsforschung in den USA. *Bildung und Erziehung*, 45 (2), 137–157.

Frey, K., Haft, H. & Hopmann, S. (Eds.) (1989). Lehrplanarbeit International. *Bildung und Erziehung*, 42, 1.

Goodson, I. & Ball S. J. (Eds.). (1984). *Defining the Curriculum: Histories and Ethnographies.* London: Falmer.

Goodson, I. (Ed.). (1987). *International Perspectives in Curriculum History.* London: Falmer.

Gudmundsdottir, S. & Grankvist, R. (1992). Deutsche Didaktik aus der Sicht neuerer empirischer Unterrichts- und Curriculumforschung in den USA. *Bildung und Erziehung*, 45 (2), 178–188.

Gundem, B. B.(1990). *Læreplanpraksis og læreplanteori: En innføring til læreplanområdet.* [Curriculum Practice and Curriculum Theory: An Introduction to the Field]. Oslo: Universitetsforlaget.

Gundem, B. B. (1992). Notes on the Development of Nordic Didactics. *Journal of Curriculum Studies*, 24 (1), 61–70.

Gundem B. B. (1993). *Mot en ny skolevirkelighet: Læreplanene i et sentraliserings-desentraliseringsperspektiv.* [Towards a New Reality of Schooling: Curriculum and the Local-National Dilemma]. Oslo: Ad Notam Gyldendal.

Gundem B. B. (1995). The Role of Didactics in Curriculum in Scandinavia. *Journal of Curriculum and Supervision,* 10 (4), 302–316.

Gundem B. B. (1996). Forholdet didaktikk-curriculum: historiske perspektiv og aktuelle utfordringer. [Didactics-curriculum: historical perspectives and present challenges]. *Didaktisk Tidsskrift. Årgang för lärarutbildning och lärarfortbildning,* 6 (1), 44–61.

Haft, H. & Hopmann, S. (Eds.) (1990). *Case Studies in Curriculum Administration History.* London and New York: Falmer.

Hamilton, D. (1989). *Towards a Theory of Schooling.* London: Falmer.

Hopmann, S. (1988). *Lehrplanarbeit als Verwaltungshandeln.* Kiel: IPN.

Hopmann, S. (Eds.) (1990). Lehrplangeschichte International. *Bildung und Erziehung,* 43, 4.

Hopmann, S. & Künzli, R. (1992). "What is Didactic?" *Beiträge zur Lehrerbildung,* 1, 98–102.

Hopmann, S. & Riquarts, K. (1992). Didaktik - didaktikk - didactics. *Nordeuropa Forum* (Nomos) 2, 21–24.

Hopmann, S. & Künzli, R. (Eds.) (1992). Didaktik-Renaissance. *Bildung und Erziehung,* 45, 2.

Hopmann, S. & Künzli, R. (1992). Didaktik-Renaissance. Zur Einführung. *Bildung und Erziehung,* 45 (2), 117–135.

Hopmann, S. (1994). *Comparative Didaktik. The Case of Heinrich Roth vs. Lee Shulman.* Paper presented at the 1994 AERA Annual Meeting, New Orleans, Louisiana.

Hopmann, S. & Künzli, R. (1994). Topik der Lehrplanung: Das Aarauer Lehrplannormal. *Bildungsforschung und Bildungspraxis,* 2, 161–184.

Hopmann, S. & Keitel, C. (1995). Editorial: The German Didaktik tradition. *Journal of Curriculum Studies,* 27, 1–2.

Hopmann, S & Riquarts, K. (1995). Starting a Dialogue: Roots and Issues in a Beginning Conversation Between the Didaktik and Curriculum Traditions. *Journal of Curriculum Studies, 27*, 3–12.

Hopmann, S. & Riquarts, K (Eds.). (1995a). *Didaktik and/or Curriculum.* Kiel: IPN.

Hopmann, S. & Riquarts K. (1995b). Didaktik and/or curriculum: Basic problems of a comparative Didaktik. In S. Hopmann & K. Riquarts (Eds.), *Didaktik and/or Curriculum* (pp. 5–40). Kiel: IPN.

Hopmann, S.; Klafki, W.; Krapp, A. & Riquarts, K. (Eds.) (1995c). Didaktik und/oder Curriculum. Beiheft 34 der *Zeitschrift für Pädagogik.* Weinheim: Beltz.

Husén, T. *et al.* (1994) *The International Encyclopedia of Education.* New York: Pergamon.

Knoll, M. (1991). Europa - nicht Amerika! Zum Ursprung der Projektmethode in der Pädagogik. *Pädagogische Rundschau,* 45 (1), 41–58.

Manen, M. van. (1991). *The Tact of Teaching.* New York: State University of New York Press.

Menck, P. (1986). *Unterrichtsinhalt oder Ein Versuch, Unterrichtsgeschen als Prozeß der Konstitution von Inhalten zu verstehen.* Frankfurt: Lang.

Neumann, D. & Oelkers, J. (1984). "Verwissenschaftlichung" als Mythos? Legitimationsprobleme der Lehrerbildung in historischer Sicht. *Zeitschrift für Pädagogik,* 30, 229–252.

Pinar, W. *et al.* (1995). *Understanding Curriculum.* New York: Lang.

Prince, J. T. (1892). *Methods of Instruction and Organization of the Schools of Germany for the Use of American Teachers and Normal Schools* Boston.

Westbury, I. *et al.* (Eds.) (1994). *The German Didaktik Tradition: Implications for Pedagogical Research.* Champaign, IL: University of Illinois at Urbana-Champaign, College of Education.

Notes on Contributors

Erling Lars Dale is a professor at the Institute for Educational Research, University of Oslo. His research interests belong to the fields of Didaktik, educational philosophy and theater professionalism. Dale is working on a reconstruction of pedagogy as a critical science and has taken an active part in the Scandinavian discussion on education. Central themes in lectures and books are educational rationality and the quality of education.

O. L. Davis, Jr. is a professor of curriculum and instruction at the University of Texas at Austin. His research interests include curriculum development, practice and theory, curriculum history and social studies of education. He has been president of numerous educational associations and has also served as vice-president, Division B (Curriculum Studies), American Educational Research Association (AERA). Davis received the Lifetime Achievement Award from this Division in 1996. He is author or editor of numerous books and articles and currently edits the *Journal of Curriculum and Supervision*.

Tomas Englund is a professor at the Department of Education, University of Uppsala and the University of Örebro (Sweden). He is director of the research group "The content of socialization and dimensions of citizenship". His current research interests center on curriculum theory, Didaktik, curriculum history, political socialization, citizenship education and the philosophical aspects of education. Englund has published in Sweden and internationally. Recent publications concern strategic evaluation of teacher education and the shift in educational policy.

Bjørg Brandtzæg Gundem is a professor of education at the University of Oslo. Her research interests and teaching are in the fields of Didaktik and curriculum studies. Gundem is the author of numerous research monographs, and she has published widely in Scandinavia and internationally. Recent books deal with curriculum practice and curriculum theory, the aims and content of schooling, and curriculum and the local-national dilemma.

David Hamilton is professor of education at the University of Liverpool. He is author of *Towards a Theory of Schooling* (1989) and *Learning about Education: An Unfinished Curriculum* (1990). His current research focuses on the beginnings of modern schooling from Quintilian to Comenius. He also serves as an executive editor of *Curriculum Studies*.

Stefan Hopmann teaches curriculum studies at the University of Postdam (Germany), the University of Oslo and the University of Trondheim (Norway). He has published widely in Germany and internationally. Hopmann's recent publications deal with: comparative research, curriculum theory and curriculum making, school history and the theory of schooling, including a reader on Didaktik and/or Curriculum.

Carlo Jenzer is director of the education department of the Ministry of Education of the Canton of Solothurn (Switzerland) and serves as a lecturer in school history at the University of Fribourg. Jenzer has been a member of several national and international commissions. His major research topics deal with school history, curriculum, school-systems, teacher training and evaluation. Jenzer is the author of *Die Schulklasse* (Lang, 1991). He has also written articles about the development of education in Switzerland.

Wolfgang Klafki held a chair at Philipps-University of Marburg Lahn (1963-1992). He took part in Deutsche Gesellschaft für Erziehungswissenschaft as a member of the executive board (1966-1980, 1982-1986), and was the Chairman from 1986 until 1988. His research interests are in the field of general theory of education, including theory of Bildung, history of pedagogical ideas, Didaktik, development of school system, school reform and school practice, and methodology of educational research. Out of more than 400 publications in 14 European and extra-European languages, the most important are: *Das pädagogische Problem des Elementaren und die Theorie der*

Katgorialen Bildung (3th/4th Edn. 1964), *Studien zur Bildungstheorie und Didaktik* (20th Edn. 1975), *Aspekte kritisch-konstruktiven Erziehungswissenschaft* (1976), and *Neue Studien zur Bildungstheorie und Didaktik* (5th Edn. 1996).

M. Frances Klein is professor emeritus of the University of Southern California where she held the Robert Naslund Endowed Chair in Curriculum. Her extensive publications include books, monographs, encyclopedia articles, and contributions to professional journals. After retirement in 1992, she was elected to the Laureate Chapter of Kappa Delta Pi and has continued writing for professional journals on curriculum theory. She currently serves as the chair of the Publications Committee for Pi Lambda Theta.

Rudolf Künzli is professor and director at Didaktikum, the teacher training center in Aarau (Switzerland). He is also a professor at the University of Zürich. Areas of special interest include curriculum history and theory, teacher education, general Didaktik and pedagogical rhetorics. His current research concerns curriculum development and administration, and the theory and history of Didaktik.

Ulf P. Lundgren has been a professor in education at the Stockholm Institute of Education where he also served as Vice Chancellor. Now he serves as Director General of the National Agency for Education in Sweden. Lundgren is chairman of the European Union Council National Committee for School and Youth Questions. He has published numerous books and articles in Scandinavia and internationally. His last book in English is *Between Education and Schooling* (1991).

Lars Løvlie is a professor in education at the University of Oslo where he teaches in the field of philosophy of education and its history. He is director of "School and Culture", a four-year research programme supported by the Norwegian Research Council. Løvlie has written articles ranging from classical educational thinkers to postmodernism. He is now writing a book on the concept of formation or Bildung in German idealism, with special reference to G. W. F. Hegel's *The Philosophy of Spirit*, and is also currently working on a history of educational thinking for students.

Peter Menck is a professor of General Education at the Universität Gesamthochschule Siegen (Germany). His research interests centre on classrooms, curriculum, the theory of instruction, history of education and content analysis of different pedagogies. His most recent books are *Unterrichtsinhalt oder: Ein Versuch über die Konstruktion der Wirklichkeit im Unterricht* (1986) and *Geschichte der Erziehung* (1993).

William F. Pinar teaches curriculum theory at Lousiana State University where he serves as the St. Bernard Parish Alumni Endowed Professor. Pinar is the author of *Autobiography, Politics, and Sexuality* (Lang, 1994) and is the senior author of *Understanding Curriculum* (Lang, 1995). He serves as an founding editor of JCT: *An Interdisciplinary Journal of Curriculum Studies*, founder of the Bergamo Conference, and editor of a book series in curriculum theory.

William A. Reid is a visiting professor of education at the University of Texas at Austin. He was previously a reader in curriculum studies at the University of Birmingham (England). He is author of a number of books and papers on curriculum questions, the most recent of which is *The Pursuit of Curriculum: Schooling and the Public Interest* (1992). Reid has served as general editor of the *JCS: Journal of Curriculum Studies*. He received a Lifetime Achievement Award from Division B (Curriculum Studies), American Educational Research Association (AERA) in 1995.

William M. Reynolds teaches curriculum theory at Purdue University. He is the author of *Reading Curriculum Theory: The Development of a New Hermeneutic* (Lang 1989), and is a co-author of *Understanding Curriculum as Phenomenological and Deconstructed Text* (1992), a co-author of *Understanding Curriculum* (Lang, 1995) and has edited *Inside Out: Contemporary Critical perspectives in Education* together with Rebecca Martusewicz (1994).

Patrick Slattery teaches curriculum theory at Ashland University in Ohio. His research and publications focus on curriculum for postmodern schooling and curriculum related to theology. He is the author of *Curriculum Development in the Post-modern Era* (1995) and is a co-author of *Understanding Curriculum* (1995).

Peter M. Taubman teaches English at Poly Prep High School in New York City. His research interests and publications center on curriculum related to gender, racial issues, phenomenology and diversity in curriculum. He is a co-author of *Understanding Curriculum* (1995).

Ewald Terhart is a professor at Ruhr-Universität, Bochum (Germany). His field of research is teacher professionalism, school development and qualitative classroom research with focus on the teaching process. Terhart has published widely in Germany and abroad.

Erik Wallin is professor emeritus of education. He held a chair at the University of Göteborg and later at Uppsala University (Sweden). During the 1980s he was Dean of the Faculty of Social Sciences at Uppsala. His main research interests are curriculum and evaluation. Since 1990 Wallin has been engaged in the research program of the Swedish Agency of Education. The title of his latest publication is *Educational Research at the Crossroads* (with Albert Tuijnman).

Ian Westbury is a professor of curriculum and instruction at the University of Illinois at Urbana-Champaign, U.S.A. He has co-edited *Science, Curriculum and Liberal Education: Selected Essays of Joseph J. Schwab* (1978), *Cultural Literacy and the Idea of General Education* (1988) and *In Search of More Effective Mathematics Education: Examining Data from the IEA Second International Mathematics Study* (1994). He is general editor of the *Journal of Curriculum Studies*.

Name Index

Subject Index